Foreign and Security Policy
in the European Union

Foreign and Security Policy in the European Union

Edited by
Kjell A. Eliassen

SAGE Publications
London · Thousand Oaks · New Delhi

First published 1998

 SAGE Publications Ltd
6 Bonhill Street
London EC2A 4PU

SAGE Publications Inc
2455 Teller Road
Thousand Oaks, California 91320

SAGE Publications India Pvt Ltd
32, M-Block Market
Greater Kailash - I
New Delhi 110 048

British Library Cataloguing in Publication data

A catalogue record for this book is available from the British
Library

ISBN 0 7619 5632 8
ISBN 0 7619 5633 6 (pbk)

Library of Congress catalog card number 98-060946

Typeset by Type Study, Scarborough, North Yorkshire
Printed in Great Britain by The Cromwell Press Ltd,
Trowbridge, Wiltshire

Contents

Preface

The aim of this volume is to try to explain why integration in the second pillar, the Common Foreign and Security Policy (CFSP) of the European Union, is proving to be such a difficult task. The point of departure for the book is a question: why do we often find that the nation-state's self-interest in this field is much more important than the possibility of developing a regional solution? The question of why this is so difficult has been investigated along three main avenues. The first part of the book examines how the reluctant growth of EU integration in the CFSP field has developed since the mid 1980s. The second part identifies national security policies and interests that often obstruct the development of a common policy in four important European countries: France, Germany, Britain and Spain. The final part discusses the future problems that will need to be addressed successfully if the EU's CFSP is to have any credibility within the fields of EU expansion and armament.

This book is published as part of a research project for the Royal Norwegian Ministry of Defence on EU foreign, security and defence policy and possible consequences for Norway. The project has produced several reports, articles and books. I am grateful for the financial support given to the project and for the interest shown by the Ministry in the publications resulting from our research efforts.

This volume is the result of a collective effort within the Centre for European and Asian Studies at the Norwegian School of Management (BI). I would like to express my thanks first and foremost to researcher Pinar Tank. Without her insistent and very energetic interest and help during the final completion of the manuscript, my task would have been nearly impossible to fulfil. I would also like to thank my assistants and staff at the Centre and in particular PhD student Marit Sjøvaag, research assistant Karin Skyllingstad and office manager Grethe Haug.

Kjell A. Eliassen

Notes on Contributors

Esther Barbé is Director of Centre d'Estudis sobre la Pau i el Desarmament at the Autonomous University of Barcelona and Professor of International Relations. She also teaches at Escuela Diplomatica in Madrid. She has been Visiting Professor at several European universities. She has published books and articles on the Common Foreign and Security Policy, Spanish foreign policy, European organizations, Mediterranean security and the theory of international relations, including *La seguridad en la Nueva Europa: Una aproximacion institucional: Union Europea, OTAN y UEO* (Madrid, 1995) and *Relaciones Internacionales* (Madrid, 1995).

Yves Boyer is Deputy Director of FED-CREST, a think-tank based in Paris dealing with international security and strategic affairs. He is Professor at the French army academy where he teaches a course on US and NATO defence policies. Having a PhD in political science from Paris University, he is also teaching at the *Grand École*, the *École polytechnique,* where he has a course on international relations and military affairs. A member of the editorial board of *Revue française de Géoéconomie* and of *Perspectives asiatiques,* he has published many journal articles. He is currently working on a collective book on the 'Revolution in Military Affairs'. He is a former IISS research associate and Woodrow Wilson Centre research fellow.

Michael Clarke is Professor of Defence Studies at King's College London and Director of the Centre for Defence Studies. He has previously held posts at the Universities of Newcastle upon Tyne, Manchester and Aberystwyth. He has been a Guest Fellow at the Brookings Institution, Washington, DC, and a Visiting Fellow at the Royal Institute of International Affairs in London. He has served as Specialist Adviser to the House of Commons Foreign Affairs Committee and the House of Commons Defence Committee and as a member of the High Level Group of Experts to advise Commissioner Van den Broek at the European Commission. His publications include *British External Policy-Making for the 1990s*, *British Defence Choices for the 21st Century* (edited with Dr Philip Sabin) and *New Perspectives on Security*. He is editor of the *Brassey's Defence Yearbook* and contributes articles and comments to a number of journals.

Pierre de Vestel is currently a PhD student at the Institute for European Studies at the Free University of Brussels. He has previously been researcher at several Belgian institutions in the field of the political economy of the defence industry.

Kjell A. Eliassen is Director of the Centre for European and Asian Studies at the Norwegian School of Management and Professor of Public Management. He is also Professor at the Institute d'Etudes Europeennes at Université Libre de Bruxelles. Professor Eliassen is former Vice President at the Norwegian School of Management and he has been Visiting Professor at several American and European universities and Associate Professor at the University of Aarhus. He has published ten books and many articles on EC and European affairs, public management and political elites, including *The European Union: How Democratic Is It?* (Sage, 1995). He has considerable experience from consultant and management development programmes in public agencies and private companies both in the Nordic countries and in Eastern Europe. He has been responsible for business school teacher training programmes and management development programmes in both Eastern Europe and Pacific Asia.

Catriona Gourlay is the Executive Director of the International Security Information Service, Europe in Brussels. She is the series editor of ISIS Briefing Papers on Security and Foreign Policy and the author of *The Security Dimension of the IGC* (ISIS Briefing Paper 58, 1996). She is a research Associate at the Institut d'Etudes Européennes at the Université Libre de Bruxelles and a PhD candidate at Manchester Metropolitan University.

Esben Oust Heiberg is a researcher at the Centre for European and Asian Studies at the Norwegian School of Management (BI). He has a BA from the University of Durham, England, and an MSc from the Norwegian School of Management. His main interest is in defence industry and security issues. He has recently completed a project for the Norwegian Ministry of Defence on 'The Transatlantic Relationship and the Defence Industry'. Previous experience includes working for DG XXIII in the European Commission, and he has also been involved in setting up a Nordic management centre at Fudan University, Shanghai, China.

Eric Remacle, PhD, is Director of the Institute for European Studies at the Université Libre de Bruxelles and Jean Monnet Professor of European foreign and security policy. He has published books, articles and reports on European security, crisis management and arms control, including most recently: *Paneuropean Security Redefined* (co-editor Reimund Seidelmann, 1998) and *L'Union de l'Europe occidentale: Phénix de la défense européenne* (with André Dumoulin, 1998). He is correspondent for Belgium of the Standing Group on International Relations within the European Consortium for Political Research (ECPR). He currently holds a NATO fellowship, jointly with Patricia Chilton (Manchester Metropolitan University), for a study to be carried out between 1997 and 1999 on Parliamentary Scrutiny of Peacekeeping Operations.

Reimund Seidelmann has been, since 1996, Professor of International Relations and Foreign Policy at the Institute for Political Science at Justus-Liebig University, Giessen and International Professor at the Institut d'Etudes Européennes, Brussels. His major areas of research are theories and methods of international relations and foreign policy, peace and security studies, European security and European integration.

Marit Sjøvaag holds an MSc from the Norwegian School of Management, where she did her Master's thesis on European political cooperation. She is currently undertaking her PhD at the London School of Economics and Political Science. Her PhD project is on state traditions and the liberalization of the telecommunications sector in France and Germany.

Arnhild Spence is a Research Fellow at the Centre for European and Asian Studies at the Norwegian School of Management. After taking her postgraduate degree in international relations at the University of Oslo, she worked for the Norwegian Institute of International Affairs, where she published on EU foreign policy and enlargement. She has also worked in the European Commission, in the European Parliament, the Norwegian Foreign Office, the Norwegian Ministry of Defence and at NATO headquarters in Brussels.

David Spence is Head of external representation policy, training, information and cooperation with the foreign ministries of the Member States administrations in the European Commission's Directorate General (External relations: Europe and the New Independent States, Common Foreign and Security Policy, External Service). He studied in the UK at Sussex and Oxford Universities and in France at the Institute of International Relations in Nice and at the Institut d'Etudes Politiques in Paris. He was Conference Advisor at Wilton Park, the British Foreign Office's conference centre, and was Head of European Training at the Civil Service College before joining the European Commission in 1990. He has published articles on European public administration and is co-editor of *The European Commission* (1997).

G. Pinar Tank is a Researcher at the Centre for European and Asian Studies at the Norwegian School of Management. The focus of her research is on security issues, in particular relating to European security, the Mediterranean region and terrorism, on which she has published several working papers. Pinar Tank has a BA honours degree (French and politics) from the University of Keele in England and an MPhil in international relations (security studies) from the University of St Andrews in Scotland.

1 Introduction: The New European Foreign and Security Policy Agenda

Kjell A. Eliassen

> CFSP is less a policy in the sense of a specific course of action, than a process.
>
> European Commissioner Hans Van den Broeck (van Ham, 1997: 309)

In an interdependent world, policies cannot flourish in vacuums. It is impossible to have an effective economic policy without simultaneously also possessing a coherent foreign policy and a credible security policy. This is an indisputable reality for all those who work with the Common Foreign and Security Policy (CFSP). What is considerably more difficult to identify are the means through which this is to be accomplished. We do not make any claims to providing the answers in this book. However, it is through asking some of the important questions that answers may be found and this is what we have sought to do in this book. We have attempted to explain why integration in the second pillar, the Common Foreign and Security Policy of the European Union, is proving to be a much more arduous task than economic integration in the first pillar.

Thus, the first part of the book examines the reluctant growth of integration, the second part identifies national security policies and interests that often obstruct the development of a common policy, and the final part discusses the future problems that will need to be addressed successfully if the EU's CFSP is to have any credibility. Briefly, then, the book is organized into separate parts based on policy, actors and issues.

Our second intention has been to illustrate the developmental process behind CFSP which is indicative of the time and the effort involved to arrive at the present state of affairs. It is perhaps knowledge of this process that provides some optimism for the future of integration in the second pillar. Commenting on its present state, Roy Ginsberg notes that 'A messy state of affairs is at least an accurate description for it avoids extremes of optimism and pessimism that serve no useful purpose' (1997: 31). The importance of the project for the future of the EU cannot be ignored for, to paraphrase a common expression, one may claim that the EU 'is only as strong as its weakest link' which, at present, is to be found in the second pillar.

What then is foreign and security policy? Foreign policy can be defined as the part of a state's policy that determines its relations with other states and with the international community. This concept covers diplomacy, alliances, military policy, trade policy etc. The broadness of the concept reflects the complex nature of politics and the multitude of connections between different policy areas. Deutsch stated that 'the foreign policy of every country deals with the preservation of its independence and security, and second with the pursuit and protection of its economic interests' (1978: 101). This makes foreign policy a multi-faceted animal.

Security policy is an even broader term. The most basic definition of security is to lower the risks. Traditionally security policy was policy answering external military threats, but as the number and intensity of links in international society have increased, security policy is extended to cover contingencies for other types of threats. Examples of such are terrorism, social unrest, domestically and abroad, and activities undermining the legitimacy of the regime.

It is quite clear that the 1989 events in Eastern Europe created an important change in European countries' security policy. Economic and material welfare inequalities, high unemployment rates, and internal conflicts were all factors contributing to the high mobility of people from the East to the West. The difficult assimilation in Western European societies resulted in increasing social unrest in EC member countries.

The political difficulties do not have to occur within one's own territory for them to have repercussions. International terrorists also attack civil targets in all parts of the world, with the 'excuse' of bringing global attention to their problem. Moral considerations play a role in deciding when states engage in other countries' internal conflicts, as for example aid to refugees and civilians in wars, and support (economical, military and moral) to certain regimes. Furthermore, the decolonization in the 1940s and 1950s influences the current situation. Former colonies, poor and badly equipped to compete in the international arena, claim rights to help from the former colonial powers.

All this has contributed to the development of a 'new' security concept. Traditionally security meant military strength, but there is a clear development indicating that security includes more areas as threat emerges from different sources. 'Nowadays . . . increasing significance attaches to a new aspect centring around internal civil strife, protection of minorities, human rights violations, ecological disaster risks, irresponsible use of new technologies etc.' (Westendorp Report, 1995: 31). The new security concept gains in relevance as the complexity of our modern society grows.

As this book attempts in part to describe the story behind the process of CFSP, we begin in the introduction by rendering a brief overview of its historical development.

History of development of idea of European Political Cooperation

Understanding European Political Cooperation as a process necessitates an overview of its history. European Political Cooperation began following the end of the Korean War in the 1950s, based on the Jean Monnet idea that Europe should strengthen its military potential against an increasing Soviet threat through defence cooperation. The European Defence Community (EDC) came into being in 1952 through the cooperation of the six member states of the European Coal and Steel Community (ECSC: Benelux, West Germany, Italy, France). It became increasingly clear that an inevitable consequence of this effort at defence cooperation would result equally in foreign policy cooperation. Italy, led by federalist Altiero Spinelli, set out to convince the other member states that federal European institutions were necessary to command a European army. The outcome of this was the European Political Community in 1953 with a constitution corresponding to the EDC Treaty.

However efforts at integration were to be short-lived, for while the EDC Treaty was signed by all the member states involved in its creation, it came to a halt in the French Parliament in 1954. This was due primarily to opposition to the supranational nature of the Treaty. Secondly, and no less important, the moves towards European Political Cooperation were taking place at a time when the Second World War was still deeply imprinted on the collective European memory. The thought of placing French troops under foreign command or the rearming of Germany faced too much opposition in the French Parliament. However, the French did indicate a willingness to cooperate at an intergovernmental level in foreign and security policy within the Community through the Fouchet Plan. This sought to coordinate the Community's foreign and defence policies outside the Community and was under discussion until the French veto of British entry.

When the EC came into being, foreign and security policies were left outside Community competency. These areas were left to national sovereignty, while the Community had the power to deal with so-called 'external relations', including economic and commercial terms for relations with third countries. Despite the clear connection between economic behaviour and foreign policy, there was no institutional framework in the EC whose competencies included analysing such effects. Nor was there any central organ to make sure that member countries' diverse bilateral agreements and actions towards third countries were consistent with each other, or at least not in conflict with joint Community action. The consequences were evident: it proved difficult to preserve the image of one coherent and unified EC actor while member states made bilateral agreements with various third countries (Regelsberger, 1988).

The European Political Cooperation (EPC) concept dates back to 1970 and the Luxembourg Report, which was made by the foreign ministers in the six member countries on request from the Hague summit in 1969. This report 'set down guiding principles and convictions which revealed both cautiousness and ambivalence over the venture into foreign policy cooperation'. On the one hand, it referred to a 'Europe composed of States which while preserving their national characteristics, are united in their essential interests'. On the other hand, references were made to a 'united Europe' founded upon 'liberty and the rights of men', and 'democratic states having freely elected parliaments'. Thus 'united Europe' was defined as 'the fundamental aim' to be achieved as soon as possible through 'the political will of its people and the decisions of their Governments' (Lodge, 1989: 228).

The goals outlined in this report were rather modest, formulated as 'greater mutual understanding of international affairs through the exchange of information and regular consultation, of greater solidarity through harmonisation of views, conformity of attitudes, and joint action when it appears feasible and desirable' (Vanhoonacker, 1992: 28). The instruments to be used were purely intergovernmental cooperation.

At the time there were signs that deepening of EC relations was desirable. Several countries had applied for membership and there was a need to tighten the existing community before these new members were admitted. The aims of the foreign policy were twofold: first, to ensure an increased mutual understanding on international problems through exchange of information and consultations; and secondly, to strengthen the member states' solidarity by harmonization of views and, when feasible, actions.

In spite of declarations and decisions to prove increasing political unity, the member countries never, during the 1970s, managed to – or wanted to – incorporate EPC into the EC. The document on European identity adopted in 1973, which stated that the Nine were to try to promote, by acting as a single entity, harmonious and constructive relations with third countries, was as close as they got to joining the two. The same document pronounces the goal of establishing a European Union within the decade (Lodge, 1989: 229).

The oil crisis of 1973 was, to some extent, a turning point for European Political Cooperation as the EC became involved in political dialogue to resolve the economic crisis, once again indicating the futility of separating economic issues from the political. This led to a gradual strengthening of the EPC so that by 1980 it was able to develop political positions, for example issuing the Venice Declaration recognizing the right of the Palestinians to a homeland. Further steps towards linking security and foreign policy were made with the signing of the Single European Act in 1986, revising the Treaty of Rome and drawing the European Parliament closer to EPC. In addition to promoting closer economic integration it also encouraged, through the provision of a legal framework, the development of political cooperation.

However, the real momentum to European security and foreign policy coordination came with the ending of the Cold War. The period of uncertainty following cast doubts on the United States' willingness to remain engaged in Europe by questioning the future of NATO. Without a dominant Soviet threat, it became increasingly difficult for American policy makers to justify spending defence dollars protecting wealthy Europeans. European nations realized that they had to take greater responsibility for their own security in an increasingly unpredictable international environment. The changes brought on by the fall of the Berlin Wall and the reunification of Germany exacerbated fears of regional conflict as hitherto repressed animosities surfaced. These fears realized themselves in the terrible reality of the Yugoslav civil war. The international system was in flux and the focus of change was in Europe. The further integration of the EU and its development of common policies in foreign affairs and security were regarded as necessary to providing a framework of stability in which to meet these new challenges. Across the Atlantic, the Americans were pressing for greater support from Europe in military operations and the willingness of Europeans to commit themselves, if not as equal partners, as active partners nonetheless. This was highlighted by American involvement in conflicts beyond European boundaries in the Gulf and in Somalia which led to discussions in Europe as to the degree of European commitment to out-of-area operations.

Perhaps the most important result of the end of the Cold War with respect to the development of CFSP was the change in security thinking. Whereas previously, the all-encompassing Soviet threat and the realist school of thinking in American foreign policy had dominated discussions on security, this began to change in response to the changing international system. A more multilateral approach to security policy began to emerge and aspects of 'soft security' were increasingly debated.

In 1990, at a Franco–German initiative, a letter was sent to the EU Presidency asserting the need to develop a Common Foreign and Security Policy. The request was further reinforced under the Italian Presidency later in the same year. Finally, the Gulf War of 1990 had been imperative in exposing the weaknesses of the lack of an integrated European approach to foreign and security policy.

Thus, the question of CFSP was placed on the agenda of the Conference on Political Union at the 1991 Intergovernmental Conference (IGC) on European Monetary Union and European Political Cooperation in Rome in December 1990. At this time, the European Council forwarded a proposition aimed at creating an institutional structure for EPC to be incorporated into the EC. Despite the differences among the member states as to the issues discussed, the development of CFSP was considered of central importance. The role of the WEU and the decision-making process were particularly divisive. It was during this conference that the first suggestion of a pillar structure was made, with three different pillars, each under the direction of a different institution and each with particular decision-making processes. However, the prevailing divisions between Atlanticists and Europeanists and between intergovernmentalists and federalists, and the pressing political problems of the day, resulted in the postponement of CFSP until the Maastricht summit in 1991.

The Conference on Political Union confirmed the tripartite pillar structure and stated, through Article J. 4.1, that the CFSP 'shall include all questions related to the security of the Union, including the eventual framing of a common defence policy which might in time lead to a common defence'. Additionally, through Article J. 4.2, it created a formal link between the WEU and CFSP by stating that 'The Union requests the Western European

Union (WEU) which is an integral part of the development of the Union, to elaborate and implement decisions and actions which have defence implications.' Both through stipulating the necessity of a common defence to ensure the security of the Union, and by identifying the vehicle responsible, the Maastricht Treaty became the end point of the formal, legal process institutionalizing European security and foreign policy integration.

While the legal framework for CFSP is now in place, its practical application has often been seen to be lacking. This has partly been attributed to the ambiguity of the language and the role assigned to it. There is no doubt that much of this ambiguity is a result of the need to reach a compromise at its creation that could prove acceptable to all the member states. Partly, however, it is due to the lack of consensus on the future role of Europe (van Ham, 1997: 307). Issues that remain unresolved are those of an institutional nature that weaken its ability to implement common policies. Let us then briefly show how these different issues are dealt with in the book.

The history, actors and challenges of the CFSP

As illustrated briefly above, the development of the institutional framework for European foreign policy and security cooperation was a long and onerous process. There is little reason to imagine that its practical implementation will transpire more rapidly. We hope through this book to describe the development of the process, its key players and the challenges it is likely to face in the coming years. As such, the book has been divided into three parts, each focusing on a particular aspect of CFSP.

The first part, consisting of chapters 2–5, discusses the development of CFSP through to the termination of the 1996–7 IGC with the publication of the Amsterdam Treaty. The first chapter in this part, 'The CFSP and the Nation-State' by Pinar Tank, attempts to place CFSP in the framework of the ever changing international environment. It is intended to explain the changes undergone by the nation-state following the end of the Cold War period by examining the growth not only of the EU as a supranational institution but also through the competing allegiances to the nation-state. Following this contribution is one by Marit Sjøvaag, explaining the history of European Political Cooperation leading to the development of CFSP. It focuses particularly on the period from 1985 to 1991, reviewing the increasing integration between the EC countries. This is followed by Arnhild and David Spence's contribution examining the difficulties experienced by European member states in their efforts to implement CFSP, noting both the challenges and the limited successes. The final chapter in this part leads us from Maastricht through to the end of the 1996–7 IGC, reflecting on the progress that was made and the ever present gap between intentions and outcomes.

The second part of the book is intended to focus on the security policies of some of the key member states involved in the development of the CFSP.

It informs on national security strategies, then reflects on the changes necessitated by member states' commitment to CFSP. It should be no surprise to the reader that the section begins with the two countries that have been regarded as spearheading the efforts at developing the CFSP. Thus, the first chapter on 'France and the European Project' by Yves Boyer starts by explaining the effects that France's difficult domestic situation has had on its support for the European project, particularly emphasizing the pressures created domestically by France's determination to forge ahead with European integration. This is followed by Reimund Seidelmann's contribution on 'The Security Policy of a United Germany', where the reasons behind Germany's support for the integration project are discussed as well as the past and future benefits they have derived through closer security ties with Europe. Closing the section are two chapters on 'British Security Policy' by Michael Clarke and 'Spanish Security Policy and the Mediterranean Question' by Esther Barbé. The first of these explains British reticence towards European cooperation in the security field owing to the benefits it derived from the status quo in European security. Esther Barbé's chapter follows the history of Spain's reluctant entry into the European security architecture through NATO up to its present role in furthering the CFSP and addressing the difficulties particular to the Mediterranean region.

In the final part of the book, we have chosen to focus on the challenges that are likely to have a major impact on CFSP in the coming years. Adequate and satisfactory responses to these issues are necessary if the second pillar is to increase its efficacy and, by extension, its legitimacy. Chapter 10 in this part, 'Security Issues Emanating from the Mediterranean Basin' by Pinar Tank, discusses the potential for instability in the countries of the Mediterranean Rim. While much of the focus has thus far been on stability to the East, stability in the South is not to be regarded as only a problem of the Southern EU states as the credibility of the EU has much to gain by being able to successfully formulate policies to increase stability in its own backyard. Looking to the East, one of the much debated issues of the new European security architecture is its expansion to include Central and Eastern European countries. The chapter titled 'Security Implications of EU Expansion to the North and East' by Esben Oust Heiberg attempts to shed some light on the effects this will have for CFSP. This is followed by a chapter addressing the issue of defence cooperation between European member states by Pierre de Vestel titled 'The Future of Armament Cooperation in NATO and the WEU'. He reflects on the present political changes in Europe that will affect the establishment of an independent European system for arms procurement and the problems it has encountered owing to the lack of momentum in European defence integration. In addition, he points out the difficulty of developing a separate European defence identity with regard to its effects on the transatlantic relationship. Finally, Kjell A. Eliassen makes concluding comments regarding 'European Foreign and Security Policy in the Future'.

In the process of selecting chapters and gathering information for this book, we have been increasingly aware of discussions that have necessarily been limited owing to the constraints of time and space. Questions of democracy, legitimacy and identity which compound the difficulties of achieving CFSP are discussed only briefly in Chapter 2, although they are at the root of the most difficult problems concerning the EU's CFSP. We have also limited our discussion of the procedural or institutional difficulties except as they relate to individual chapters as there is already a considerable specialized literature on this topic. Finally, with respect to the approach we have taken in this book, we hope to be able to present, through the following contributions, a balanced view as each chapter has reflected the conceptual framework of the author. As we have an international list of contributors, we hope that this has also served to highlight some of the different perceptions of the CFSP and its future role.

2 The CFSP and the Nation-State

G. *Pinar Tank*

The end of the 1996–7 Intergovernmental Conference on the European Union did not result in the envisaged revisions to the second pillar – the Common Foreign and Security Policy (CFSP). It was hoped that the Amsterdam summit would conclude with a commitment to strengthen the political foundations of the European integration process. However, the focus of the summit was very much on the first pillar, reinforcing the greater importance attributed to monetary union as the engine in the integration process. There is a historical precedent in the failure of the French Parliament to ratify the EDC Treaty in 1954, indicating that future integration was more likely to be successful in the economic domain and met with resistance in the areas of foreign policy and security. This chapter attempts to examine why there is a much greater resistance to integration in the second pillar(not to mention the third). In doing so, it will by focusing first on the nation-state in general, addressing its composition and the role of sovereignty as an integral element. There is little doubt that increasing interdependence has affected the role of the nation-state, in some cases diminishing it and in others strengthening it through strategic alliances. The phenomenon of interdependence and its effects are therefore significant to any discussion of the nation-state. This leads quite naturally to a discussion of whether the European integration process is taking on a federalist structure as desired by pro-European advocates or whether it remains at the level of intergovernmental cooperation. In order to do this, it is necessary to analyse the potential cleavages resulting from national differences among the nation-states. Finally, it must be noted that the ambiguous, and from time to time difficult, relation between the nation-state and CFSP is the backdrop against which most of the discussions concerning its future development take place.

Composition of the nation-state

The Common Foreign and Security Policy provides challenges to the nation-state structure which can be better understood by first understanding the

(handwritten margin notes: ELEMENTS THAT COMPOSE THE NATION STATE: ① TERRITORY ② COMMON LANGUAGE ③ CULTURE ④ RELIGION ⑤ COMMON ECONOMIC GOALS; ABSTRACT; SOVEREIGNTY; JEAN BODIN 1576; HOBBES)

elements that compose the nation-state. Among the objective elements forming the nation-state are included a common territory and its defence. The question of territory, however, can also provide a divisive element if groups feel greater allegiance to a particular region over and above that which is defined by the borders of the nation-state. Several examples of this abound, from the democratic secessionist movement of Quebec to the more militant variety of the Basque separatists. Another necessary element in the composition of the nation-state is that of common language, though it need not necessarily be a factor as in the case of Belgium, or of Switzerland with its three languages. Further, there are the elements of culture and religion which can equally result in either integration or disunity. Finally, a nation-state has common economic goals and must be capable of redistributing welfare by intervening on behalf of the national interest.

All of the aforementioned factors serve to objectively define the nation-state, but it is the abstract elements that ensure its survival. Primary among these is the belief in the sovereignty of the nation-state. The concept of sovereignty is first mentioned in the writing of the French political thinker Jean Bodin, who in 1576 defined it as 'the state's supreme authority over its citizens and subjects' (Stoessinger, 1973). Thomas Hobbes, also believing in the predominance of the state over the individual, claimed that the power of the state must be unconstrained in its actions both within and beyond the boundaries of the state. Historically, sovereignty was a concept that was used to justify the monarchical consolidation of state power (state sovereignty).[1] While the above definition of the state's power internally over its citizens is still valid today, it has also has been modified in tandem with the acceptance of democracy to include an element of consent so that, within the nation-state, sovereignty is considered to be a right given to the state by its citizens. Externally, sovereignty has meant the pursuit of the national interest and it has been distinctively more resistant to change. The process of yielding sovereignty to other states has not had as much success externally as the process of yielding sovereignty to the consent of the governed has had internally – a reality depicted by the CFSP process.

While, on the one hand, a loss of sovereignty for the nation-state has been the stated argument behind some member states' unwillingness to integrate further in foreign policy and security matters, on the other, the demise of sovereignty in the modern world has also been used to explain the necessity for further integration. According to Michael Newman's (1996) analysis, 'sovereignty' has been used emotively throughout the EU debate to justify the aims of both the Eurosceptic and the integrationist camps, obscuring its definition to meet their intended aims. The contradiction between these two views on sovereignty clearly indicates the difficulty inherent in using such a complex and diffuse term to justify the arguments either for or against integration. Sovereignty has historically been linked to the sanction of power, whether given by the people, as in the case of popular sovereignty, or vested in the state beyond any higher authority as in the case of legal sovereignty. Thus, there has evolved over time a connection between power and sovereignty that is at the root of the supranational debate surrounding the EU. However, sovereignty can be more clearly and simply defined as an attribute of statehood with the result, as Newman indicates, that it is then not used as a doctrine to legitimate arguments for or against European Union.

The second defining element in a nation-state is the equally diffuse concept of nationalism. Nationalism is, contrary to popular belief, a modern, developed concept rather than a permanent element in political life. Its development in Europe dates to the end of the eighteenth century with the growth of cultural nationalism through the reformation of European languages and the exaltation of national myths. This served to lay the foundations for movements of national statehood. Briefly, nationalism can be described as the collective consciousness forming the cornerstone of national identity as created through common past myths and future hopes. It is a sense of allegiance to, and identification with, a particular group. It is described by Charles Kupchan (1995) as 'an ideology that calls for the merging of the sentimental nation with the functional state. The state is purely administrative; it provides goods and services to its citizens. The nation is purely emotive; it provides a sense of belonging and community to its members.' As noted above, the modern nation-state in the nineteenth century and through the twentieth has been an evolutionary concept and the elements that compose it have not always been inherent to its definition. The spread of mass education along with the imposition of a standard language (Horsman and Marshall, 1994) have been fundamental to commanding the allegiance of citizens within a defined border. In practice, the nation-state was regarded as the model best suited to organizing international relations in both the nineteenth and twentieth centuries.

Finally, contained in the nation's history is its 'personality' with failures and successes determining its future development. Important to bear in mind is that the collective identity is composed of individual perceptions projected onto the nation. So 'man may seek compensation for the lack of a personal future in the reflected glory of a nation's collective future' (Stoessinger, 1973). This has had a particular impact in international relations after the end of the Cold War era.

Within the European Union and particularly with regard to the CFSP, nationalism has been interlinked with sovereignty in providing both resistance to political union and protection from the dangers of excessive nationalism through integration. As with sovereignty, it has been manipulated to justify the arguments of the European Union debate, alternately conveyed as essential to the survival of the nation-state or as detrimental to the survival of the nation-state in the international system. On the other hand, the integrative function of nationalism is often disregarded although interestingly enough, according to Charles Kupchan, one of the reasons that the European Union has managed to advance to its present level of political and economic integration is the strong sense of national identity in the member states. States with highly developed national identities (a strong

[Handwritten top margin: NATIONALISM, SOVEREIGNTY AND LEGITIMACY ARE NOT ORGANIC AND HAVE EVOLVED OVER TIME.]

sense of legitimacy and sovereignty) are more capable of devolving their sovereignty to supranational institutions than those that are struggling with their identity and autonomy (Kupchan, 1995). There is, thus, the potential for European Union policy makers to capitalize on this aspect of national-ism rather than regarding it as a danger to integration *per se*.

Finally, the success of the nation-state and its capacity to persevere depend in the long run on its legitimacy. The concept of legitimacy is closely tied to state sovereignty, relying on a justification for state authority over society. For this to occur, it must provide for the welfare of its citizens and satisfy their demands. In responding to the needs of its citizens, the state must not contradict the prevailing values in liberal democracies such as those of democracy and government by popular consent. Legitimacy is thus defined as 'the expectation of freedom from intolerable value conflict, and is, therefore, the expectation of the compatibility or consonance of values' (Deutsch, 1978: 56). The legitimacy of the European Union in general and the CFSP in particular is often linked to questions of democracy and sovereignty. Additionally, Weiler points out that legitimacy depends on the existence of a *demos*, or in other words, a polity 'for which and by whom the democratic structure and process is to take place' (1997: 250). For while legal legitimacy exists where national parliaments have yielded some of their sovereign powers to the EU, social legitimacy is still lacking. Its evol-ution depends partly on the subjective perceptions of its members that they belong to a distinct group of people with a clear identity and partly on the accessibility of decision making within the polity (Wallace and Smith, 1995).

[Handwritten left margin: WEILER LEGITMACY DEPENDS ON THE EXISTENCE OF A DEMOS, A 'POLITY' DEMOCRATIC STRUCTURE AND PROCESS IS TO TAKE PLACE]

Sovereignty, nationalism and legitimacy are all factors that construct a feeling of national identity which interprets the past, accepts the present, and plans for the future. As indicated above, none of these concepts are organic. They have all evolved over time. This leads to the conclusion that time and political will could lead to the construction of a European identity which could provide the basis of solidarity in foreign and security policy. A union of European member states based solely on pragmatic reasons, for example of economic gain, will be a 'frail process susceptible to reversal' as it is not 'reinforced with deep ideological or philosophical commitment' (Haas, 1967).

[Handwritten: 'A FRAIL PROCESS SUSCEPTIBLE TO REVERSAL' IF BASED SOLELY ON ECONOMIC GAIN.]

The nation-state and the growth of interdependence

The centrality of the nation-state was particularly affirmed after the end of the Second World War with the rise of the theory of realism in international relations which remained dominant throughout the Cold War period. This theory depended on states as the major actors in international relations and defined power in terms of military security, securing the national interest, as the goal of all states operating in an anarchic international environment.

[Handwritten left margin: STATES ARE NO LONGER CONFINED TO SELF INTEREST.]

However, whether this remains to be the case as we approach the twenty-first century is debatable. Several changes have made it such that the state-centric approach is becoming increasingly unsuited to the evolving world order. Doubts as to the descriptive adequacy of realism were already gaining ground in the 1970s with the evolution of pluralist theory. Pluralism began challenging the realist approach by claiming that states were not necessarily the most important actors in international relations and that they were not always driven to action by the need to guarantee national security, challenging the supremacy of 'high politics', the competition between states to attain greater power, over that of 'low politics', the securing of economic and social welfare for citizens. Finally, it questioned the realist belief that competition, endemic violence and insecurity describe the international world order, citing the rise of institutions and procedures that indicated growing collaboration, interdependence and cooperation between national governments in their efforts to improve the material well-being of their citizens (Hanrieder, 1978). In a pluralist view, security issues, based on sheer military power, were of secondary importance to economic issues. The traditional barrier between international and domestic policy was becoming less defined, so resulting, in Hanrieder's words, in a 'domestication' of international politics. The ability of national governments to protect the material interests of citizens, in turn, served to maintain their legitimacy.

With the end of the Cold War period came both greater integration among the states of Western Europe, evident in the signing of the Maastricht Treaty, and elsewhere greater fragmentation of nation-states freed from the oppression of superpower hegemony. Both these processes served to weaken the traditional role of the nation-state. The increased globalization and integration of nation-states have been most evident in the spheres of finance, production and commerce (Horsman and Marshall, 1994). Traditional manufacturing is declining in the developed world and being replaced by the service sector and knowledge-based industries making their way into the international market. Additionally, it is the *Fortune* 500 companies that are increasingly responsible for a substantial amount of global production. The technological revolution has also had the effect of making borders irrelevant as data transmissions allow interactions among financial markets at opposite corners of the globe. Financial markets have also robbed the nation-state of some of its economic sovereignty with their influence on the making of monetary policy. An example of this was the August 1993 reaction to France's decision to espouse a policy of economic liberalism through a strong currency linked to the European monetary system, which was subsequently sabotaged by foreign exchange markets. Economic liberalism as interpreted by twentieth century capitalism has encouraged the growth of private ownership, reduced trade barriers, and replaced the state with the market as a distributor of economic goods (Horsman and Marshall, 1994). The growth of interdependence corresponds to the federalist vision of Europe that claims that a state-centred international system is an anachronism owing to the pressures both internal, for example through separatist movements, and external through the necessity of economic interdependence. In this perspective, the European Union presents a new supranational entity that needs stronger democratic institutions in order for it to develop into a federation. Nonetheless, the federalist vision is still counterbalanced by the realist view, which claims that states will remain the only real actors at the international level and that the development of a supranational European Union replacing the position of the member state is an illusion.

Although it cannot be claimed that the nation-state is an insignificant actor on the international stage, it is undoubtedly facing challenges both internally and externally that undermine its position. This makes it particularly sensitive to yielding power to the European Union in the second pillar. Indicative of this are the cleavages to be found within the European Union between the competing member states' national interests. Esther Barbé (1997a) notes three categories of cleavages that divide the member states of the EU with regard to the CFSP. The first group consists of the states' perspective on the European construction (either federalist or intergovernmentalist), and the second on whether their sympathies lie in the Atlanticist or Europeanist camp. The final cleavage is to be found in their world view, and divides in reality into several smaller categories including their size (small/large), their location (Baltic/Mediterranean) and their historic interests or loyalties. In addition to the internal cleavages, there are the external factors found at the international systemic level.

The first two sets of cleavages affect the depth of European security cooperation, determining to what extent an independent European defence identity is to be endorsed. Thus, there is the divide between the Atlanticists who maintain that intergovernmental cooperation within already established security organizations such as NATO is the best option available, and the Europeanists who see the eventual development of a unified European approach in security and foreign affairs, independent of American involvement. The final cleavage among the member states that creates divisions in their approach to CFSP is formed by their world view or their relationships to countries beyond the Community framework. As an example, some CFSP efforts have been undermined through historical ties to other nations that have impeded agreement on common policies. Britain's close relationship with the United States and France's historical animosity towards a US dominated foreign policy, illustrated by its absence from NATO until 1997, have resulted in their opposing outlooks when discussing the development of CFSP. The colonial past of countries such as France has had a particular impact on their desire to focus more energy on developments in the southern Mediterranean. Likewise, Spain's links with Latin America and Portugal's past involvement in both Africa and Asia result in their unique perspectives in foreign policy *vis-à-vis* these regions (ibid.). Another equally salient national consideration has been that of geographic proximity, resulting in differing views as to the policies to be followed in the formation of foreign and security policy within the EU. An indication of this has been Germany's desire to focus on projects to develop Eastern Europe competing with the Mediterranean countries' wish to encourage the development of a satisfactory policy for the southern Mediterranean. Both these policy initiatives are based on the perception of challenges that will directly affect these regions. Another consideration is that of size, with small countries such as Luxembourg consolidating their strength through alliances with larger countries. Conversely, larger countries such as the UK which already possess a significant international position and defence capability are not as willing to become party to a Community framework in foreign and security policy.

In addition to the internal differences among member states, there are also the external factors that have influenced the momentum of the CFSP process. Prior to its inclusion as Title III in the Single European Act of 1987, European Political Cooperation remained separate from the European Community treaties. This initial stage between 1970 and 1987 has been further divided by EU scholars into three plateaux (Barbé, 1997a; Regelsberger, 1988) which are described briefly here. First, from 1970 to 1974, member states established working procedures while facing the pressures of détente between the USA and USSR and the oil crisis. Secondly, from 1974 to 1979, once the working procedures became more familiar, increased confidence in cooperation in security and foreign policy among the European states was evident, for example, through their unified opposition to the United States' position in the Middle East and the Camp David process (Barbé, 1997a: 132). However, the positive momentum ended in the final period from 1979 to 1987 when the member states increased from the original nine to twelve and negative developments surfaced on the international scene such as the end of détente and the overtly antagonistic feelings between East and West, evident in the Soviet invasion of Afghanistan and President Reagan's 'evil empire' references to the Soviet Union. All these factors contributed equally to straining the relations among the European member states and stagnation in the European security integration process, forcing it to yield first and foremost to American policy in NATO.

By 1987, however, the Community was strengthened with Spain's and Portugal's accession and a gradual easing of East–West tensions. Therefore, the Single Act was signed in 1987 amidst an atmosphere of greater optimism both within the Community and in the international political climate generally. The fall of the Berlin Wall in 1989 removing the previous bipolar structure of international relations brought about the opportunity, if not the necessity, for further integration in the CFSP. It simultaneously accentuated differences among the nation-states, discussed above, that had been restrained under the previous bipolar confrontation. A turning point came with the Gulf War in 1990 which was imperative in exposing the weaknesses of the lack of an integrated European approach to foreign and security policy. However, the external event that had the greatest impact on European security and foreign policy integration was the reunification of Germany in 1990. As an immediate consequence of this, European member states, led by France and Germany itself, sought to integrate Germany further into the European security architecture and began a venture to transform EPC into a Common Foreign and Security Policy within the framework of the European Union. It was agreed that a CFSP would be discussed during the Conference on Political Union at the 1991 IGC on European Monetary Union and European Political Cooperation starting in Rome in 1990. It was in 1991 during the Maastricht Treaty that the tripartite structure was legally endorsed with CFSP in the second pillar. The pillar structure was a compromise solution owing to resistance in part from those countries opposed to qualified majority voting and in part from those objecting to the development of a 'common defence' in competition with NATO.

The importance of national considerations was equally apparent during the 1996–7 IGC. The divisions focused on two issues: British resistance to Franco-German deepening of European defence cooperation, and the smaller states' resistance to increasing the voting powers of the larger member states. Finally, British resistance with regard to WEU integration into the EU necessary to strengthen the defence capability of CFSP resulted in a compromise aimed at closer EU–WEU ties 'with a view to the possibility of the integration' of the two (*International Herald Tribune*, 18 June 1997).

As illustrated above, the differences among the nation-states throughout the formulation of a CFSP have made it a complicated and uncertain process. Although it may be too idealistic to assume that there will ever be complete agreement on foreign and security policy issues, Van Ham states (with reference to a common defence policy): 'It is clear that a European CDP will remain based on the sovereign decision of each member state . . . an effective CDP . . . presupposes that there is sufficient European solidarity and readiness among participating states to share responsibility' (1997: 321).

Although the member states have been reluctant to yield power to the second pillar, as it has been perceived as robbing the nation-state of its sovereignty, there are other challenges that presently exert pressure on the unity and sovereignty of the nation-state. Within the European Union, there are the challenges that arise from the growth of regionalism and ethnonationalism that provide an alternative allegiance for citizens. Additionally, beyond the borders of the European member states (and to some extent within), the growth of militant and politicized religious movements threatens the unity of the nation-state. Should some of these challenges remain unresolved or worsen, they are likely to spill over in the form of refugee flows which will increasingly strain the cultural homogeneity of the traditional European nation-state. The nation-state is thus faced with some challenges following the end of the Cold War that have weakened its traditional power. The following section examines these challenges, both within and beyond the borders of the EU, and the role that the CFSP may play in strengthening the nation-state.

Ethnonationalism and intrastate war

International systemic factors such as the steady growth of greater economic interdependence and the rise of alternative allegiances have collaborated to weaken the power of the traditional nation-state. This has led to the rise of ethnonationalism in the post Cold War period. Particularly destructive is the increase in intrastate conflicts of an ethnonationalistic content. At the same time, an alternative to the nation-state is not yet found in the EU as European integration has not been capable of capturing popular support. Citizens have not transferred their allegiance from the nation-state to the EU. Nor has the European Union adequately addressed the poor level of available information. So while citizens of the nation-states hold national governments responsible for their welfare, decisions regarding their futures are often being taken elsewhere, with apparently minimal national control. This, in turn, has led to the oft cited 'democratic deficit' in the European Union.

A loss of legitimacy for the national authorities has the potential to encourage the search for alternative sources of allegiance. These can often be found in regional or local sources, potentially resulting in forms of intrastate struggle as evidenced in the Yugoslav civil war, or through militant religious movements as evidenced in the growth of political Islam on the southern shores of the Mediterranean. Both affect the European Union's CFSP and are already highlighting the North–South cleavages of national interest to be found among the member states (Barbé, 1997a).

Intrastate conflict, especially in the Balkans and the former Soviet Union, has been a direct consequence of the end of the Cold War. Once the need for unification in the face of a common enemy became obsolete, suppressed internal animosities resurfaced. As the *SIPRI Yearbook* for 1995 notes, 'In 1994, among the thirty-one major armed conflicts in twenty-seven locations around the world, no "classical" interstate war was waged. All of them were intrastate conflicts. However, there were interstate components in several conflicts, such as Nagorno-Karabakh, Bosnia and Herzegovina and Tajikistan' (SIPRI, 1995: 1).

The likelihood exists that intrastate wars will increase as social and political orders experience upheaval. In part, this is due to the decline in interstate wars in the post Cold War world which are capable of diverting attention from economic difficulties and unifying nations against an outside threat to national security. There are several reasons for the decline of traditional interstate wars. These include the global sanction of territorial aggression, and the discreditation by advanced industrial countries of *bellicisme* – the ideology glorifying war. Additionally, economic power has been affirmed as a more effective means of pursuing national objectives while military force has been shown to be decreasingly cost-effective both internally and externally (where territorial aggression is concerned). Finally, due recognition is given to the need for democratic cooperation by citizens in complex and interdependent societies if they are to function successfully (Evans, 1994).

The likelihood of continued intrastate wars between ethnic groups is supported by the number of multination states and multistate nations. Only 20 per cent of the world's states are ethnically homogeneous while 40 per cent have five or more significant ethnic populations. These figures are on the increase owing to migrations and refugee movements. The spiralling economy provides an environment for exploitation by political opportunists engaging in ethnonationalistic propaganda. One of the security challenges faced by the European Union will be developing effective responses to violent intrastate conflict, a challenge that has been insufficiently addressed in the past. This will require a move away from traditional thinking in security that places the sovereignty of the state over and above that of the individual. The shift toward the protection of individuals over states was recognized as early as April 1991 when acting UN Secretary-General Javier Perez de Cuellar noted 'the shift in public attitudes towards the belief that the defence of the oppressed in the name of morality should prevail over frontiers and legal documents' (Evans, 1994: 8). By the same token, encouraging economic development, promoting the rule of law, seeking the protection of human rights and supporting the growth of democratic institutions are also increasingly being recognized as security policies. The realization that security is multi-dimensional places emphasis on preventive measures. 'Cooperative security' has been used as an umbrella term upholding consultation over confrontation, reassurance over deterrence, transparency instead of secrecy, prevention over correction and interdependence in place of unilateralism (Evans, 1994 : 7).

The end of the Cold War has also unveiled the growing dissatisfaction experienced by countries on Europe's southern periphery where the growth of political Islam provides an indication that the nation-state is struggling to maintain its internal authority. If irredentism resulting in intrastate war can be, in part, attributed to the search for a suppressed national identity then Islamic fundamentalism would appear to be a similar quest for a lost cultural identity. Intrastate conflicts often result from the failure by the nation-state to meet the expectations of its citizens at a national level, thereby impelling them to seek regional or ethnic affiliations. Political Islam presents a similar alternative to the nation-state. Thus, the tenets of Western culture are being replaced to some extent by the ideology of militant Islam in countries where dissatisfaction over living standards has provoked a crisis of identity. Political Islam has the additional strength of presenting a competing ideology in the perceived 'ideological vacuum' brought on by the end of the Cold War. The Islamic world view provides an alternative to the Western model of international order, replacing the competition of nation-states with the cooperation (theoretically, at least) of a community of believers. This has been a particularly seductive alternative in the countries of the Mediterranean Basin, where capitalism and Western culture have not been capable of fulfilling their promises. The effects of the rise of militant fundamentalist movements on the southern shores of the Mediterranean is examined in greater detail in Chapter 10.

Addressing intrastate conflict: a role for the EU's CFSP?

The strengthening of both economic and democratic institutions on the European periphery will assist in diminishing the threat of intrastate conflict. Studies done by Rudolph Rummel (1994) in the *Journal of Peace Research* state that around 151 million people have been killed by governments from the beginning of the twentieth century to 1987 (in addition to the 39 million that have died from war or civil war). The majority of these deaths were instigated by governments against their own citizens, with totalitarian governments leading by 84 per cent, followed closely by authoritarian states. Deaths perpetrated by democracies formed a relatively minor percentage.

European Union efforts at diminishing intrastate conflict include the Stability Pact for Europe negotiated as a joint action of the EU Common Foreign and Security Policy in November 1993. Learning from the lessons of the former Yugoslavia, the Pact consists of an agreement on borders and minority rights with particular focus on Central and Eastern European countries. The EU recognized the challenge these problems presented and linked economic assistance and future membership to successful negotiation. The aims, principles and operational arrangements of the Stability Pact as well as a document on regional round tables were adopted in May 1994 by 52 Conference on Security and Cooperation in Europe (CSCE) nations. At the final conference in Paris in March 1995, the Pact and 100 bilateral agreements were signed by all Organization for Security and Cooperation in Europe (OSCE) states, whereupon implementation of the Pact was transferred to this organization (Evans, 1994: 27). The first important negotiation agreement was a peaceful resolution to the Hungarian–Slovak minority problem, declaring the inviolability of their respective borders and denouncing any territorial claims.

These efforts indicate that European security organizations are increasingly recognizing the need for effective prevention of intrastate conflict and are following the principle that 'prevention is better than cure'. Cooperation in the face of this threat through various agreements and organizations has been instigated but needs to be further improved in the future. It is important for the European Union to be able to present a united front in the face of future security threats, particularly those that can be prevented by strategic long-term planning.

With regard to the Mediterranean Rim, the EU has the potential for strengthening democratic institutions as well as promoting economic stability. It has indicated its commitment through the Barcelona Declaration in 1995 followed up by the Euro-Mediterranean Conference in Malta in April 1997. More specifically, the opportunity to improve the credibility of the CFSP should not be ignored. An issue on which it has already taken action is the joint action on dual-use goods which promoted the development of a more stable international political scene through prohibiting the sale of armaments to rogue states. This was done despite its clash with the first pillar in the form of the EU's common commercial policy (Ginsberg, 1997: 29).

However, focusing only on soft security can result in criticism when more decisive action is needed, as in the case of EU policy in the former Yugoslavia. If the CFSP develops a stronger capability in hard security as well as in soft security by taking greater responsibility in regional conflicts, then it may strengthen member states' sovereignty rather than detracting from it by preventing the growth of alternative allegiances.

Conclusion

Both the rise of intrastate conflicts and alternative ideologies such as political Islam indicate the inability of the nation-state to capture the faith of the citizen. While traditionally the nation-state was capable of uniting people through a common language, religion or culture, increasing globalization, in a world where borders have become fluid and nation-states less homogeneous, has incited some citizens to look elsewhere in defining their identity and placing their allegiance. But will this herald a greater allegiance for 'supranational' organizations such as the European Union? Undoubtedly among the elite for whom crossing borders physically and mentally presents no dilemma – and on the contrary allows many advantages – there are many who could espouse a 'European' nationality. However, to the ordinary citizen who does not directly observe any benefit from a united Europe, there is little to entice their allegiance. Alternatives are to be found, for example, in regional allegiances. In essence, the European identity lacks a distinctive ideology. Nor has there been sufficient effort to legitimize the power that the EU wishes to dispose of through the consent of the citizens of Europe. Even Jean Monnet realized the importance of a European identity towards the end of his life when he stated that were he to begin again, he would start with culture (Baleanu, 1994).

The pressures exerted on the nation-state through the first pillar are an additional reason for resisting further integration in the second. Not only are there differences of national interest that make it difficult to achieve a unified approach in foreign and security policy, but there are also international systemic factors that make states unwilling to yield power in second pillar issues to the European Union. Considerations of national interest have consistently undermined attempts at joint action, diminishing the credibility of the CFSP.

In conclusion, while fragmentation and integration are contradictory impulses, both serve to weaken the nation-state. Fragmentation within the nation-state destroys the unity and sovereignty of national power, and integration at the European level threatens to further diminish the nation-state's role. A strengthened CFSP could in actuality serve to promote greater regional stability and lessen the pressures placed on the nation-state. However, essential to its success will be the consent of the governed, without which nation-states cannot yield greater sovereignty to the European Union. The development of a real European security and defence identity requires a vision of a common future as much as the institutional machinery to ensure its competency. This depends greatly on the ability of European citizens to regard European integration as a legitimate and desirable goal for the member states, which in turn depends on efficiency and transparency in all the pillars.

Note

1 Although there are many forms of sovereignty that could be discussed here, including legal sovereignty, popular sovereignty, national sovereignty and shared sovereignty, I have addressed only state sovereignty in relation to the nation-state. For a more complete analysis of each form of sovereignty see Michael Newman (1996).

3 The Single European Act

Marit Sjøvaag

Political cooperation in Europe has long traditions, although economic issues have always been at the core of cooperation in the European Communities. However, the boundary between 'economic' and 'political' is becoming increasingly blurred, and political ends are often achieved through economic means. There exists an ambiguity in most member states about what they want to achieve in the international arena and how much national sovereignty they are willing to give up in order to reach these goals. In order to get a fuller understanding of these problems and their impact on the negotiations leading to the Treaty on European Union, it is useful to give a brief overview of the history of political cooperation in the European Communities.

The scope of this chapter is to question whether one can, for the specific period 1985–91, show a change in the level of interdependence between the EC countries in high politics. Further, if such an integration has occurred, it is interesting to study *how* it took place. One should bear in mind that six years is indeed too short a period to test or to build theories of political cooperation and integration among nations, but it will prove a useful basis on which to discuss the successive events, especially the 1997 IGC held in Amsterdam. However, let us first look at some central and useful concepts.

The Single European Act (SEA) was signed in 1986 as the first major revision of the Treaty of Rome and entered into force in 1987. It settled a plan for the completion of the internal market and introduced majority voting, and is widely considered a turning point for the integration process in Western Europe. From a period of severe economic difficulty in the early 1980s, European countries had an economic upturn from the mid 1980s which facilitated the introduction of measures to promote closer economic dependence.

In addition to its major impact on economic integration, the SEA also gave a new impetus to European Political Cooperation (EPC). 'For the first time in its history, political co-operation received a legal basis' (Regelsberger, 1988: 9). The SEA provided the EC with a legal basis for the internal market, rules for majority voting, an outspoken commitment to further social and economic cohesion, a new role for the European Parliament through the co-decision procedure and, not least of all, a framework for further development of concerted action in the area of foreign policy. This first major revision of the EC constitutional basis, the Treaty of Rome, 'brought together in one "single" act a treaty on European co-operation in the area of foreign policy and institutional and procedural reforms' (Nelsen and Stubb, 1994: 43). The period just after 1985 saw a positive development in many EC related matters, and an increased 'Europification' as more attention was being paid to the EC level and its significance for day-to-day business in Europe.

Decision making in the EPC was to take place on an intergovernmental basis, but with an opening for majority voting in some limited areas. There was a fairly pragmatic view among the member countries on how to develop this field, and its inclusion in the Treaty did not imply any supranational decision-making procedures. Attempts to achieve such ends (Tindemans Report from 1975, Genscher–Colombo initiative in 1981, and EP's Draft Treaty on European Union from 1984) have not been successful. The highest authority for EPC was the European Council, and between their meetings the Council of Foreign Ministers (CFM). There was established a permanent secretariat. The Presidency represented the Community in all external relations, and the Commission was represented in the EPC framework. The SEA opened for discussion the 'economic aspects of security' and set down that development in EPC should be incremental.

The SEA underlines the intergovernmental character of EPC as well as the member states' ambivalence in the field. The British had always been positive towards security cooperation but were reluctant to accept supranationality in any form. Franco-German proposals, however, gave direction to foreign policy deliberations. 'The idea of a permanent secretariat to assist the presidency for EPC was to find favour, but the anxiety expressed about its role and duration reaffirmed member states' concern about the relationship between EPC and the EC' (Lodge, 1989: 232). Title III in the Treaty, on foreign policies, refers to the member states as 'High Contracting Parties', avoiding reference to supranational structures. However, both the Commission and the Council are obliged to ensure consistency between European Community actions and EPC. The Single European Act confirmed already existing goals for EPC and institutionalized existing practice (Regelsberger, 1988). The most important results of the SEA were the establishment of a permanent secretariat in Brussels, and the opening up of the possibility for discussions on related issues such as security policy and industrial and technological aspects of defence. This opening of discussions on security matters included both economic and political aspects of the member countries' actions.

Institutional provisions of the EPC were not significantly altered with the SEA. The European Council remained the apex of the hierarchy. A forum for coordination of member states' foreign policy, the Council of Foreign Ministers (CFM), a body for political cooperation, the Political Committee (PoCo), and the Group of Correspondents, constituted the main units in the structure. The permanent secretariat for EPC was established, subordinate to the Presidency of EPC, and performing instrumental and administrative tasks for this. The secretariat had potential for developing into more than a purely administrative organ, for example by coordinating external activities. The fact that leadership of the EPC follows the Troika arrangements, as in other Community areas, implies that a permanent secretariat can play an important stabilizing role and preserve the needed continuity for longer periods than the Troika arrangements allow. Such an institution will obviously have much potential for influencing policy making. According to some observers, the legal codification of EPC was formally no more than a 'symbolic gesture' and its daily working did not change, except for the establishment of the EPC secretariat. The true value, however, of the legal binding is to be found in the recognition of political cooperation as a necessary step on the way to a European political union (Regelsberger, 1988).

The European Commission has always played a central role in the EPC, especially in controlling and ensuring coherence and consistency between the EC and EPC. As the complexity of the economic means and ends in the EC increased, the Commission became more important, and the 'practical distinctions between the EC and EPC competence (were) steadily eroded not through a deliberate EC ploy to augment its competence but by necessity and by the need for the Commission both to present its views and to ensure that the creeping extension of intergovernmental EPC activity (did) not emasculate EC competencies' (Lodge, 1989: 232–3). The fact that an increasing proportion of instruments used in foreign policy areas fall into the category of economic means (trade agreements, sanctions) underpins the Commission's importance as coordinator and 'invisible hand'.

The SEA enables legitimate discussions on security in a broad sense within the EPC framework. Enlarging the Community from six to twelve has increased the number of issues to be discussed under the heading of 'security'. Denmark's adherence to the Nordic Union, Britain's avowed Atlantic allegiance, as well as the historical ties between member states and their former colonies, all contributed to the complexity of EC foreign policy. This complexity on the one hand, and growing economic integration with the setting up of EMU on the other, explains the ambivalence of the member states that was expressed in the SEA.

Political union was a goal for the EC and it was believed that increased cooperation and interdependence in economic matters as well as the presence of the EU in the international community (e.g. CSCE, UN) would lead to political cohesion. However, there was an apparent lack of instruments to implement this kind of common foreign policy. EPC remained a system for intergovernmental decisions by consensus. Notably, new security commitments under the SEA did not have any direct operational implications for either the WEU or NATO.

The breach of the Berlin Wall

Four years after the SEA, at the end of 1989, the most outstanding development in European history after the Second World War took place, namely the breakdown of the communist regimes in Eastern Europe. This completely changed the scene in Western Europe's foreign policy arena. When the Soviet Union disappeared, the Western world lost a well-identified enemy, and the security policy picture became much more fragmented and complex. Suddenly the member countries of the EC had very different relations to the countries in Eastern Europe, for geographical and historical reasons. Germany in particular had special relationships with its close neighbours. This development has undoubtedly had a great impact on political cooperation in the EC. Studying the impact of such a shock as the political earthquake in Eastern Europe on political cooperation in the EC can tell us much about the rigidity and the stability of EPC. 'The events of 1989 shatter many of the common-sense assumptions that political scientists have made about the political process in Eastern Europe, whilst for international relations scholars they provide a unique opportunity to examine the utility of the main theories of system stability' (Smith S., 1994: 2).

Even though the members of the EC slowly and somewhat reluctantly developed towards the embryo of a common foreign policy, they were not at all prepared for the political earthquake of 1989, the revolution in Eastern Europe symbolized by the fall of the Berlin Wall. The event inaugurated a new era in international and inter-European relations. This event came to strengthen a perception in Europe of the need for further and deeper political cooperation. The main reason for this was the change in the security picture from a clearly bipolar structure to fragmentation and confusion regarding loyalties. Central and Eastern European countries (CEECs) felt a security vacuum and a power vacuum after the breakdown of the Warsaw Alliance and proclaimed their primary goal as a 'return to Europe' (Delrapport til Europa-utredningen). Economic poverty and severe societal problems were other arguments for developing stronger ties with Western Europe, the EC and NATO, but there is no doubt that security constituted a major part of the rationale for seeking closer relationships with and membership in Western organizations (Simic, 1993).

CEECs have huge, unresolved conflicts among ethnic groups that require solutions or will cause disasters – as we have seen in the former Yugoslavia. For Western Europe, this implied new refugees on West European territory as well as people in need of aid at home. Industry in these countries is largely outdated and polluting, a problem national borders do not stop. Insufficient control of the economy leads to growth in the black markets, which might result in drug trafficking, trade in arms and an undermining of the welfare system.

From the Central and Eastern European countries' vantage point the difficulty was, and is, finding a balance between adhering to the West and keeping Russia satisfied. Nobody would gain from Russian isolation. Countries like Poland, Czechoslovakia and Hungary had little possibility of safeguarding their security on a purely national level, with their limited resources and geopolitical location. These countries support the integration process both in the EC and within the Atlantic Alliance. 'A multilateral structure of NATO military forces and the Alliance strategy, including extended nuclear deterrence, is an important form of control over German military potential' (Handl, 1993: 228). Not only is controlling Germany important, but for CEECs it is vital to ensure a place for Russia in the European security picture.

Western European countries responded to this qualitatively new situation by realizing their need for closer political integration. An eventual extension of the EC with CEECs required a political entity that the possible newcomers could adhere to, but even without the perspective of enlargement, there were an important number of new threats demanding joint action from the EC. This demand had long been present in the economic field: already, in 1988, Jacques Delors had been asked by the European Council to put forward concrete proposals for the progressive development of an economic and monetary union, and the decision to hold an intergovernmental conference on the subject was formally taken at the December 1989 summit (Vanhoonacker, 1992).

The developments in Eastern Europe, and especially the reunification of Germany, spurred proposals that a summit be held on political union in parallel with the IGC on EMU. The decision on this point was taken in June 1990. During the first months of 1990, several reports and memoranda were launched, from many of the member countries. It is useful to sketch the content of some of these.

Positions and proposals before the conference

The European Parliament launched on 14 March 1990 a report pleading for an extension of the scope of the upcoming IGC to include issues like rationalization of EC instruments for external relations, better Treaty provisions in the social and environmental fields, more efficient decision making, and legislative power to be shared between the Commission and the European Parliament (Vanhoonacker, 1992: 216). One week later the Belgian government asked for the convening of an IGC on political union in a memorandum. Such a conference was to aim at 'strengthening the effectiveness and democratic character of our institutional mechanism, codifying the subsidiarity principle and increasing the impact of our external action' (Belgian Memorandum, 21 April 1990). But the real impetus for the process on a political union conference came with the joint Franco-German letter to the Irish Presidency. This letter proposed that the IGC treat the 'democratic deficit, more efficient institutions, unity and coherence between the actions of the Twelve in the economic, monetary and political field and, last but not least, the development of a Common Foreign and Security Policy' (Laursen, 1992: 5).

At an extraordinary summit in Dublin in late April 1990 it was not possible to reach a full agreement on convening a second conference. The UK and Portugal in particular expressed little determination for committing themselves to this task. Discussion continued at the ordinary summit in Dublin two months later, in late June 1990. During this meeting it became very clear that while some of the member countries aspired to words like 'federalism' and 'federative union', especially Italy and France, it was absolutely impossible for Britain to accept any decision which would impose a Common Foreign and Security Policy (CFSP).

It is interesting to note that the two countries that used the most extreme federalist language in this summit were the same that had been accused of 'playing below their pre-match write-up' by MEP David Martin. He classified the member countries' positions in May 1990:

> The star players in the European team at the moment are Belgium, Germany and Spain. The Atlantic Alliance of Britain, Ireland and Portugal is reluctant to take the ball. The midfield is made up of Luxembourg, Denmark, Greece and The Netherlands. But those who take the field with the most promise and consistently play below their pre-match write-up are Italy and France. If the goal of Political Union is to be reached, these two countries will have to take their courage in both hands and play a team game. (*Agence Europe*, 24 May 1990)

The Iraq conflict starting in August 1990 gave new energy to those arguing in favour of a tightening of the political union, but not enough to ensure convergent views among the member countries before the start of the IGC. France and Britain both held that national governments should 'be free to take national foreign policy initiatives' (Laursen, 1992: 9). Germany also supported the view that CFSP initiatives should first and foremost find acceptance in the European Council before it was possible to implement them through decisions in the CFM. This German move was not entirely consistent with earlier statements about a federative goal, as the European Council is a consensus decision-making institution. It is possible that Chancellor Kohl had other motives in this period (Laursen, 1992).

So far this discussion has concentrated upon the member states' position regarding the degree of supranationality in the field of foreign and security policy, and mostly their feelings toward federation or the opposite – pure intergovernmentalism. Obviously, there were nuances in this picture. A conference on political union would also treat questions on the WEU's role, the democratic deficit, the subsidiarity principle, and institutional provisions. These questions are connected. Voices positive towards a federative structure often use the argument of democratic deficit to render the European Parliament more powerful. The subsidiarity principle is important with regard to efficiency and democracy, as well as being at the core of federalism. Institutional provisions are the machinery at the centre of the process, the translation of ideas and solutions into reality.

Furthermore, issues like economic and social cohesion and a citizens' Europe were elements in the debate. These are not directly linked with foreign and security policy, but are seen to play a role in the bargaining game. Here, however, it is natural to concentrate upon propositions and proposals regarding CFSP.

Italy, who held the Presidency in autumn 1990, when the conference opened, considered it high time to 'extend the competencies of the Union to all aspects of security without limitations' (Italian Proposal, 18 September 1990). The EC was, however, not ready for this *saut qualitatif* and the Italian Presidency launched the following propositions on common security policy:

- industrial and technological cooperation in the military sphere
- the transfer to third countries of military technologies, export control and non-proliferation
- a security dimension within the Conference on Security and Cooperation in Europe (CSCE) framework
- the Union to have competence in disarmament negotiations and confidence-building measures, in particular within the CSCE framework
- participation and coordination of military initiatives, notably in the context of UN-mandated actions.

Negotiations at the 1991 IGC

The 1991 IGC on EMU and EPU was formally opened in Rome in December 1990. According to the guidelines set down by the European Council, the Conference on Political Union was to concentrate on five different headings:

1 Democratic legitimacy: with a special emphasis on the EP's role and competencies.
2 Common Foreign and Security Policy: the European Council proposed a coherent institutional structure for the EPC to be incorporated in the EC, including the right of initiative for the Commission and an opening for majority voting in the Council, as well as a gradual extension of Community competencies to the field of defence. The view that such coherence between EC and EPC was necessary had been supported already in October by a majority of the member states during a European Council meeting.
3 European citizenship: i.e. inclusion of citizens' rights in the Treaty.
4 Extension and strengthening of Community action: in fields such as social policy, the environment, economic and social cohesion, research, energy, culture and education. The principle of subsidiarity should be included in the Treaty.
5 Effectiveness and efficiency: evaluation of decision-making rules and implementation procedures, and a strengthened role for the European Council.

The debate on democratic legitimacy is closely linked with a debate on federal structures versus intergovernmental cooperation systems. Germany has always pronounced its sympathy for supranational structures, while the

French attitude has been more in the direction of a confederation. The British want to keep the EC as an institution for economic harmonization and cooperation in line with the principles for free trade. Denmark was positive towards increasing the powers of the EP in areas like environmental and social policy, fields where the Council of Ministers has had a low level of activity. But Denmark was still hesitant towards granting powers to the European Parliament in the fields of foreign and security policy.

Different member states had different issues at the top of their agenda. Spain insisted on the development of a European citizenship; Denmark opted for more Community activity in fields such as environmental and social policy; Portugal wanted closer integration in the EC at the economic and social levels. These tendencies underline the 'What's in it for us?' attitude often found in bargaining situations. The UK was clearly against most of the proposals promoting closer integration, and in favour of measures that would ensure smooth functioning of the internal market. Germany insisted on the principle of subsidiarity, alongside its joint proposals with France.

The discussion on CFSP became the dominant theme in the debates. Between the continental 'Europeanists' on the one side and the 'Atlanticists' on the other there was a significant breach, stemming from their disagreement in relation to the degree of supranationality that EC institutions were to have and the role of NATO. France, Germany and Italy proposed a merger between the WEU and the EU in 1998 when the Brussels Treaty expires. Until then, the WEU would be the centre for security and defence policy making in Western Europe, but the European Council was to lay down defining principles as to the content of the security concept.

The UK and The Netherlands were especially provoked by these suggestions. Britain would accept nothing but consensus decision making in the security field, and NATO in its view was and should continue to be the most important defence organization in Western Europe. The British therefore saw the WEU as playing a bridging role between the EC and NATO, possibly with identical representatives in the WEU and the EU.

It seemed difficult to find a solution for all parties to agree on. In April 1991 the Presidency of the European Communities presented its proposal for a Draft Treaty 'based on the dominant tendencies' expressed in the discussions. The pillar structure was introduced, where the provisions of the EEC, of the CFSP, and of cooperation in justice and home affairs constituted three different dimensions with different institutions and decision-making rules. The European Council was given the responsibility for providing political guidelines and impetus in all three pillars. There was an opening for majority voting in cases of joint actions unanimously decided upon in the European Council.

The proposal was met with opposition from many sides. The Commission, The Netherlands and Belgium disapproved of the pillar structure principle where two large and important areas were exempted from supranational procedures. Britain, Denmark and Ireland reacted negatively to majority voting in CFSP matters. The Commission presented its amendments to the Draft Treaty in May 1991, stressing the usefulness of a 'tree structure', that is a unified structure in which implicitly there lies (in accordance with what is expressed in the Treaty of Rome) a federal goal.

Negotiations on CFSP up to the Maastricht summit seem to have focused on three subjects:

1 the question of supranationality versus intergovernmentalism, including majority voting
2 WEU's role, especially in relation to NATO's role
3 the defence question.

Divisions were visible between Britain and Denmark as the proponents for purely intergovernmental solutions, and more federalist countries such as The Netherlands and Belgium; between large and small countries; and between Atlanticists who wanted NATO as the major European defence organization (Britain and Portugal), and those who promoted the WEU as the European defence alternative (France, Germany). The Community took one step further, however, in October 1991, when all member countries agreed to include an article on defence in the Treaty. But in spite of this, tension was running high in the last weeks before the Maastricht summit. Agreements were a long way off in many key areas. Several countries as well as the Commission and Jacques Delors himself threatened to veto or denounce the Treaty. 'Contrary to the negotiations on EMU, where the finance ministers more or less reached an agreement prior to the summit, the final form of the provisions on EPU would only be decided upon in Maastricht' (Laursen, 1992: 20).

The project of establishing a European political union also met public resistance. *The Economist* reported on the two unions, the economic and the political, that 'the first deserves support. The second, like most mauls, should be stopped before it causes serious injury' (2 November 1991). The EPU plan was conceived of as hammered out in a hurry, without taking the time that was necessary to find support among the general public, or among the politicians operating at a national level. The project was seen to 'derive from yesterday's federal dream and pay too little attention to tomorrow's reality' (*The Economist*, 2 November 1991). The increasing number of member states in the EC would undoubtedly complicate decision making based on unanimity, and in parallel the chances of a transfer of real legislative powers to the European Parliament would decrease. The European Community should thus remain a regime for intergovernmental cooperation where, according to these arguments, any attempt to create a credible common foreign policy, defence policy or immigration policy would fail.

Underlying the cited argument is resistance against a European federation. On the other side of the political spectrum, the federalists too, who wanted a logical, democratic, all-European structure, were sceptical about the solution that seemed feasible at the IGC. 'To federalists . . . it was obvious that this half-baked compromise would not work' (*Financial Times*, 5 May 1995). But several elements both internally in the EC and in the international environment inhibited the fulfilment of a federation in 1991. The conflict in the former Yugoslavia and the turbulence in Eastern European countries required much political attention and have been cited as factors explaining why so much political work and discussion was postponed until the Maastricht summit.

The Maastricht summit

During the two days of the Maastricht summit in December 1991, the UK manifested its position as the least integrationist country of the Twelve. With opt-outs on both EMU and social policy (or opt-ins for the Eleven, as the British prefer to call it), the Community had implicitly agreed to the development of a multi-speed EC/EU.

The Conference on Political Union resulted in a three-pillar structure of the Community, with EEC/EMU, CFSP, and cooperation in justice and home affairs as the three pillars. The European Council was given the competence to decide what areas should become areas of joint action. Once an area is placed in this group, the General Affairs Council could decide that some implementation should take place with majority voting. This was the only opening for majority voting in CFSP in the Maastricht Treaty. And even though the Commission had required the right of initiative, the central decision-making bodies within CFSP remained the CFM and the Presidency.

The following were decided as areas of joint action:

1 the CSCE process
2 the policy of disarmament and arms control in Europe, including confidence-building measures
3 nuclear non-proliferation issues
4 the economic aspects of security, in particular the control of the transfer of military technology to third countries and the control of arms exports.

Regarding the WEU, the Treaty stated that the Union shall 'assert its identity on the international scene, in particular through the implementation of a CFSP which shall include the eventual framing of a common defence policy' (Treaty on European Union 1992, Title I, Common Provisions, Article B). The WEU is asked, as an 'integral part of the development of the EU', to elaborate and implement decisions with defence implications. Hence, the WEU was clearly assigned the role of Community instrument in security and defence policy.

Furthermore, it was agreed that the development of this aspect in the EU should be an incremental process, and that the WEU should be strengthened in the context of a common defence policy within the EU which would in time lead to a common defence. It is worth noting that the development of such an EU common defence would take place within the NATO framework as NATO's 'European leg'. From this rose the problem of mismatch of the group of members in the two organizations. Some countries were members of the EU and not of the WEU (Denmark, Greece and Ireland), some were in NATO but not in the EU (Iceland, Norway and Turkey). A 'solution' was found in that WEU membership was offered to all member countries of the EU, while NATO members outside the European Union became associated members of the WEU. Denmark and Ireland, which did not wish to join the WEU as full members, received observer status.

The member states of the European Community, now the European Union, had divergent views not only on the policies to be laid down in the Treaty and those to be left outside, but also as to the actual outcome of the conference. The French said that the WEU with the Maastricht Treaty was made subordinate to the European Union, while the British said the precise wording in the text means it is not. France 'got its review of defence arrangements in 1996' (*The Economist*, 14 December 1991), while the British obtained that the future arrangements for the WEU should be compatible with NATO. This reflects that the IGC more than anything else was what its name implies, namely an intergovernmental conference, where the actors, the member states' governments, searched for solutions that could be interpreted according to need. And the need for interpretation was mainly determined by their domestic situations. The Maastricht Treaty had to be ratified by national parliaments, and in Denmark and Ireland referenda were held. As history illustrates, lack of legitimacy at home (for example, in Denmark where the people refused the original Treaty text) threatened the whole agreement.

The position and actions of France at the IGC

We have seen that the political process in the EC leading up to a Conference on Political Union in 1991 was very much a result of cooperation and joint initiatives from Germany and France. History and a traditionally strong Franco-German axis in European cooperation are not sufficient explanations of this fact. What factors, domestic, intra-EC and international, can help in explaining the development?

The impetus for the Conference on Political Union was the development in Eastern Europe. The changing security situation increased the need for greater political cooperation, notably in the field of foreign and security policy. But the more specific motivations were rather different for France and Germany. President Mitterrand stated in his New Year's speech on 31 December 1989 that in his view Europe should develop towards a confederation of all European states (Martial, 1992: 115). De Gaulle's ancient idea of a Europe stretching from the Atlantic to the Urals can be seen lurking in the background of Mitterrand's statement.

At the time, the French saw the EC as being linked to the Cold War, i.e. as a system of powers balancing each other on Europe's territory. Following this logic the breakdown of the communist systems rendered the EC rather obsolete. For France it became of utmost importance to strengthen its ties with Germany, to hinder Germany from expanding and becoming the dominant power of Europe.

The change in the geopolitical picture of Europe, where the political centre of gravity indicated a tendency to move from Paris towards Berlin, increased the importance of inventing a new architecture for Western Europe. This new structure would have to ensure that France remained in a central position. 'The establishment of a confederation; the preservation of sovereignty; the containment of Germany; the pillars of French foreign policy were no different from those that had been defined by de Gaulle' (Martial, 1992: 117).

Reunification of Germany in 1990 rendered the idea of a European confederation less urgent, and France changed its strategy. European cooperation was to be developed with several pillars: one in which political integration would enhance Germany's links with the EC; another with an institutionalization and broadening of the CSCE and the Council of Europe; and the last with the strengthening of the country's national defence capabilities.

Changes in the international security position were not the only factors responsible for French action at the beginning of the 1990s. President François Mitterrand had by 1990 been in office for nine years. Unemployment was high and rising. The number of immigrants to the country and persons belonging to minority groups reached high levels, resulting mainly from the French policy of *droit de lieu*, where citizenship is linked to place of birth (as opposed to *droit de sang*, where citizenship follows from ancestors' nationality). The sense of national identity was eroding. President Mitterrand's initial negative response to German reunification and the inclusion of Eastern European countries into the European Community was felt to be a burden on French diplomats already struggling to secure the image of a strong, active and determined France.

> Underlying all this is a vague fear that France is slipping into an irreversible decline; that it will soon no longer count among the world's leading powers. Maintaining France's 'rank' in the world . . . has become a national obsession . . . More than any other western nation, France has been shaken by the break-up of the old world order. (*The Economist*, 19 October 1991)

Facing this situation, President Mitterrand reached the same conclusion as Jean Monnet: the best way to ensure a strong and influential France was to promote further political integration. In April 1990 he, together with Chancellor Kohl, sent a letter to the Irish Presidency proposing a Conference on Political Union to be held in parallel with the Conference on EMU. As they expressed it, 'it is time to transform relations as a whole among the member states into a European Union' (*Agence Europe*, 20 April 1990). They also stressed the need for ensuring 'unity and coherence of the union's economic, monetary and political action'. This move can be interpreted as a French move creating closer links between economic and political activities, to prevent Germany's strong economy and the Bundesbank from driving the economic integration process on their terms alone.

A good example of how important the temperature of the Franco-German relationship was for the process of political integration in the EC is the freezing of the process in 1990, when Helmut Kohl went into negotiations directly with President Gorbachev on German membership in NATO. France did not appreciate this move and put its foot down with respect to further activity. 'The French assumed that the way to guard *la gloire* was through Europe. Now they fear that the biggest role in Europe, and the greater part of the glory, will belong instead to Germany' (*The Economist*, 19 October 1991). France now had three possible strategies for her foreign policy:

1 isolation, which would mean a return to balance of power politics
2 broadening the scope of other institutions, such as the CSCE, in order to keep the security issue outside the EC
3 intensifying the efforts towards building a European political union (Martial, 1992: 119).

Keeping the security question outside the EC framework was not feasible. Such a solution would have required an all-embracing structure resembling a European confederation, which clearly was out of the question owing, among other things, to the many problems in Eastern Europe. Even with a very narrow security concept the idea seemed impossible to implement, not only because of Eastern Europe, but also because of the relationship with the US.

French foreign policy, then, was to work for a political union in order to contain Germany from becoming the dominant power, and at the same time to improve strategic nuclear capabilities and capacities. This meant that France prepared for the worst, on its own terms. The two approaches seem contradictory and can be interpreted as a sign of France's scepticism towards how serious Germany was in promoting political integration. It is also another example of how difficult it is for an independent country to give up its last stronghold of military strength.

If formal power were to remain in the states in the short term, both France and Germany agreed that a common security identity should be developed within the framework of a political union. The WEU was envisaged as taking on the role of central institution for implementing decisions with defence implications, and with time the WEU should be fully integrated in the EU. The relationship with NATO constituted a major problem in the negotiations. France's relations with the US have always been less warm than the British bonds across the Atlantic, and so it was natural that

France advocated the development of a security identity within the EC/EU. Given France's firm belief in keeping and securing national sovereignty, it can also be easily understood why it outlined that this process should take place gradually.

The French goal of establishing a European security identity was not fulfilled in Maastricht. However, France ensured her position as an important European power, and by accepting statements about military integration in the EU system, which Germany wanted, she obtained from Germany, in return, agreement to the French idea of developing the WEU as 'an integral part of the European Union'. The alliance with Germany made them a forceful couple.

Germany and German unification

'Are you afraid of Germany? This is not the way discussion about the European Community's future usually begins in polite society. And yet it is the (too often hidden) question that lies behind the current push for a more federal Europe' (*The Economist*, 12 October 1991). Strengthening German ties with Western Europe has been one of the fundamental aims of the EC ever since the establishment of the European Coal and Steel Community (ECSC) in 1952, on both the French and the German side. A unified Germany reopens the ancient debate on strategic security in Central Europe, and the country's geographical position easily makes it a threat to the European balance of power. Its economic strength is above question and it is vital for Western countries, especially France, that this power is not converted into military strength. Germany also has an interest in keeping a low profile in order not to provoke its friends in the EC. The EPC has been a useful vehicle for Germany as a forum for concerting its foreign policy with the other member states. The scepticism towards Germany was overcome when its foreign policy aims were presented as (and have actually been) in agreement with other Western European countries, which have played the role of 'guarantors' for Germany. Without political cooperation in a Western European framework, Germany would have met severe constraints in its relations with other states, such as the USA and the Arab world (Pijpers, 1991: 25–7).

Germany saw in 1990 the fulfilment of one of her long-standing priorities in foreign politics: the reunification with Eastern Germany. The elements of German foreign policy remained remarkably constant in the postwar period: security, reunification, political rehabilitation, and economic reconstruction in the context of Western Europe and the Atlantic Alliance (Van Wijnbergen, 1992: 49). Foreign and security policy had a very different standing in Germany compared with the other Western European countries, owing to the Second World War. Resistance from the Western world regarding German security policy led to strong restrictions on her foreign policy means, and opinion within Germany, both in political elites and among the general public, created a real need to keep a low profile in order not to create unnecessary doubts about the state's intentions. In the process of political recovery, a strong integration with Western Europe was considered indispensable, even if this meant curtailing the country's freedom of action. The Federal Republic had to 'rely on a multilateral framework to express its foreign policies. The process of European integration provided the German government with the framework it was searching for' (1992: 50).

The EC was not the only Western organization in which Germany participated. Membership in NATO created a strong basis for German security policy, a situation which determined the relation between the country's security policy and its foreign policy. While foreign policy was expressed primarily in accordance with French views, and to a large extent was clarified with France, it did not always correlate with American standpoints. France hesitated to accept Germany as an equal partner in the Atlantic Alliance.

Western Germany wanted reunification with Eastern Germany, and had to relate to the superpower of the Eastern bloc, the Soviet Union. The USSR was obviously not very enthusiastic about the Federal Republic's strong integration into Western Europe. This German dilemma between its commitment to the West and the strong historical bonds with the East remained unsolved throughout the postwar period.

Security policy was more problematic in Germany than in many other EC member states, because of the conflict between what the country really wanted to achieve and the limited means it had at its disposal. With the reunification emerged old fears of the superpower Germany, fears that were addressed within the EC framework. But there existed another aspect that further complicated the discussion on security in Germany and Western Europe, namely the country's geographical position. The German question of today is not simply what to do to ensure that Germany does not become a dominant military power; it is more pressing to find solutions to the new security threats emerging in the East. European security in the future will be threatened by conflicts among ethnic groups and growing nationalism in the East, rather than by 'traditional' East–West conflict (Simic, 1993). Today's institutions – NATO, the EC/EU, the CSCE, the WEU – are not adapted to solve these kinds of conflict. Germany's physical proximity to these areas increases the necessity of solving these problems.

The reunification of Germany in October 1990 changed the relative power structure in Western Europe. Ever since 1945 Germany had depended upon international relations and international structures to express her preferences in foreign policy. As long as the country remained divided by the Iron Curtain the centre of gravity of Europe was located to the west of Germany, which created a 'one-sided dependence' politically speaking. The reunification changed this situation in that, together with the general opening of Eastern Europe, it moved the geographical and political centre of European affairs. 'People said Paris is no longer the centre of

Europe but Berlin is' (Martial, 1992: 115). The geographical centre of a Europe stretching from the Urals to the Atlantic became relevant and Germany strengthened her position as a central European power. It was therefore of utmost importance to Germany to keep positive relations in three directions simultaneously: towards France, towards NATO, and towards the newly liberated Eastern European countries.

The Franco-German axis remained vital to European cooperation, as the joint proposals in 1990 and 1991 confirmed. Ever since the time of Chancellor Adenauer (1949–63) a positive attitude in France has been regarded as vital to German political recovery, while France has deemed it necessary to have Germany contained in the Western bloc. 'It is hard to imagine that an initiative within the EC will survive without the support of these two major actors' (Van Wijnbergen, 1992: 51). This is not to say that France and Germany have always been of the same opinion. De Gaulle was far less integrationist than the Germans, and more hostile to enlargement (as an example, British membership of the EC was vetoed by de Gaulle from 1963 until his death in 1969). However, there has always been an understanding that Germany was the economic giant within the Western European framework, while France had the role as the political weight ensuring sincerity and credibility *vis-à-vis* third countries. In a situation where political and social stability was of greater value and maybe even more indispensable than pure economic resources, Germany had strong interests in underlining her willingness to 'stay put', firmly anchored within the European Community.

During the intergovernmental Conference on Political Union, Germany and France dominated the scene with their joint propositions. This might have puzzled some observers, especially since it showed that Germany was willing to go back on some of its federal ideas which it had defended for so long. It is interesting to note that not only was Germany willing to accept an intergovernmental solution in the field of Common Foreign and Security Policy, but she would do this without going back on issues that would weaken the chances of governing regarding currency. Even though Chancellor Kohl threatened to use his veto power on the EMU if he did not get the support needed for a common defence, there was a willingness in Germany to 'offer up chunks of the sovereignty it has just regained through unification' (*The Economist*, 12 October 1991).

The Franco-German joint proposals put forward a more prominent role for the European Council, including giving more power to an institution for intergovernmental cooperation, another sign that Germany had loosened her requirements of establishing a European federation immediately. However, at the time, Helmut Kohl seemed to have other priorities besides fulfilling all the criteria for the EU to become a real federation. 'The prospect of American troop withdrawal from Western Europe, and consequently the increasing importance for France's *force de frappe*, made Germany's priority the obtaining of a French commitment to common defence' (Van Wijnbergen, 1992: 57–8).

In October 1991 came the last Franco-German joint proposal including Draft Treaty Articles based on earlier proposals, where it was agreed to strengthen the Franco-German brigade as a first step towards a European army. Germany, however, did not want this proposal to disturb its relationship with the Atlantic Alliance, and Chancellor Kohl could be heard watering down the idea in the Bundestag and at the NATO summit in Rome in November 1991.

The German role in NATO deserves a brief comment. There was a growing discrepancy between the role that Germany played in NATO, and the country's economic resources. The USA especially saw this as unsatisfactory and noted that Germany should undertake a larger part of the responsibilities in building a European defence. In order to achieve this, one would have to overcome both French and British fears, and also fears in Germany itself. Chancellor Kohl 'expressed his preference for the eventual representation of the EC in the Security Council' (1992: 53) and thereby once again stressed that Germany had its place in an integrated Europe.

As a logical consequence of this view, Germany wished to expand the role of the EC in foreign and security policy matters, although without letting go of the US presence. Political integration in Western Europe became a core matter for Germany. Other features that would enhance political integration were increased powers to the European Parliament, improving the democratic deficit, and extending the Community security policy to areas like immigration and asylum policy. The principle of subsidiarity was to ensure increased democracy and efficiency.

During the SEA negotiations the federal government discussed the extent of the Länders' authority to the EC, without the Länders' direct involvement in the debate. This was taken very negatively by the Länder which threatened not to ratify the SEA in the Bundesrat. The key word was 'subsidiarity', and it explains why the German government insisted on including this principle in the Maastricht Treaty. Without it, the domestic situation would have become exceedingly difficult.

As institutional provisions, Germany wanted a strengthened European Parliament, including involvement in appointing the Commission President, ensuring that the Commission got non-exclusive right of initiative in CFSP matters, extending majority voting, and the principle of subsidiarity. These provisions were considered so important to Germany that Chancellor Kohl threatened not to sign the Treaty on EMU unless they were accepted.

In the history of the development of the EC, Germany has a positive record. Chancellor Kohl has been characterized a 'true believer' (*The Independent*, 28 June 1991) who will continue to ensure a positive German attitude towards European integration. However, the domestic situation creates constraints on his space of action. 'The opposition of the Länder, the SPD in the Bundesrat, and more particularly the Bundesbank has brought a growing awareness of the costs of European integration and Germany's role in the process as paymaster' (Van Wijnbergen, 1992: 61).

Britain's minimalistic approach

The Economist, under the heading 'Sprechen sie Maastricht', defines 'unanimity' as the official EC term for British veto (14 December 1991). This 'definition' is obviously less than exhaustive, but it does contain a grain of truth that calls for a smile.

Britain has always been sceptical about the project of the European Communities. It did not join the EC from the beginning, but rather established the European Free Trade Association (EFTA). It was not until 1961 that Britain applied for membership in the EC. Owing to resistance by de Gaulle, Britain became a member only in 1973.

Like Germany, Britain had strong foreign policy ties to be maintained in three directions. Like Germany, it wanted to remain close to the USA, which for Britain has constituted the ultimate element in the country's security policy in the postwar period. Fear of American isolation drove Britain to develop links that could secure an American presence in Western Europe. Germany's second foreign policy stakeholder was France, while for the UK it was all of Western Europe that needed attention. But unlike in Germany, Eastern Europe was not an issue in the UK. The Commonwealth, however, has always constituted an important actor in British foreign policy.

The Commonwealth is an association of former British possessions, like the colonies and crown colonies. Britain has the leading role among these countries. Since 1945, British power has drastically declined. The bipolar power structure, decolonization and decreased economic strength have also changed the scene for British foreign and security policy. It seems as though the major difficulty for the British is not to secure their military independence, but to realize their new situation in which they are relatively less important than some decades ago. In such a situation, symbol politics gain relevance.

The UK has a constitutional principle of parliamentary sovereignty. This might explain why almost any transfer of power from Westminster is perceived as a loss of national power and hence must be hindered. The country, however, and especially the Conservative government, was strongly in favour of a free market economy, and supported and even engaged in the construction and completion of the internal market.

Before the Conference on Political Union, Margaret Thatcher had announced that 'the United Kingdom will never accept a Political Union which imposes a joint foreign and security policy. If a conference on Political Union is held, the United Kingdom will attend, although it will not be of any use' (*Agence Europe*, 25 and 26 June 1990). The British government never really went back on this strategy, although in the end it accepted a Common Foreign and Security Policy.

European integration was a sensitive matter in Britain's domestic politics. Although many were sceptical about European integration there was a growing fear that Britain might become isolated if it did not join the process.

The attempt to create a viable alternative to the EC did not succeed and this lack of good alternatives resulted in the attitude of 'constructive critical approach' (Wester, 1992: 193). The British Labour Party was much more positive to Europe than the Conservatives, a fact credited to the presence and work of Jacques Delors. Labour was in favour of extended majority voting, and of giving more power to the European Parliament which they thought would 'fill a gap that Westminster could not fill' (Wester, 1992: 194), but regarding a CFSP they were in line with the Conservative government.

During the IGC in 1991 Britain strongly opposed proposals that would decrease national sovereignty and argued for the principle of subsidiarity which they saw as a protection against centralization in Brussels. Although both subsidiarity and the principle of vertical division of powers are central features of federalism, Britain strongly opposed a federal Europe. The word 'federal' was removed from the Treaty text because of British opposition.

In line with this view, the British opted for continued legislative power in the Council of Ministers. Their solution to the problem of democratic deficit was to let the EC remain an intergovernmental institution where each government is responsible to its own, democratically elected parliament. The European Parliament, however, should have extended power and a strengthened role in one particular area, namely in monitoring the Commission which is a non-elected institution. Of primary importance was controlling the Community's expenditure. Thatcher had in the 1980s worked hard to 'get her money back', as she saw British money being poured into an inefficient Southern European agriculture. Monitoring expenditures is of special importance to the British as they feel they pay more to the Community than the Community returns to them.

Britain's position regarding a Common Foreign and Security Policy was in line with her foreign policy objectives. The American presence in Europe was indispensable, and British sovereignty was to be protected by all means. By and large, this leads to a negative attitude towards CFSP: they would rather have a development within the framework of EPC. Proposals included reinforcing the EPC secretariat, improving the coordination between the Political Committee (PoCo) and the Committee of Permanent Representatives (COREPER), and increasing the use of working groups in order to lighten the workload of the PoCo. The European Parliament was not to have any formal power. The British government was strongly in favour of the pillar structure, which they regarded as a clear distinction drawn between areas where the EC has supranational competencies, and CFSP and justice and home affairs (Wester, 1992: 196–8). They had to accept the nomenclature of France and Germany who insisted on the term CFSP, but, owing to British insistence, 'even once (the member states) have agreed on a common policy, countries will be allowed to act on their own "in case of imperative need"' (*The Economist*, 14 December 1991).

There is little doubt that Britain was the least integrationist country at the summit in Maastricht, and Prime Minister Major had stated before going there that the other member states could not rely on Britain's fear of failure in order to push things through. The UK originally said no to a single currency, no to a common social policy, and no to a supranational security policy. Diplomatic and bargaining 'creative solutions' resulted in Britain opting out of the single currency, and the other eleven 'opting in' for social policy without Britain, and a CFSP where consensus decision making in the Council of Ministers is the rule. When the British adopted a somewhat softer attitude towards CFSP during the IGC, this must be attributed to American signals that they saw it as favourable if Western Europe took more of the economic and political responsibility for its own defence.

The UK did not play a leading role in shaping Europe's future at the 1991 IGC. Its minimalist approach to European integration is clearly a brake to the development of relations between the other eleven, which for example in social policy have been seen to make substantial progress without the EU interfering. British opt-outs in 1991 laid the ground for a resurrection of the old debate over a multi-speed Europe, a situation that might isolate the British. Two problems are therefore decisive for the UK's relations with the EC. The first is the possibility of being isolated; the second is the dilemma between American/Atlantic and Western European allegiance.

Concluding remarks

I started out by questioning whether any significant integration had taken place in matters of high politics between 1985 and 1991 in the European Community, and I have shown an increase in the interdependence between the EC member states. In 1985 European Political Cooperation achieved a Treaty basis through the Single European Act, but the Treaty text reflected the pragmatic views of the member states. Decision making in the EPC field remained purely intergovernmental: in the Treaty, the member states were referred to as 'High Contracting Parties', and the European Council remained the responsible institution. Signs of forthcoming integration include an opening of discussions on both the economic and the political aspects of security, and giving the Commission the responsibility of ensuring consistency between EC and EPC matters.

The fall of the Berlin Wall altered the environment in which European foreign and security policy was shaped. The events in the former communist regimes from 1986–7 onwards, with the fall of the old regimes, is undoubtedly the single factor that had the most forceful impact on the EC security situation. Germany was naturally the new centre around which a large part of the discussion evolved: the country had special relations to preserve with France, the former communist countries of Eastern Europe, especially the DRG, and the USA with the Atlantic Alliance. The security policy of Western countries was to a large extent based on and shaped by the Cold War and the bipolar structure. France had seen German commitment to the EC as vital for security reasons, and UK security policy was based on a strong US presence in Europe. This was the case also for many of the smaller countries. With the opening of Eastern Europe and the prospect of momentous future enlargements of the EC, the pressure to secure the existing stability and prosperity within the Community increased.

The lessons of the 1991 negotiations indicate that it will be difficult to agree on new institutional structures. Already in Maastricht the tendency was clear: the member states fought for institutional models that they were familiar with from their own domestic situation. France proposed a European-level Senate, Germany was positive to a federal structure, and the UK was afraid to lose its constitutional parliamentary sovereignty. It is interesting to note that even a change in government in Britain has not altered this situation, as was evident at the 1997 Amsterdam summit.

4 The Common Foreign and Security Policy from Maastricht to Amsterdam

Arnhild and David Spence

Looking back at the Maastricht Treaty negotiations, former British Foreign Secretary, Lord Howe, has reflected ruefully that

> Almost five years later, things look rather different. The Qualified Majority Voting provisions have never been used. Relatively few joint actions have been undertaken. The CFSP budget is bogged down in controversy, immobilised between an unwillingness of individual countries to fund it, and a reluctance to let the European Union fund it for fear of the power which that might give to the European Parliament. One is reminded of Charles Peguy's comment: 'Everything begins in mysticism and ends in politics.' We have certainly been brought down to earth. (Howe, 1996)

His view echoes the thoughts of many soon after the entry into force, on 1 November 1993, of the Treaty on European Union. European Political Cooperation (EPC) had been transformed into the Common Foreign and Security Policy (CFSP) of the European Union. But, already within six months of its implementation, Commissioner van den Broek (1994) was claiming that 'while the Treaty is clear on goals, it has rather less to say, and then only tentatively, on how to achieve them ... nor is there any clear direction given on achieving a balance between external policy, as defined under the second pillar, and the other so-called traditional Community instruments.'

Van den Broek's assertion formed part of the concerted lobbying by the European Commission, aimed at upgrading CFSP, leading first to its report to the Reflection Group (European Commission, 1995a) established to draw up the guidelines for the intergovernmental conference (IGC) of 1996 and subsequently to its opinion to the IGC itself (European Commission, 1996a). Yet, it is important to stress that the Commission was not a lone critic in the wilderness. The Maastricht negotiators had included articles in the Treaty bearing witness to its own shortcomings, thereby illustrating that member states themselves were clearly aware of the deficiencies of the Treaty, if unable to resolve them.[1] They had actively to seek convergence between their national interests if their stated objective of a Common Foreign and Security Policy was to be realized in areas where European presence matters.[2] In practice they hardly did. Some observers even argue that the transformation of individual national interests into a genuine European foreign policy became even more unlikely as a consequence of the

Cold War's end: 'There are ... a number of cross-cutting elements which suggest that in the future the member states are likely to be seriously divided on the issue of foreign policy priorities now that the discipline imposed by the Cold War has evaporated' (Allen, 1996: 301).

Judging by the outcome of the 1996–7 IGC, member states continue to find solutions hard to reach. Just as the Maastricht Treaty was replete with 'deliberate ambiguities', the Amsterdam Treaty reflects a continuing theme of the Maastricht Treaty negotiations – 'distracted political engagement and inattention to detail as well as continuing symbolic and substantive differences'(Forster and Wallace, 1996: 426). This chapter reviews the implications of a transformation deemed already at the outset to be insufficient by academic and media pundits and by the European Commission. Its purpose is to assess the relative success and failure of the Maastricht arrangements. The chapter does not only concentrate on the legal provisions and the operational illogicalities of the Treaty. It juxtaposes fact and theory in order to test the assumptions and conclusions of the Treaty's detractors. In doing so, it concentrates specifically on one of the major innovations of the Maastricht Treaty, the 'joint action', reviewing three operations in order to test the utility of this new tool.

Internal contradictions of the CFSP: a case of built-in obsolescence?

The previous chapter underlined how, after the Single European Act, EPC was formally considered the coordinating mechanism for the foreign policy interests of EC member states. Nevertheless, the fact that EPC was not adequate to meet the challenges facing Western Europe in the 1990s was of no contention. The creation of the Common Foreign and Security Policy was thus meant to represent a qualitative leap forward by which the member states would attempt to position the European Union adequately to meet the challenges and grasp the opportunities posed by the end of the Cold War. These challenges included the disappearance of the East–West divide in Europe which opened new prospects for EU enlargement.

The European Union, formerly a Western European integration project, was fast becoming the focal point for pan-European unification. The reduced role of the superpowers on the European continent opened the opportunity for the EU to exercise a central role in a new European security order. The European response to the Gulf conflict of 1990–1 had illustrated that the Community needed, yet lacked, a common view of its security interests. The crisis in Yugoslavia, and the reluctance of the US government initially to take the lead in its management, represented a window of opportunity for the EU to demonstrate its 'actor capability'[3] on the international stage. The essential aim was to move beyond the most frequent policy output of EPC, namely political declarations: the 'declaratory diplomacy' given by one participant in the process the unflattering label of 'procedure as a substitute for substance' (Nuttall, 1992) and described by one foreign minister as 'immobilised decision-making underpinning lack of will' (Howe, 1996). Public opinion supported a genuine foreign policy based on a wider range of policy instruments and more sophisticated decision-making rules and the outside world expected Europe to speak with one voice. Yet, while this may have been the expectation of public and pundits alike, as Hill (1993) has argued, there was a 'capability–expectation gap'.

The Maastricht Treaty was a fudge. As one of the early treatises on the Treaty stressed: 'The intergovernmental structures of the CFSP and cooperation on justice and home affairs will produce too many disappointments. Classic intergovernmentalism is a prescription for suboptimal decisions' (Laursen and Vanhoonacker, 1992). The European Union which emerged from the IGC of 1991–2 consisted of three separate pillars: the European Community, the Common Foreign and Security Policy, and cooperation in the field of justice and home affairs. The significance of the pillar structure for CFSP was that policy making was to be largely shielded from the institutional mechanisms and traditions of the European Community (first pillar). This meant exclusion of involvement of the European Parliament, the European Court of Justice and, in particular, the increasingly transparent decision-making processes of the EC with their evolution in most EC policy areas to qualified majority voting and the indispensable involvement of the European Commission. With CFSP defined as a separate pillar of the Union, cooperation was to operate on intergovernmental lines. Decisions were now to be taken by the Council of Ministers, as Article C of the Maastricht Treaty put it, in 'a single institutional framework', rather than the 'Foreign Ministers of the Member States meeting in the framework of the Council', as it had hitherto been termed. But the formal change was replete with implications. These were hardly recognized and certainly not formally admitted at the outset. They seem to have escaped those responsible for the Treaty, even if their legal advisers were aware of the realities (Eaton, 1994). The paradox was that there was a fundamental ambiguity; a single institutional framework was an objective countermanded by the pillar structure in theory and, as later became clear, by policy making in practice.

The principle of consistency in an inconsistent world

The Treaty ascribed different roles to the institutions in each of the three pillars, but this created problems of consistency. External representation of the Union is, for example, a function shared by the Presidency and the Commission, with different bureaucracies involved. While the Commission is responsible for external representation in areas falling within the competence of the EC, the Presidency represents the Union in CFSP. In terms of the assertion of the Union's identity, the shared responsibility for external representation was not helpful. Few outside the Union (or inside it for that matter) comprehend the difference in institutional focus between trade policy and foreign policy *per se*. Significantly, the fact that the Commission's role remained untouched as external representative of the Union in areas of Community competence posed anew the issue of the demarcation line between foreign policy in terms of trade and economic affairs and the potentially 'high political' policies implied by the CFSP (Smith, 1997). What matters to public opinion is clearly the political success of an EU external policy, not whether it is defined as a joint action under CFSP or a measure under external trade policy. Yet, the outside world continued to be obliged to relate to two different institutional bodies, the Commission and the Presidency, with the composition of the Presidency and the Troika changing every six months and most member states lacking embassies in most countries of the world and thus passing responsibility for representation in those countries to other member states.

It was the Presidency's role to represent the Union in matters of CFSP, whether in international organizations, international conferences or bilateral relations outside the Union, though the task of keeping the European Parliament informed fell to both the Presidency and the Commission (Article J.7). The Commission traditionally reported to the External Relations Committee in the European Parliament. It now began to appear before the Foreign Affairs Committee and it was not long before calls were heard for the creation of a European Foreign Service. The inconsistency of the Treaty had thus begun to create pressures for spillover. The integrationists metaphorically rubbed their hands, but the lesson they wished to draw was certainly not obvious to the intergovernmentalists.

One of the objectives of the pillar structure was to guard CFSP from the jurisdiction of the European Court, yet Article M of the Maastricht Treaty provides that nothing in the Treaty on European Union should affect the Treaties establishing the European Communities. Thus, action in the field of CFSP or justice and home affairs (Titles V and VI of the Treaty) may not impede the operation of the EC, and the Court of Justice would be entitled to rule on whether such action did represent an impediment. Likewise, the Commission would be entitled, consequent on its role as guardian of the Treaties (Usher, 1997), to call upon the Court to rule in such cases. Since the Treaty also further provides that the Council should 'ensure the unity, consistency and effectiveness of action by the Union', there is incontestably a drift into the Community institutional framework, itself further reinforced by the use of Community instruments in joint actions under CFSP, which is further elaborated below. A key element in the evolving jigsaw of the CFSP, the consistency of EU action, was thus fraught with ambiguity.

Under these conditions the political significance of any joint action or other foreign policy initiative of the EU has often been lost in procedural and structural confusion. This affected the decision-making process as such and thereby the external image of the Union. Official intergovernmental debate often concentrated on issues of irrelevance and incomprehensibility to domestic support for the policy substance. Thus, while the Treaty seemed clear, the implications in practice were not.

One clear element of progress in the Treaty was the creation for the Commission of a right of initiative in CFSP, thus formally recognizing the important role of the Commission in policy formation. This built on its sole right of initiative in first pillar matters, where hitherto the only practical instruments of EU policy were to be found, namely the use of trade policy as a foreign policy tool. Curiously, however, the Commission was to prove reluctant formally to use its new right. Holland (1997: 6) argues that member states took fright at its prominence in the initial policy making in the joint action on South Africa. This might have led the Commission to prudence. Counterbalancing the Commission's expanded role, the Treaty also added some new constraints on member states. They were to inform their EU partners of developments in international organizations, where the others might not be represented. This also applied in the specific case of the UN Security Council, where periodic membership might be involved. France and the UK, the two permanent members, were enjoined to ensure the defence of the positions and interests of the Union (Article J.5(4)).

A further major inconsistency lay in the lack of serious financial provision for the operation of CFSP (Monar, 1997). Paradoxically, the Maastricht Treaty stipulated that operational expenditure may be charged to the Community budget (Article J.11), thus automatically negating the exclusively intergovernmental nature of CFSP and triggering involvement of the Commission, as well as the Council of Ministers and the European Parliament as the 'budgetary authority'. Since most financial transfers from the Community to third countries fall within the category of 'non-obligatory expenditure', where the Parliament has the last word in the budgetary procedure, it is difficult to imagine how the architects of the Treaty proposed to keep the Community institutions from influencing decision making in the second pillar. Indeed, no sooner had the policy come into force then member states began to argue for the use of Community funds to finance a joint action, thus triggering Community decision-making mechanisms. As the Commission put it: 'The hybrid structure of the Treaty, with decisions under one pillar requiring funding under another, has introduced an additional source of conflict. The complexity of the present system gives rise to procedural debates instead of debates of substance' (European Commission, 1995a: 64).

Shaping the tools of the CFSP

One of the central issues debated in the 1990–1 Conference on Political Union was whether to treat all foreign policy matters on the same footing or to give priority to issues where significant common interests were at stake. In the latter case, deeper cooperation (a CFSP proper) would be appropriate, while the handling of other issues would continue to resemble the EPC model practised under the Single European Act. 'Joint action' was the key term for upgrading the areas where member states have important common interests. 'Common positions' were defined as systematic cooperation between member states on any matter of general interest (Article J.2). The distinction was intended to facilitate the process of gradual transition from EPC to CFSP, with its higher commitment to common policies. It seemed simple, yet it became a much debated issue. As the Commission pointed out: 'This distinction has not been followed in practice. The result is confusion about the role of the different instruments. "Positions" can extend to cover both fundamental orientations and concrete actions. "Actions" can be limited to *ad hoc* or administrative measures' (European Commission, 1995a: 64).

The next paradox in the new practical arrangements was the provision for economic sanctions on third parties to come under the auspices of CFSP. Under EPC there had already been several instances of ministers taking decisions which required subsequent EC legislation after a proposal from the Commission to act. The question had been whether it was right and proper for the Commission to be *instructed* by the Council to make specific proposals within the framework of the EC Treaty. In practice, action had been taken, for example, against Iraq after the invasion of Kuwait, Argentina in the Falklands–Malvinas issue and, most recently, Serbia. In these cases recourse had been made to Article 224EC (crisis measures to limit the effects of international situations on the internal market) and a mixture of EPC and Article 113EC (common commercial policy). The Maastricht Treaty Article 228a established the need for a common position within the framework of CFSP to be adopted by unanimity and a Community decision (normally a regulation) to be adopted by qualified majority. Alarmingly, there seemed to the Commission's lawyers to be an element of Council instruction to the Commission involved. This would have implications for the Commission's sole right of initiative in the field of trade policy.

Several common positions on economic sanctions have been adopted since the entry into force of the Maastricht Treaty. The majority were aimed at the former republic of Yugoslavia, but other countries such as Sudan and Haiti have been subject to economic sanctions adopted in the form of common positions. The Commission was constrained on several occasions to point out to member states that economic sanctions may well need to be imposed for foreign policy reasons, but this cannot legally entitle the Council to *instruct* the Commission to make proposals in this area. The implications for the independence of Community law led the Council to produce a *mode d'emploi* in March 1995, thus saving the honour of EC law and the institutions involved (Willaert and Marqués-Ruiz, 1995: 42).

Thus, in practice it has proved hard to differentiate between joint actions and common positions, and the difficulty has been compounded by the lines of demarcation drawn between the first and second pillars. In the period of *élan* following the entry into force of the Maastricht Treaty the Council adopted joint actions on a wide range of issues, of which the former Yugoslavia formed a large part (seven decisions, six of which concerned the convoying of humanitarian aid in Bosnia–Herzegovina). Other joint actions pertained to South Africa, the Stability Pact, the Middle East peace process, non-proliferation of nuclear weapons, Russian parliamentary elections and dual-use goods. Because the former Yugoslavia was then and has since been such a prominent preoccupation of the CFSP, the joint action on convoying humanitarian aid to Bosnia–Herzegovina is analysed in some detail later in this chapter. The case illustrates most of the procedural themes outlined above.

Decision-making rules

Joint actions were to involve complicated decision-making procedures. According to one observer, the provisions on majority voting were so hedged about with conditions that it was unlikely that a vote would ever be taken (Nuttall, 1997). The Treaty prescribed that the European Council was to set guidelines for the Council, whereupon the Council was to decide unanimously whether an issue should be the subject of a joint action and, importantly (so it was believed), whether subsequent decisions within the area might, as Article J.3(2) foresaw, be taken by qualified majority. Yet, the European Council admitted its inability to shape an effective decision-making framework when it agreed a special Declaration (no. 27) to the Treaty on voting in the field of CFSP, whereby 'with regard to decisions requiring unanimity, Member States will, to the extent possible, avoid preventing a unanimous decision where a qualified majority exists in favour of that decision'. This principle of so-called 'constructive abstention' has continued on into the Amsterdam Treaty, as Gourlay and Remacle underline in Chapter 5. In practice, hitherto there has been no visible effect on CFSP decision making. On the contrary, the universal application of the unanimity rule is still a major impediment to the development of CFSP and a reason for member states either to act unilaterally or to seek international coalition partners outside the EU.

The security aspect of CFSP

The Single European Act had introduced security policy as a part of political cooperation, specifically concentrating 'on matters of technological and industrial conditions necessary for their security' (Article 6b), though announcing readiness to 'coordinate positions more closely on the political and economic aspects of security' (Article 6a). In the Maastricht Treaty, by contrast, the member states pronounced their intention to include all questions of security, 'including the eventual framing of a

common defence policy which might in time lead to a common defence'
(Article J.4.1). For this purpose the Western European Union (WEU) was
now deemed to be 'an integral part of the development of the Union' and
was requested in the Treaty to 'elaborate and implement decisions and
actions of the Union which have defence implications' (Article J.4.2). In
this way the Maastricht Treaty distinguishes between the security of the
member states, which falls within the Union framework, and their defence,
which is formally maintained by WEU/NATO. This arrangement was particularly convenient for those of the EU members who adhered to a policy
of neutrality – a not inconsiderable factor at the time, given the imminent
start of enlargement negotiations to include three more neutral states in
the EU.[4] The policy was also compatible with participation in so-called
Petersberg tasks (peacekeeping, humanitarian and rescue operations etc.)
but, intriguingly, incompatible with the mutual defence commitment contained in Article 5 of the WEU Treaty which now became the defence arm
of the EU.

The issues initially identified as possible areas of joint action in the
security field were the operation of the Organization for Security and
Cooperation in Europe (OSCE), disarmament, arms control, nuclear non-
proliferation, and economic aspects of security (control of transfer of military technology and arms export to third countries). None of these areas,
which are largely overlapping, touch upon the core areas of security, i.e. a
common defence capability, nor were they likely to contribute to the
development of a European security and defence identity (ESDI) in any
meaningful way. The areas identified only suggested that the members of
the Union would seek to develop a common approach in the field of economic aspects of security (economic sanctions, non-proliferation through
export control etc.) and in 'soft security' areas such as confidence- and
security-building measures within the multilateral framework of the OSCE.
Since a majority of EU members were already allied in NATO, and all of
them were members of the Conference on Security and Cooperation in
Europe (CSCE), they had, of course, a long-standing tradition of working
together in these areas.

Three joint actions were launched in the security field under the Maastricht Treaty. These concerned the non-proliferation Treaty, anti-person-
nel mines and the control of dual-use goods. In terms of developing the
links with WEU, the EU requested the WEU to implement one joint
action, involving it in the EU administration of Mostar with a WEU police
contingent as an integral part of the EU operation. This was, however, not
a 'defence aspect' of a joint action in real terms. The joint action on the
EU administration of Mostar is an issue to which this chapter returns
below. The case illustrates the dilemma facing member states in terms of
what 'security' was to imply and underlines how successful action requires
not only political will but operational machinery in addition to procedural
commitments.

Some interim conclusions on the nature of CFSP

The analysis so far underlines hindrances to successful policy making. First, a striking feature in the overall functioning of CFSP was the discrepancy between political decisions of intent outlined by the European Council and the actual policies pursued by the EU. Whether the fifteen governments participating in the 1996–7 IGC drew the necessary practical consequences of the lessons learned is an issue addressed by Gourlay and Remacle in Chapter 5. It is certain that while the Treaty was intended to boost the visibility of the Union, it also involved obvious paradoxes which were to prove a hindrance to the practical implementation of CFSP. If CFSP has proved a disappointment to those who hoped the European Union would now assert its identity on the international scene, one conclusion might sensibly be that one cannot simply decree political will by creating new procedures. The adoption of Treaty reform may be a necessary, but is certainly not a sufficient, condition for improved policy output.

Secondly, CFSP may not have grown beyond European Political Cooperation with a limited number of joint actions, which hardly heralded a coherent pattern of foreign policy. Yet this was not due to an insufficient level of activity. On the contrary, since the entry into force of the Maastricht Treaty, the level of activity within the EU has exploded. The number of meetings at all levels of decision making has been augmented and the amount of information and views exchanged by foreign ministries through the dedicated security telegram network, known as COREU, has increased significantly. But, despite this enhanced activity, it remains the case that the policy output of CFSP is not fundamentally different from EPC. Political declarations are still the main vehicle. Joint actions have only exceptionally taken the form of major policy initiatives.

Thirdly, inadequate external visibility has clearly been an obstacle to establishing a credible CFSP. The composition of the Presidency still changes every six months and the Presidency is not easily identifiable as a visible and continuous player on the international scene. Even if it were, the EU has not yet developed a coherent range of foreign policy interests and the Presidency and Troika inevitably operate under a strict mandate from the Council in relations with third parties. Such mandates are, of course, based on the lowest common denominator of policy. In order to represent the Union, there has to be something substantial to represent. The narrow margin of manoeuvre of the Presidency adds to the difficulty of representing the Union, particularly in crisis situations. All these factors undermine the credibility of CFSP and, at the same time, the foreign policy influence of the EU.

Finally, however, a word of caution to the sceptic is perhaps in order. Procedure may well pose as a substitute for policy in CFSP developments. Yet, the practice of collaboration between foreign ministries of Western Europe has undoubtedly forged a basis upon which a European foreign policy might see the light of day (Spence, 1998). It is no longer true that national foreign ministries decide policy in terms of a strictly defined national interest. There is a growing European reflex buttressed by countless meetings in Brussels of officials at all levels and their political masters. Indeed, the mere fact that the Brussels focus has been enhanced by the creation of a Brussels-based venue for CFSP and WEU affairs, with its concomitant fusing of first and second pillar working groups, might lead to the conclusion that the *engrenage* principle still applies, that spillover may yet be at work and that the neo-functionalists may yet prove right.

CFSP in practice

Three joint actions illustrate the wide scope of foreign policy areas engaged in by CFSP: convoying humanitarian aid to Bosnia–Herzegovina, the Stability Pact and the EU administration of Mostar. They exemplify foreign policy behaviour of an active, initiatory nature, as intended for CFSP, while illustrating EU involvement in different phases of crisis management. Each of them serves to underline different themes of the chapter so far.

Joint action on convoying of humanitarian aid to Bosnia–Herzegovina

The political decision to provide humanitarian aid to Bosnia–Herzegovina was taken by the European Council in October 1993, when the heads of government and state instructed the Council to take all necessary steps to ensure that humanitarian food aid reached its proper destination before the winter. However, in implementing this political decision, the Council encountered a number of problems of a practical and conceptual nature, mainly emanating from the pillar structure of the Maastricht Treaty. How was this joint action to be financed? How would the financial resources operate? How could the policy instruments governed by the first pillar be mobilized in support of this joint action under CFSP? Because there was no clear answer to these questions, the practical implementation of the political decision of the European Council was severely delayed. The Council spent four months discussing whether to cover the cost of the operation through the Community budget or on a shared national basis. It was finally decided to cover 50 per cent of the allocated ECU 48 million from the Community budget while 50 per cent would be shared between member states. In the meantime, the winter was over and the population no longer had an urgent need for reinforced humanitarian aid. In the end the money intended for humanitarian aid in Bosnia–Herzegovina was transferred to another operation, the administration of Mostar.

The case of humanitarian aid to Bosnia–Herzegovina illustrates the imbalance between political intentions and the considerable difficulties in efficient implementation of decisions by the EU institutions. In a crisis situation the time aspect is of course crucial. If the gap between decision and implementation becomes too large, as it clearly was in the case of humanitarian aid to Bosnia–Herzegovina, the contrast between intentions and realized policy can easily become an international embarrassment to the EU and undermine its credibility.

Joint actions rely on a swift analysis of the situation, followed by an assessment of how the situation relates to the interests or values of the EU. One of the deficiencies of the CFSP under the Maastricht Treaty was that the preparatory phase of decision-making was practically non-existent. This is largely explained by the pillar structure of the Treaty. In the first pillar, when the Commission prepares a proposal for the Council, the research into common interests takes a central place in the preparatory work. In CFSP, by contrast, there is no independent body able to act independently of the national interests of member states. In policy areas where the Commission has the legal right and obligation to defend the interests of the Union, the common interest identified would normally amount to something more than the sum of national interests. In CFSP, however, no institution has been responsible for identifying the common interest.[5]

The Commission has no national axe to grind. Yet, since it does not prepare the ground for CFSP decisions, obtaining the required unanimity of all member states is more complex than in the first pillar context. And this the more so since the Presidency of the Council may (despite the theory) represent the interests of a particular member state. There is obviously a job to be done in systematically building a convergence in substance among the national interests of the member states. This is one of the primary functions intended for the new planning and analysis centre. On the other hand, it is difficult to envisage how one could solve the problem of different national perceptions resulting from diverse historical, geographical and other idiosyncratic conditions.

There are several conclusions to be drawn from the humanitarian aid case. Some were translated into concrete proposals for reform in the framework of the 1996–7 IGC, discussed in greater detail in the following chapter. Suffice to say that unless the functional deficiencies of CFSP were properly addressed by the IGC, it is hard to imagine how CFSP could function in an enlarged European Union. However, in order to balance the impression of CFSP as deficient and malfunctioning, it is useful briefly to review two other joint actions, at least one of which was considerably more successful.

The joint action on the Stability Pact

The French initiative to create a Stability Pact for Europe was among the first areas subject to a CFSP joint action.[6] The purpose of the Stability Pact was to solve border disputes and minority problems between countries in Eastern and Central Europe, with a view to promoting regional stability. Negotiations were conducted in two regional round tables. In addition to the general objective of peaceful settlement of sensitive border issues, the round tables sought to guarantee the rights of ethnic minorities situated in the territories of neighbouring countries.

Although projection of stability on the European continent in itself was a perfectly sound justification for the initiative, the CFSP joint action on the Stability Pact was not entirely disconnected from the prospect of Eastern enlargement of the EU. The enlargement aspect might have persuaded some initially reluctant EU members, such as Germany, that the Stability Pact was a good idea.[7] For several of the countries concerned, the EU enlargement perspective certainly persuaded them to take active part in the round tables and to make a positive contribution towards the completion of the Pact. The prospect of EU membership as a reward for cooperation on the Stability Pact thus contributed to the success of this joint action.

Compared with other joint actions adopted within the framework of CFSP, the Stability Pact marked a move by the EU towards preventive action as opposed to other joint actions aimed at resolution of existing crises. The experience from the former Yugoslavia had, if anything, illustrated the shortcomings of the EU in the area of crisis management. Whereas several other CFSP joint positions and actions took the form of a reaction towards external events, the Stability Pact set out to create the conditions for peace and stability among a group of countries, at the initiative of the European Union itself. The initiative was driven by a major member state and it was uncontroversial in the sense that it did not mobilize strong divergent national interests in any of the member states. These factors were central to its success. Because it was a European initiative, not triggered by a crisis or another external event, it allowed for proper planning and implementation. The Stability Pact thus had a number of factors on its side: it was an EU initiative, managed by the EU from beginning to end;[8] cooperation by the parties was highly motivated by expectations of future EU membership; and the action did not mobilize divergent vital national interests among existing member states. Such favourable conditions have so far been rare ingredients in CFSP. An improved planning and analysis capacity at the European level, as envisaged in the Amsterdam Treaty, might contribute to creating similar, seemingly necessary, conditions in future joint actions.

The joint action on EU administration of Mostar

During the three and a half years of war in Bosnia, the city of Mostar became a central war theatre involving all three of the main ethnic groups: Serbs, Croats and Muslims. In this particular aspect of the war, the only thing these groups had in common was their territorial claim on Mostar. Having managed to keep a united front against their common enemy, the Serbs, Croats and Muslims soon started fighting each other once the Serbs had been ousted. However, they accepted an American designed compromise in March 1994, which set up a Muslim–Croat Federation. This agreement put a temporary end to the fighting in Mostar. The EU Council decided on 16 May 1994 to carry out a joint action which would support the administration of Mostar. On 23 July 1994 the EU administration of Mostar was established, with the aim of overcoming the ethnic division between Muslims and Croats through a process of technical and economic reconstruction and political and social reunification.[9]

The EU was to undertake an entirely civilian operation, limited to two years' duration, with the emphasis on reconstruction and reconciliation. The operation could best be characterized as 'peace building', a post-conflict action to identify and support structures tending to strengthen and solidify a political settlement in order to avoid a return to conflict.[10] With no means of enforcement, the EU team naturally depended on the goodwill and cooperation of the parties on the ground. The creation of a single, unified police force, composed of both parties to the conflict, was a central objective of the operation. For the first time under the Maastricht Treaty, the EU requested the WEU to assist in the implementation of a CFSP joint action when a unified police force was created with the support of 182 WEU police officers. Their job was to ensure public safety and freedom of movement between the two parts of the city to which the parties had agreed. The city had been divided under the previous leadership of the Croat republic of Herzeg–Bosna between Croats and Muslims. The EU appointed administrator, Hans Koschnick, became the head of the Mostar city municipality and directed his efforts, under the instructions of the EU Council, towards the aim of a single administration of a single, multi-ethnic city.

Among the conditions for the EU administration of Mostar was an end to military activity in the area, that the area would be demilitarized[11] and that the parties would cooperate fully with the EU in the fulfilment of its mandate.[12] Unfortunately, none of these conditions were fulfilled in practice. This made it virtually impossible for the EU team to succeed. Both Muslims and Croats came under repeated attacks from their common enemy, the Serbs, who had taken up positions in the hillside surrounding the town. Apart from destroying the infrastructure of Mostar, the Serb shelling served to destabilize the situation on the ground and to undermine the safety of civilians and EU personnel. Efforts at peace building were clearly premature in this situation of open conflict. It also became clear that the freedom of movement and a central municipal authority, which were among the objectives of the EU administration agreed to by the parties, were not supported by the local Croatian leadership. Mostar was effectively divided in two, and non-cooperation by the parties, primarily the Croats, made it impossible to grant freedom of movement. This of course represented a major obstacle to other forms of reconciliation among the parties.

The EU possessed no sanctions which could have induced more cooperative behaviour. The Croatian side gradually came actively to obstruct the EU administration. The single police force soon ran into trouble as local police refused to respect the authority of the EU administration. Cooperation with the WEU police force was not a success story either. WEU personnel were prepared to take orders from the WEU's political authorities only, not from the EU administration. The command structure had clearly not been agreed by the EU and WEU in advance of the operation. Under

the prevailing circumstances, the city of Mostar was not under EU administration in any meaningful way. The non-cooperation and obstruction of EU
efforts reached a climax in February 1996 when Croats attempted to assas-
sinate Koschnick as he was arbitrating border issues between the parties. It
resulted in Koschnick's resignation.

A key objective of the EU administration was to organize democratic
elections before the expiry of its mandate. The arrival of IFOR in January
1996 provided a security framework which made free movement possible.
This was a necessary prerequisite to the organization of the elections and
greatly assisted the EU in its task. The EU financed reconstruction process
brought more tangible results than the process of reconciliation. The EU
allocated ECU 150 million over a period of two years – a substantial contribution to the 50,000–60,000 inhabitants of Mostar. The Muslim dominated
eastern part of town was subject to a major reconstruction effort aimed at
bringing living conditions up to a level comparable with the Croat west. The
restoration of water and electricity supplies and the rebuilding of bridges
were among the most important tasks of the EU administration.

Virtually all the premises upon which the EU based its administration of
Mostar were false. The premature attempt at peace building was doomed
to failure, because peace was not established and the parties did not want
reconciliation. The joint action was thus carried out in extremely difficult
and dangerous circumstances, requiring continuous and firm political
leadership. The rotating Presidency was unable to exercise such leadership.
The EU did not have enforcement instruments, thus leaving the EU
administration virtually powerless over the local police force or other actors
on the ground. The fact that the EU became involved in Mostar therefore
arguably bears witness to a lack of analysis of the situation.[13] Huge human
and financial resources were invested in this joint action over two years, yet
the parties remain far from reconciled. The overall result of the operation,
despite considerable progress made in the area of economic and technical
reconstruction, was failure. The main mistake was to embark on a peace-
building exercise in something which amounted to a war theatre. A more
thorough prior analysis of the situation on the ground, provided by the
newly agreed planning and analysis centre, might ensure that similar misin-
terpretations are avoided in the preparation of future joint actions
(Vanhoonacker, 1997).

Conclusions

Despite the formal appearance of progress, the European Union's capacity
for effective foreign policy making after Maastricht remained extremely
limited. The EU proved unable to manage, let alone settle, the international
issues it selected for joint actions and there is little evidence to suggest that
its future performance will be more effective.

The ambiguities and contradictions of the Maastricht Treaty might suggest that inability to act is a result of procedural deficiencies alone. However, this chapter has argued that political will to act cannot be decreed by the creation of procedures as a context for action. On the other hand the existence of a procedural framework clearly helps create the reflex and thus potentially the will for policy makers to assess the European interest and the likely benefits of common action in cases of crisis. A successful CFSP would appear to be predicated on conditions of three kinds: analytical, procedural and operational.

As far as foreign policy analysis is concerned, the existence of a planning and assessment unit now seems imperative. The proposed Council unit is intended to analyse international affairs, predict crises and make policy prescriptions for EU operational involvement for use by the Council. Gourlay and Remacle discuss in Chapter 5 the ways in which the Amsterdam Treaty meets this need. As for procedures, there seems virtually unanimous agreement by observers that a condition for successful decision making is a move from unanimity to qualified majority voting. The EU's arcane decision-making procedures, in particular given the three-pillar structure, need fundamental revision if efficient and above all integrated foreign policy management is to be brought about. It may not be sufficient to reinforce Article C of the Treaty and to change the constellation of the Troika, as Gourlay and Remacle discuss. Unless the deadlock brought about by the mix of diverse objectives, procedures and instruments of the three pillars is broken, the outlook for policy is bleak. Governments were certainly less bold in their decision not to let CFSP slide into the first pillar than they were in letting part of the third pillar and the Schengen Agreement so slide. Importantly, it is again clear to most observers that a Europe of 21 member states, and still enlarging, will not be able to take effective decisions if unanimous decisions are still required.

The third condition for successful change highlighted by this chapter is a rationalization of the instruments of foreign policy. There are two issues here. The first concerns the European security and defence identity (ESDI). As long as Europe's notional capability in world affairs is not matched by military capability, with armed forces operating within an agreed transatlantic framework, the EU's ability to rise to the challenge of crisis will clearly remain low. It will remain low despite the overall encouraging developments in European security which preceded the Amsterdam Treaty signature: the signing of the NATO–Russia Founding Act, the agreement on EU and NATO enlargement, and the official approval by the US government of a ESDI. It remains to be seen whether the current process of enabling the WEU to conduct military operations within the framework of combined joint task forces (CJTFs) will add substance to the ESDI concept.

The second issue in the area of foreign policy tools is the integration of foreign economic policy and CFSP – a process under way, institutionally at least, by virtue of the fusion of Council working groups in these hitherto diverse areas. However, the problems surrounding the links between the first and second pillars, not least the issues of the financing of CFSP and the automaticity of the link between first pillar law and the political custom of the second pillar, remain unresolved. This chapter has hopefully demonstrated the need for further change if member states wish to close the capability–expectations gap.

Notes

1 Articles B, J.4(6) and N bound the member states to reconvene in 1996 'with the aim of ensuring effectiveness of the mechanisms and the institutions of the Community'.

2 The concept of EU presence in the international arena is used by several authors on CFSP to define a role for the European Union which falls short of an effective or authoritative international actor (see Allen and Smith, 1990; Hill and Wallace, 1996). For further insight into the actor concept, see Sjoestedt (1977).

3 This concept is developed by Sjoestedt (1977).

4 Austria, Finland and Sweden joined Ireland in the neutralist camp of the EU in January 1994.

5 It remains to be seen if the establishment of a planning and analysis centre within the Council secretariat, as laid down in the Amsterdam Treaty, will enhance the preparation of CFSP decisions.

6 Two joint actions concerning the conference launching the Pact were adopted on 20 December 1993 and 14 June 1994.

7 The reticence was largely due to a concern that the Pact would compete with the OSCE as a forum for settlement of such minority and border issues.

8 Until its implementation was transferred to the OSCE in 1995.

9 An excellent background study on Mostar is provided by Reichel (1996).

10 This definition, which builds on the UN Secretary-General's 'An Agenda for Peace', is included in NACC (1993).

11 The UN Protection Force (UNPROFOR) carried out a demilitarization prior to the arrival of the EU team, but the lack of follow-up and verification made this action ineffective.

12 A memorandum of understanding on the EU administration of Mostar was signed by the parties on 5 July 1994, defining the mandate for the EU and WEU involvement.

13 Interview with Commission officials.

5 The 1996 IGC: The Actors and their Interaction

Catriona Gourlay and Eric Remacle

After the signing of the Maastricht Treaty, or the Treaty on European Union (TEU), the reform of its second pillar appeared a necessity for two reasons. First, the negotiation on the creation of the Common Foreign and Security Policy (CFSP) had frustrated many governments and international events showed the obvious inefficiencies of this policy. Second, the Brussels Treaty establishing the Western European Union (WEU) was facing its 1998 deadline, when its signatories would have the right to denounce it. These were the two incentives for bringing into the TEU itself a provision for a revision of CFSP, and more explicitly of Article J.4 on defence, at the next intergovernmental conference (IGC) to be convoked in 1996 under Article N of the TEU.

The Corfu session of the European Council on 24–5 June 1994 decided to establish a Reflection Group, which began work in June 1995 under the chairmanship of the Spanish Secretary of State for European Affairs Carlos Westendorp y Cabeza. Since the Reflection Group was composed of representatives of the fifteen member states, plus the Commission and two representatives of the European Parliament, its work looked like a first round of pre-negotiations on the agenda of the IGC. The final report of the Reflection Group was transmitted to the European Council for its Madrid session on 15–16 December 1995 at which it also decided to open the IGC in Turin on 29 March 1996.

The Westendorp Report is primarily an attempt to give more visibility and, if possible, transparency to the IGC process. It divides the challenges of the IGC into four main baskets: the reform of the EU; the citizen and the Union; an efficient and democratic Union; and the Union's external action. This fourth chapter of the report details the agenda and some scenarios for reforms in the fields of external relations, foreign policy and defence (Remacle, 1996). It is divided into three sections. The first deals with the questions related to 'globality and coherence': definition of the objectives of the Union; relationship between the first and second pillars; consistency of the policies carried out in these different pillars; interest in an international legal personality of the Union; and clarification of the instruments of CFSP (common positions and joint actions) (Reflection Group, 1995: par. 145–51). A second section deals with CFSP itself and identifies four possible developments: creation of an analysis cell; reform of decision making, especially relaxing the unanimity voting system; personification of CFSP by the appointment of one person in charge of its management and direction; and CFSP financing and the role of the European Parliament (par. 152–65). A third section elaborates some reflections on the new tasks related to crisis management, on possible European operational instruments and on the links between these developments and their impact on national sovereignty and the Atlantic Alliance. It also refers to scenarios about the future relationships between the EU and the WEU (par. 166–77).

This chapter will focus on the way these issues have been discussed during the whole IGC. First, the positions of the actors (governments and institutions) will be summarized. Secondly, the evolution of the negotiation (for CFSP and defence) will be detailed. Concluding remarks will give a general assessment.

Positions of the actors at the beginning of the negotiation

States are traditionally referred to as 'actors' in foreign policy. We will nevertheless not use that 'Westphalian' definition for two reasons. First, as emphasized by William Wallace, 'States do not make politics: government does' (1971: 25). Secondly, although Treaties are signed and ratified by states, non-state actors at a subnational or transnational level have increasingly been involved in European and world politics (Risse-Kappen, 1995). Therefore the analysis of actors in the negotiation will be divided into three parts. The first summarizes the positions of governments of the member states. The second develops the views of institutions involved in the negotiating process (European Commission, European Parliament, Western European Union). A concluding section will propose to apply the concept of an 'evolving web of actors' to the pattern of negotiations which led to the Amsterdam Treaty.

Positions of governments of the member states

It would of course take a whole book to summarize the positions of all fifteen member states on CFSP and defence during the whole negotiation (Laursen and Vanhoonacker, 1992; 1994). Much has been written about national foreign policies of European states (Hill, 1996) and other contributions to this book introduce British, French, German and Spanish security policies. This section will therefore focus exclusively on the comparison between national positions and on the coalitions of states which appeared during the negotiations about the four main questions related to the reform of CFSP and WEU: aims of CFSP, visibility of CFSP, decision making and procedures, and defence and WEU.[1]

Aims of CFSP   The aims of CFSP described in Article J.1 of the TEU were discussed by some member states in order to strengthen or enlarge them. Crisis management was seen as a common objective to be strengthened through more coherent and less diverging actions, especially by the Finnish and Swedish governments.

But the main proposal came from Greece which, owing to its border problems with Turkey, asked to introduce a guarantee for external national borders and a mutual assistance and solidarity clause into the new Treaty.

Visibility of CFSP: analysis unit and Ms/Mr CFSP   The idea of an analysis and planning unit was raised at an early stage of the negotiation. All governments publicly backed this idea, but with different views about the role of the unit and its position in the administrative structure of the Union. This was related to the debate about the opportunity to create a new function of Ms/Mr CFSP. France clearly urged such an appointment. For President Jacques Chirac, 'The European Union must strengthen its representation and defend its interests better. For this purpose France proposes the creation of a high level representative, appointed by the Council for three to five years, who would provide Europe with a face and a voice' (*Libération*, 1996). In the French view, this would imply the strengthening of all means to be used by that high representative, especially the Secretariat-General of the Council, and the clarification of the link between CFSP and the Community's external policies (Istituto Affari Internazionali, 1996: 46). This personality would not be the Secretary-General of the Council. Inspired by old French conceptions of foreign policy already developed in the Fouchet Plan (Bloes, 1970), this proposal was highly controversial among the other European governments.

For those who were reluctant to strengthen the EU's role on the world scene, this proposal looked too much like the embryo of a European Foreign Ministry and too close to the French design of *l'Europe puissance*. For those who considered that the European construction should remain built on the Community method and institutions, it appeared too intergovernmental and undermined the European Commission's and Council's role. These criticisms corresponded with different views on the future of the European project in this field. Three groups of states can be identified by the resulting cleavages.

The first group could be called 'orthodox Europeanist'. Benelux countries[2] proposed the most Community-based approach: full use of the right of initiative by the Commission in CFSP; creation of an analysis unit; appointment of Ms/Mr CFSP by the Council in consultation with the Commission; creation of a group of representatives permanently stationed in Brussels who could meet between meetings of the Political Committee. Greece was very close to the Benelux countries since it favoured the creation of the unit jointly by the Council and the Commission and did not support the idea of any personification of CFSP, for practical reasons and because of a mistrust of individualized posts.

A second group was more 'pragmatic' and insisted on an enhanced role for the Council in CFSP. Austria and Germany supported the idea of more visibility, emphasized the need for a clear framework based on transparency and accountability, and envisaged the possibility of giving foreign policy tasks to the Secretary-General. Ireland, Italy and Spain shared this position, insisting at the same time on a greater visibility and responsibility for the Council Secretariat, preferably at senior official level.

A third group included the 'pure intergovernmentalists'. Supporting the creation of an analysis unit in the framework of the Council, Denmark and Sweden insisted on the central position of the Council, while Finland emphasized the role of the Presidency. For those three countries, in regard to the appointment of a Ms/Mr CFSP, she/he should have a low profile and receive a mandate from the Council. The UK and Portugal also wanted to prevent Ms/Mr CFSP from limiting on the scope of the Presidency. For Britain, 'the terms of reference for this office would need to be carefully answerable to the Council of Ministers, representing the collective view of Member States, not deciding them' (Foreign and Commonwealth Office, 1996: par. 41).

In this context, a compromise was possible on the basis of the creation of the post of Ms/Mr CFSP with a senior official profile and clear linkage to the Council. With the exception of the Europeanists, this compromise satisfied most of the actors concerned. French and German foreign ministers met several times[3] in order to finalize the compromise which not only dealt with the concept of the High Representative (see hereafter for the evolution of the negotiation) but also agreed the nationality of the first person to be appointed.[4]

Decision making in CFSP   Three groups of states can also be identified in this debate. However, the coalitions differ from those in the debate on Ms/Mr CFSP.

On the one hand, a majority of member states (Austria, Benelux, Finland, Germany, Italy, Spain) promoted a step-by-step introduction of qualified majority voting (QMV) in CFSP (except for military issues) instead of unanimity. Intermediary options like 'reinforced' QMV, 'consensus minus one (or two)' and 'constructive abstention' were also introduced.

A second group was composed of those who did not want to give up their *de facto* veto power, especially the UK and some small countries like Denmark, Greece, Portugal and Sweden. For some of them, only the 'consensus minus one' formula was quoted as an acceptable compromise.

A third group, including France and Ireland, favoured some extension of QMV without undermining sovereignty on key issues. Joint French–German proposals about constructive abstention and the possibility of resorting to QMV for implementation delivered progress on that question (French–German Foreign Ministers Seminar, 1996).

Defence and WEU   Defence issues had been considered as one of the main areas of unfinished business in Maastricht. The IGC should, in particular, reform Article J.4 of the TEU in order to clarify the relationship between the EU and the Western European Union (WEU) and the position of neutral states (Austria, Finland, Ireland, Sweden) and Denmark which are the five observers at the WEU, the last being, in addition, the only member state to get an opt-out in common defence policy according to the 1992 so-called Edinburgh compromise.

Four positions were defended by member states during the IGC, again on the basis of coalitions other than those formed for previous debates.[5]

A first group promoted a federalist approach where the EU would become competent in military affairs, and which would allow full integration of the WEU *acquis* into the EU legal basis. In particular, Germany presented a phased concept of integration of the WEU into the EU where the IGC would make four commitments (Auswärtiges Amt, 1996):

1 a clause in the EU Treaty stating the principal objective of this integration
2 a responsibility for the European Council to adopt guidelines for the WEU
3 a political solidarity clause (which would be binding for non-WEU members)
4 the integration into the Treaty of the Petersberg tasks (humanitarian, rescue, peacekeeping operations, as well as combat missions including peacemaking).

Belgium generally adopted the same position and emphasized the convergence between NATO's acceptance of the concept of combined joint task forces (CJTFs) and the prospect for the IGC to integrate the Petersberg tasks into the EU Treaty (Dehaene, 1996). Greece also favoured the incorporation of WEU into the EU as soon as possible in order to fulfil its purpose of introducing a mutual assistance clause into the second pillar objectives.

A second group was composed of so-called neutral states. At an early stage in the negotiations, Finland and Sweden promoted the idea of EU–WEU reinforced cooperation and the integration of Petersberg tasks in the EU Treaty (Memorandum from Finland and Sweden, 1996). This would allow them to be associated fully in all decisions regarding the preparation of collective security operations. Full equality between member states was important in that respect. They would retain their neutrality with respect to defence of the territory and did not envisage applying for WEU or NATO membership. Integration of the WEU into the EU was therefore not supported. The two other neutral states supported the Finnish–Swedish position, but held different views. For Ireland, integration of the Petersberg tasks was acceptable, but not in the field of combat missions, and closer relationships between the EU and the WEU were not rejected (Irish Government, 1996: par. 4.88). In contrast, Austria was more open to such developments: it favoured convergence between EU and WEU and asked that the EU directs or instructs the WEU. In addition, the coalition agreement provided for the exploration of all security options, including the question of full membership in the WEU, and for the presentation of a governmental report on these options to the Austrian Parliament during the first semester 1998.

The third group is the orthodox Atlanticist one. It partly shared the same views as neutral countries about the maintenance of the WEU, but from a different perspective. In the case of Denmark, the Finnish–Swedish Memorandum got a chilly reception in Copenhagen. Denmark wanted to keep its opt-out in defence policy and preferred to rely only on NATO. Any change from this position would create domestic political trouble. Of course the main Atlanticist position was also defended by the UK, which considered that

> the WEU should be maintained as an autonomous organization with its own Treaty base and that its operational capabilities should be developed to enable it to operate effectively in peacekeeping, humanitarian and other limited crisis management tasks . . . We have proposed a number of measures to promote closer cooperation between WEU and EU bodies, from back-to-back or coordinated meetings of Heads of State and Government to better coordination at working level. (Foreign and Commonwealth Office, 1996: par. 47)

The WEU obviously would play the role of an instrument for Atlanticizing the EU, but not for Europeanizing the Alliance. These views were shared in Maastricht by The Netherlands and Portugal. Nevertheless, during the last IGC, these two countries partly softened their Atlanticist position and adopted a more Europeanist view. They had new reasons to do so: first, singularity is, in the longer term, more difficult for small countries than for a big power like the UK; secondly, being candidates of the single currency and signatories of the Schengen Convention, they need to be involved in all 'core groups' of the EU if they want to influence all its policies; thirdly, the changes in domestic politics led to new cabinets more ready to integrate a Europeanist approach in defence (Socialist–Liberal in The Hague, Socialist in Lisbon); fourthly, The Netherlands and Portugal succeeded each other at the Presidency of the WEU in the second semester of 1994 and the first semester of 1995. Therefore, although defending an Atlanticist line, they did not back the London position as strongly as they did in Maastricht. Portugal considered that the WEU should continue to exist autonomously after 1998 but that a reinforcement of links with the EU was required and a long-term incorporation of WEU into the EU was possible. The Dutch government also supported a reinforced partnership between WEU and EU, proposed to invite the Secretary-General of WEU to the EU's Foreign Affairs Council and to some meetings dealing with the Community's external relations, and envisaged a long-term personal union between Ms/Mr CFSP and the Secretary-General of the WEU (Adviesraad Vrede en Veiligheid, 1996).

Portuguese and Dutch approaches seemed therefore closer to positions of the fourth group, consisting of the countries which are not keen to incorporate the WEU into the EU but recognize the necessity of a closer relationship in order to strengthen the European defence capability and give more autonomy to the European pillar within NATO. This group comprised France, Italy, Luxembourg and Spain. Their intermediate position was acceptable, as a first step, to the promoters of the integration of WEU into the EU in the longer term, and was compatible with the position of the neutral states. Therefore it represented the basis for the final compromise. Although it leaves the main disagreements about defence issues unsettled, it allows closer cooperation in the implementation of Petersberg tasks and keeps all options open for a next IGC. The UK and Denmark seemed to receive less support from other member states than at Maastricht, although the neutral states supported them about the non-integration of the WEU into the EU. Nevertheless the likely evolution of the position of some neutral states towards NATO could undermine that *ad hoc* coalition in the foreseeable future.

Positions of extranational institutions

Article N of the Maastricht Treaty provided not only that the EU Council should convoke an IGC for reforming the Treaty, but also that every institution should provide a report assessing the Treaty and possibly suggesting proposals for its reform. The views of the institutions are of interest for evaluating the implementation of the TEU and because they also reflect the strategies of these institutions *within* the decision-making and bargaining process. Since these institutions are not central in the Treaty reform negotiations which are essentially intergovernmental, they used this opportunity for promoting their own views as 'extranational'[6] actors in the European construction, to secure further powers and find allies in the negotiations.

Since the reports presented by the Council of Ministers and the Court of Justice have less interest for a study focused on CFSP, we shall concentrate the analysis on the Commission and the European Parliament. A comment will also be made on the Western European Union's first direct contribution to an IGC at an early stage.[7]

The European Commission   The European Commission's central role in the external relations of the European Community has been frequently emphasized by analysts as a key feature in the development of the Community's position on the world scene (Edwards and Regelsberger, 1990; Holland, 1993a; Smith M., 1994). By contrast, since the beginning of the European Political Cooperation (EPC) in the early 1970s, it has always been difficult for the Commission to get powers in the core of foreign and security policy (Nuttall, 1994: 288). Although the 1987 Single European Act institutionalized the EPC on a legal basis, it did not crucially change the Commission's powers in foreign policy, with the exception that it conferred to both the Commission and the Council 'each within its sphere of competence' the responsibility of ensuring consistency between the external policies of the EC and the policies agreed in EPC.[8] This role was confirmed by the Maastricht Treaty[9] which also gave a non-exclusive right of initiative to the

Commission in the newly established second pillar, the so-called Common Foreign and Security Policy (CFSP).[10]

The Commission's opinions in the preparation of the 1996 IGC are characterized by a mix of cautiousness, inspired by its secondary role in foreign policy, and of integrationist proposals for institutional progress. As early as March 1991, the Commission's draft proposal for the CFSP Title of the Treaty on European Union (TEU) had been considered audacious, with its promotion of: equality between the Presidency and the Commission; qualified majority voting in foreign and security policy; association of the Commission with defence policy; and the inclusion in the Treaty of the *acquis* of the Western European Union (WEU), implying the creation of a Council of Defence Ministers and a mutual assistance clause similar to Article V of the modified Brussels Treaty.[11] However, since these aggressive Delors-style integrationist proposals had frightened almost all member states and simply failed, the behaviour of the Santer Commission before the 1996 IGC appeared softer and more cautious. In the meantime, the concrete experience of the CFSP, especially during the Yugoslav crisis, had also confirmed the intergovernmental nature of the CFSP. The opinions of the Commission for this IGC were focused on the need to improve efficiency rather than on a political federalist project for the future Union.

Two main documents were released by the Commission during the IGC process. The first was published before the launching of the Reflection Group (European Commission, 1995a) and made an assessment of the functioning of the Union under the TEU rule. The second took into account the results of the work of the Reflection Group and developed more detailed proposals for the amendments to be discussed by the IGC itself (European Commission, 1996a). Both documents mentioned four aims of the external policy of the Union.

The first is *efficiency and coherence*, implying the need to deal with all external policies including Community matters (development, sanctions, common commercial policy) and CFSP as such, as well as (in)coherencies between the three pillars.[12] The 1995 document raised especially the question of the overlapping between common positions in the second pillar and Community policies towards third countries in the first pillar. It emphasized the Commission's role in promoting coherence through the drafting of communications to the Council and the Parliament about integrated policies towards some regions of the world involving matters of the two pillars (1995a: par. 156). It also explicitly quoted the examples of economic sanctions and export controls of dual-use goods as negative cases of contamination of the first pillar by procedures coming from the second (1995a: par. 137). The 1996 document revisited this concern through the demand for more responsibility for the Council and the Commission and effective cooperation between them (1996a: par. 24).

Secondly, the Commission emphasized the need for more *Community method* in the management of external relations in general and in the representation of the Union in particular. It asked therefore for more visibility of its own role in some international fora and negotiations[13] and for a reform of the Troika (1995a: par. 163). In an additional communication issued in March 1997 and especially dedicated to its own composition, organization and functioning, the Commission also stressed the necessity to appoint among the Commissioners one Vice-President for External Relations who would represent the Commission in the new Troika for CFSP (European Commission, 1997: 4). This was conceived as a way to limit the dispersion of the external relations portfolios within the Commission and to cooperate efficiently with the High Representative for CFSP to be appointed by the Council.

Thirdly, an *institutional reform of the CFSP* was detailed. This included: creation of an actual Presidency/Commission tandem for preparation, implementation and representation of CFSP decisions, implying a reinforcement of the Presidency (1996a: par. 28 and 32(1)); establishment of a 'joint analysis cell' (1996a: par. 29); clarification of the difference between common positions and joint actions (1995a: par. 151(1), 152 and 154(2); 1996a: par. 30(1)); use of qualified majority voting as the rule in CFSP;[14] the possibility of reinforced cooperation or coalitions between willing states acting on behalf of the Union (1996a: par. 31(3)); the possibility to mandate some individuals to perform *ad hoc* tasks in the implementation of decisions (1996a: par. 32(2)); and financing by the Community budget (1996a: par. 33).[15]

Last but not least, in *defence matters*, the Commission wanted more utilization of the WEU by the EU and more subordination of the WEU to the Union (1995a: par. 159–61). In the 1996 document, it insisted especially on the building of a European security and defence identity (ESDI) in the framework of NATO and through the development of the CFSP with common defence as its final aim (1996a: par. 34). To this end, four proposals were made: introducing in the Treaty the so-called Petersberg missions; organizing the participation of defence ministers in the Council; fixing a timetable for the progressive integration of the WEU into the Union; and integrating the armaments sector in the Treaty and creating an armaments agency (1996a: par. 35).

In conclusion, the Commission's positions, through the emphasis on coherence and efficiency, promoted two main objectives: contributing to the development of a more integrationist and Community-oriented profile for CFSP, and consequently reinforcing its own role in that policy. However, in comparison with 1991, the Santer Commission was markedly more cautious than the Delors Commission because of its weaker position in the negotiation.[16]

The European Parliament   CFSP is one of the topics that has been regularly addressed by the European Parliament since the Single European Act. Sometimes qualified as an underdog of the EPC and CFSP (Grunert, 1997: 109–31), the Parliament has been especially active in its permanent monitoring of the Treaty reform process. In the field of CFSP, it has organized, as provided for in Article J.7 of the TEU, annual assessments and debates on the implementation of CFSP which provided it with opportunities to launch proposals during the IGC.[17] The Parliament has also promoted transparency through the organization of public hearings in the Foreign Affairs and Security and Disarmament Committees (Public Hearing of the Subcommittee on Security and Disarmament, 1996), and through the publication by its Directorate-General for Research and its Task Force on the IGC of updated briefings on positions taken during the IGC on all issues, including CFSP and defence.[18] Finally, the Parliament always dedicated a chapter to external relations, CFSP and defence in its resolutions about the Treaty reform, the Reflection Group and the IGC.[19]

Although there is a wide spectrum of positions within the European Parliament, the majority of its political groups traditionally defend integrationist positions. The accession of the Greek Nea Demokratia and of the Spanish People's Party together with the association of the British Conservatives to the Group of the European Peoples' Party (EPP), as well as the reinforced weight of the British Labour and the German Social-Democratic Party within the Group of the Party of European Socialists (PES), have strengthened both biggest groups of the Parliament, but at the same time obliged them to soften their traditional pro-federal approaches. Complex compromises within and between the two groups led to a relatively moderate Resolution based on the Bourlanges–Martin Report which was adopted in May 1995.[20]

In this Resolution, the Parliament emphasized almost the same *aims for CFSP* as the Commission but went further in some areas, namely: coherence between the different pillars, a military guarantee of the Union's borders, and transfer of the WEU competences to the Union. In *institutional* terms, it favoured: qualified majority voting, coalitions of the willing, strengthening the Commission's role in initiating and implementing CFSP, the creation of a joint planning and analysis unit between the Commission and the Council, and democratic control of CFSP by the European Parliament and national parliaments. As far as the *content of the policies* was concerned, the Parliament promoted the abolition of Article 223 of the TEC, which blocks any cooperation in the field of armaments production and exports, and expressed an interest in a European contribution to conflict prevention through the establishment of a civilian peace corps which would train monitors, observers and mediators in crisis areas.[21] The same ideas were also defended in the Matutes Report on the annual assessment of the implementation of CFSP, which not only emphasized the importance of qualified majority voting and the development of a common defence policy, but also proposed that the Union focus not only on Eastern Europe and the Mediterranean but also on Latin America and the Asia/Pacific area. During the discussion of that report, the question of *cooperation between neutral countries and WEU/NATO countries in* the field of common defence policy was highly controversial between the European Peoples' Party and some Social Democrats and Greens (*Agence Europe*, 1995b: 3). When the

Matutes Report was adopted, the reference to an *assistance clause* similar to Article V of the WEU Treaty was deleted at the initiative of the former Finnish Defence Minister MEP Elisabeth Rehn (*Agence Europe*, 1995d: 4). This mixing of Europeanist, leftist and neutralist views in the Matutes Report showed the impact of the change in the composition of the Parliament after the accession of the three neutral EFTA countries. Nevertheless, during the work of the Reflection Group and of the IGC, the position of the Parliament became progressively more similar to those of the governments and the Commission and more in conformity with a Europeanist approach.

This was especially true for the Resolution adopted on 16 January 1997 after the Dublin European Council. In this Resolution, the Parliament welcomed the introduction by the Presidency of a *political solidarity clause* and asked for the introduction of a financial solidarity clause (European Parliament, 1997: par. 26). As far as the *institutional dimensions* of CFSP were concerned, it supported the idea of creating a policy planning and early warning unit and asked that it be responsible to the Commission (1997: par. 27). It also insisted on the role of the Commission and on qualified majority voting (1997: par. 28). In the field of *security and defence*, it supported the integration of the Petersberg missions into the Treaty, coalitions of the willing in the defence field, as well as a common armaments policy. It further asked for the subordination and progressive integration of the WEU into the Union, and proposed a facultative protocol on mutual military assistance (1997: par. 33–4). Four months later, these positions were reaffirmed in the Resolution on the development of perspectives for security policy of the Union, which also asked the Commission and the Council to make a feasibility study on the *creation of a European corps mixing military and civilian units* for carrying out peacekeeping and peacemaking operations.[22]

In taking these positions the Parliament appeared to react to proposals from member states or the Presidency rather than to build on its own initiatives. In the field which interests it directly, i.e. democratic control of CFSP, it did not get more powers than those already fixed by Article J.7 of the TEU. Nevertheless, it struggled for a 'normal' resort to the Community budget for financing CFSP since 1993 and finally got a victory at Amsterdam on this issue, through the signing of an inter-institutional agreement with the Council and the Commission on the financing of CFSP.[23] Besides, although it still plays the role of an underdog, the European Parliament gives to CFSP an added value through the provision of transparency in a policy area often clouded by secrecy and *raisons d'état*.

The Western European Union (WEU) In Declaration 30 of the Maastricht Treaty, the WEU countries declared their intention to contribute to the 1996 IGC in their sphere of competence.[24] They reaffirmed that objective at the Noordwijk and Lisbon sessions of the Ministerial Council on 14 November 1994 and 15 May 1995 which launched the internal process of drafting such a contribution (Council of Ministers of the Western European Union, 1994: par. 16; 1995a: par. 26). Of course, since it is issued by an intergovernmental body, this contribution did not present the same autonomy as positions of extranational actors like the Commission or the Parliament who intervene more freely in the debate. Consequently, it reflected more directly the evolution of the positions of member states and the bargaining and compromise building among them.

The contribution of the WEU to the IGC was prepared under the Spanish Presidency (second semester 1995). For the first time in the history of the organization, the same country chaired both the EU and the WEU simultaneously. There was, therefore, a meaningful interaction between the drafting of the WEU contribution and the report of the Reflection Group chaired by Carlos Westendorp. Based on a first reflection document published by the Spanish Presidency on 4 July 1995 (Ministerio de Asuntos Exteriores, 1995), the WEU contribution was adopted by the Madrid Ministerial Council on 14 November 1995.

Like other contributions of EU institutions, the document first assessed the implementation of the TEU, especially in regard to Article J.4 of the TEU. It noted that the relationship between the EU and the WEU could be improved (Council of Ministers of the Western European Union, 1995b: par. 19–21), and was positive about the cooperation between WEU and NATO and about the operational development of the WEU itself (1995b: par. 22–40). In a second chapter, the organization describes the future framework of European defence and security (1995b: par. 43–9) and emphasizes the need for a European security and defence identity (ESDI) based on the development of the WEU. This stronger linkage between ESDI and WEU, which was not yet clear during the 1991 negotiations,[25] was established at the Brussels Atlantic summit in January 1994. It resulted from the success of the reforms launched by the WEU in Maastricht and carried out in 1992 and 1993. These included: transfer of the WEU Secretariat-General to Brussels, participation of observers and associate members in the WEU, development of cooperation between WEU and NATO, operational development of the WEU, and merger of the EUROGROUP and IEPG into the WEU structure.[26]

The core of the document was the presentation of three options for the future of the WEU, with the variations between them reflecting the divergences between the member states.

Option A is based on a *reinforced partnership between an autonomous WEU and the European Union* (1995b: par. 50–8). According to this scenario, promoted by the UK, things would continue as before but with a higher level of cooperation. The WEU and the EU would remain separate organizations and the members of the EU would continue to have different levels of participation in the WEU. Priority would be given to the Petersberg tasks. The EU institutions would not be involved in defence affairs and a WEU summit would be created in parallel to the European Council.

At the opposite end of the spectrum, option C favours the *integration of the WEU into the EU* (1995b: par. 76–92). The EU would take over the functions of the WEU and the WEU Treaty of Brussels would end in 1998.

It would require an amendment to the Treaty to allow national defence ministers to meet in the Council when required. The associated partners of the
WEU would become associates of the CFSP, and the EU and NATO would
make a joint declaration on cooperation in a Treaty annex. Promoted by
Belgium and Germany, this scenario included two options for implementation: either the transfer of all WEU responsibilities to the CFSP, with the
possibility of an opt-out on the defence dimension (option C.1); or a differentiation between common defence policy introduced in the Treaty text
and a protocol on common defence annexed to the TEU and signed by the
willing countries (option C.2).

Option B was conceived as the intermediary solution, promoting *intermediate changes with a view to institutional convergence* (1995b: par. 59–75).
The EU would be given some authority over the WEU, but the two organizations would remain separate. Working groups and high-level civil servants
would cooperate closely. WEU ministers, including defence ministers, and
the Secretary-General of the WEU could attend General Affairs Councils
of the EU when crisis management would be discussed. This would require
the EU to avail itself of the WEU on a more systematic basis than described
in Article J.4 of the TEU. Three mechanisms were considered as possible
options for improving the mechanism of the WEU's instruction: general
guidelines of the European Council (option B.1), instructions of the
General Affairs Council (option B.2), or a legally binding link between both
organizations (option B.3). Promoted by France and The Netherlands, this
approach was seen as a pragmatic way to proceed towards a stronger European defence identity without undermining NATO and provoking a negative public reaction in the neutral states. The WEU Assembly also
supported this approach since it would permit the use of the WEU as an
integral part of the European Union without weakening the WEU's position (including the parliamentary control function of the WEU Assembly),
and strengthen the European security and defence identity without any drift
towards 'communautarization' of defence.[27]

The WEU's role in the EU debate enhanced the value of participation in
this organization and obliged Denmark and the neutral states to react by
adopting their own positions on security and defence in order to be present
in the discussion. Rather than a direct *spillover effect* (extension from one
sphere of competence to another one *within* the Union), this trend can be
compared to a *vortex effect* (mutual interference between developments in
the EU and in other organizations).[28] In contrast to the Commission and
the Parliament, the WEU, being an intergovernmental body, left the scene
of the IGC to its member states and did not intervene as an institution at a
later stage, with the exception of the adoption by the WEU Council on 22
July 1997 of the WEU Declaration annexed to the Treaty of Amsterdam.[29]

An evolving web of actors

The EU is characterized by an entanglement of national and supranational
institutions. It operates neither as a political market, characterized by

arm's-length transactions among independent entities, nor as a hierarchy in which the dominant mode of regulation is either the national governments or the supranational institutions. Rather the EU exemplifies a network form of organization, characterized by horizontal ties and complex relationships between actors. Consequently, the process of an intergovernmental negotiation can best be described as one of complex bargaining, demonstrating flexible coalitions of state, supranational and non-state actors in ever changing constellations. Moreover, as the competencies of the Union have increased, the process of intergovernmental decision making has become markedly more complex than the bargaining demonstrated in the early stages of European construction.

Even in the area of foreign, security and defence policy, where the Union plays a limited role and the authority of the member states is well established, the negotiations have been influenced by various coalitions of non-state actors and the dynamics of the simultaneous negotiations on the first and third pillars. Consequently, the negotiations generated an enormous number of proposals which were subject to multiple and multi-level modification and to cross-pillar *package deals* between state actors.

Negotiations on the CFSP chapter, however, were self-contained until the final Amsterdam summit. This led to some reforms being discarded at the last minute (i.e. flexibility clause, legal personality of the Union) while other amendments were introduced without prior discussion by the representatives of the member states during the negotiations (e.g. the Luxembourg compromise on national interests). Some governments make no secret of their bargaining aspirations. For example Greece, which was in principle opposed to introduction of qualified majority in the CFSP, publicly stated that it was prepared to soften its position if the compromise included the right of veto where 'vital national interests' are at stake (Istituto Affari Internazionali, 1996: 48) and if the protection of external borders were to be included in the CFSP objectives. The British government is also well known for its negotiation tactics based on 'tension strategy' and final *quid pro quo* bargaining. Since it was the only country satisfied with status quo it also held a strong negotiating position.

Compromises are often based on a preliminary *rapprochement* between some leading states, a role which is traditionally played by France and Germany although, with regard to CFSP, their positions sometimes diverge. This was not, however, the case during this IGC, where Germany and France presented joint proposals on the issue of Ms/Mr CFSP and the extension of qualified majority voting. Moreover, on issues of defence and the relationship between EU and WEU they were able to broaden the coalition to include Belgium, Italy, Luxembourg and Spain.[30] Nevertheless the Paris–Bonn axis was unable to overcome the strong resistance to these proposed changes which was most clearly demonstrated by Britain and backed by Denmark and the neutral states.

For a number of reasons it is, of course, easier for relatively large states like Britain to maintain a 'no' position for the duration of an IGC. In addition to domestic political forces which strongly influence these states' positions,[31] there are several other factors which generate negotiating constraints and incentives for smaller states. For example, the constraints on the military budgets of smaller states effectively render them dependent on interstate cooperation to ensure military operability. Similarly, the *de facto* linkage between the pillars encourages compliance with mainstream positions. This was obviously the case for Italy, The Netherlands and Portugal who moderated their Maastricht pro-UK positions in order to get closer to the Europeanist 'core group' which was in favour of EU–WEU integration. Thus, the potential of being part of so-called 'reinforced cooperations' (EMU, WEU, Schengen) becomes a stake in itself for those who want to retain their influence in the permanent bargaining of the Union. The joint Finnish–Swedish proposal to introduce the Petersberg tasks in the Treaty illustrates a similar phenomenon. In this case, the Swedish–Finnish initiative helped limit the marginalization otherwise associated with their neutrality and observer status in the WEU. Paradoxically, as with the Schengen Agreements, this initiative involved the use of an intergovernmental body in order to promote deeper integration among a smaller group of states. Nevertheless, it is consistent with the Europeanist goal of promoting further integration since it obliges Denmark and the neutral states to discuss and decide military affairs with WEU states within the EU framework.

In sum, the negotiations did demonstrate some indirect *spillover* or *vortex* effects resulting from a convergence of the foreign policies of member states. The French *rapprochement* with NATO's military structure is a case in point. The national developments are not, however, to be seen as the outcome of any institutional integration or trend towards supranationalism in foreign policy. They result from the formation of alliances of similar positions during the negotiations in accordance with James Rosenau's (1970) adaptation theory[32] rather than Ernst Haas's (1958) neo-functionalist approach. The interests and stated positions of actors therefore shifted as the result of their adaptations to new external environments and domestic constraints.

The complexity of the IGC negotiations was increased by the involvement of different kinds of non-state actors. In such a negotiation, these 'non-state actors' potentially comprise all civil society as it 'exists through self-organized activity, not dependent on the agency of the State for its initiation and day-to-day management, but on the free association of individuals' (Chilton, 1995).[33] According to this wide definition, non-state actors might include political parties, trade unions, pressure groups, commercial interest groups, voluntary associations, clubs and charities. These groups may, in turn, be part of broader political associations organized around a political idea or statement of principle. In general, these can be classified as various movements which include: peace movements, human rights movements, federalist movements, green movements, development movements, democratic movements, movements within trade unions, movements within political parties, movements within churches, women's movements and youth movements (1995: 197). During the IGC, three kinds of non-state actors have been involved in the discussion: transnational groups, supranational institutions and NGOs. Transnational organizations often share common interests with other non-state actors in so far as they all seek to ensure that the agenda is not entirely dictated by member states. The relationships between the Commission, the European Parliament and NGOs is a case in point. Nevertheless, a common status as non-state actor is not sufficient to ensure cooperation in all areas of the debate. For example, development, human rights and peace NGOs were closely aligned to the positions of the Commission and the Parliament with relation to the promotion of conflict prevention policies or the creation of a peace corps, while they often did not share the institutions' positions on military affairs, which were closer to those of the WEU and defence industries' interest groups.[34]

Transnational non-state actors, while not directly involved in the IGC, have an indirect impact in so far as their advocacy serves to support the positions of certain governments. For example, the federalist positions taken by the European Commission, the European Parliament, and by numerous think-tanks and movements who argued that defence identity is a natural and necessary component of a comprehensive political union, effectively reinforced the proposals of the Europeanist governments in the negotiation. By contrast, many peace and development NGOs were sceptical about an increased role for the EU in matters of defence. These non-state actors often supported the position of the neutral states, arguing that EU foreign and defence policy would always be restricted by its decision-making procedures which would invariably result in policies reflecting the lowest common denominator.

In general, NGOs have idealistic interests which do not necessarily favour a specific institution. Thus NGO support for any institution is usually conditional on that institution's furtherance of goals such as universally respected human rights, the alleviation of global poverty, or the furtherance of conflict prevention policies. This is true for the concerns voiced about the EU's democratic deficit, although NGOs have traditionally been divided on the issue. For some, the only way to deal with democratic deficit in CFSP is to strengthen the scrutinizing powers of the European Parliament (notably through the budget procedure), while others argue that accountability in this domain is best maintained at a national level.

It remains difficult to assess the impact of non-state actors on the intergovernmental negotiations. The principal objective of institutions such as the Commission and the Parliament was clearly to maintain and, where possible, reinforce their limited influence in CFSP. While their institutional role was not effectively eroded, neither was it dramatically enhanced. CFSP after Amsterdam remains essentially intergovernmental and will continue to suffer from chronic tensions between the Commission and the Council.

As far as NGOs are concerned, few of their specific demands were codified in the final Treaty, but there is ample evidence that the member states, the Council and other EU institutions were made aware of the concerns these actors highlighted. The case of conflict prevention is a good example. While it is not mentioned in new Article J.1 of the TEU as a specific goal of the CFSP, it was adopted as a political priority by the Dutch Presidency, the Commission and the Parliament in parallel with the IGC. In 1995, DG1A of the Commission established a Conflict Prevention Network (CPN) on the basis of a proposal by the Parliament. This network, coordinated in close cooperation with the German foreign policy foundation *Stiftung Wissenschaft und Politik* in Ebenhausen, is tasked with collating and coordinating expert analysis on regional zones of potential crisis. Similarly, in March 1997, the Presidency organized an informal meeting of the development ministers in Amsterdam and supported an open conference of 1,500 European and African NGO representatives dedicated to conflict prevention. The culmination of these efforts included a Council common position concerning conflict prevention and resolution in Africa[35] which stated that the EU's policy 'shall also focus on preventing the outbreak or recurrence of violent conflicts, including, at an early stage and post-conflict peace building'.[36] The Council also agreed a Resolution on coherence in May 1997 which explicitly recognized that coherence of policies is a permanent concern covering many areas, and which sought to address some of these issues with regard to: peace building, conflict prevention and resolution; food security; fishery and development; and migration and development (Resolutions, 1997c).

These two examples of Council initiatives demonstrate that, though not directly referred to in the Treaty texts, some proposals have been addressed by the institutions. In this case, the issues spilled out of the IGC negotiations themselves onto fertile ground in the Council.

In what follows we will describe the dynamic development of the negotiations in an attempt to illustrate the interactions of member states and the evolution of the final compromises.

The negotiation on CFSP: objectives, means and structures

The IGC negotiations to revise the Treaty on European Union (TEU), otherwise known as the Maastricht Treaty, were convened at the Turin summit on 29 March 1996 during the Italian Presidency.

The principal negotiating forum was a group of national representatives appointed by foreign ministries, around which working groups on specific subjects carried out more detailed discussions. The representatives met for one day approximately every two weeks during the Italian Presidency until the first opportunity for major review of progress at the European Council in Florence in June 1996. Thereafter the Irish Presidency increased the pace of negotiations with the representatives meeting for two days a week and ministers meeting approximately once a month. These representatives' meetings were scheduled to deliver 'successive approximations' of draft text for Treaty revisions. The goal was to agree a complete draft of

Treaty revisions for discussion at the Dublin European Council in December 1996.

The following phase of the negotiations, described by the Irish representative, Noel Dorr, as the decision-making phase, was conducted under the Dutch Presidency and scheduled to be concluded at the Amsterdam European Council in June 1997. While the proximity of the UK (and unexpectedly French) general elections to the June deadline led many to believe that the IGC might drag on until the Luxembourg European Council in December 1997, the proposed time frame was adhered to.

Reporting of the IGC negotiations was largely limited to infrequent summaries of progress by the secretariat of the conference of representatives. These briefing notes do not reveal any details about national negotiating positions or intergovernmental bargaining. The following summary of the evolution of the debate therefore offers no insights into the precise execution of intergovernmental decision making. Rather it outlines the gradual formulation of widely agreed compromises on the main issues.

This section will discuss the development of the negotiations with regard to: the principles and objectives of CFSP; the determination of major policy guidelines and clarification of policy instruments; the proposal for a new policy planning and early warning unit; ways of relaxing the unanimity requirement; the role of the European Parliament; and the implementation and financing of CFSP. The next section covers the security and defence negotiations. It does not include a discussion of proposals to introduce greater flexibility into the second pillar or to give the Union a legal personality, since both of these proposals ultimately failed and have been discussed elsewhere.[37]

Principles and objectives of CFSP

The first proposal for amending the objectives of the CFSP was introduced by the Greek delegation in advance of the Florence European Council in June 1996. It called for the safeguarding of the territorial integrity of the Union and the inviolability of its external borders to be included in Article J.1.2 as a CFSP objective. While Greece felt that it deserved stronger support from the EU over its various disputes with Turkey (a concern heightened by its ongoing clash with Turkey over two islands), other EU member states were reticent about adopting such a commitment given Turkey's membership of NATO. In its progress report the Italian Presidency indicated that this proposal had failed to receive widespread support, a development which was confirmed by the draft text compiled by the Irish Presidency for the Dublin Council in December 1996. This Presidency suggested that the various concerns expressed could be taken into account in the following amendment to Article J.1.2 where an objective of the CFSP shall be: 'to safeguard the common values, fundamental interests, independence *and integrity* of the Union *in conformity with the principles of the United Nations Charter*'.[38] This amendment can be read as a reference to

Article 51 of the UN Charter which allows for legitimate self-defence, but clearly does not go as far as Greece would like.

It was only at a meeting of IGC representatives on 26–8 May 1997 that further changes were agreed which at least partially addressed the continued concerns of Greece. In the consolidated Draft Treaty texts prepared on 30 May explicit reference was made to supporting principles of international security, *including those on external borders* (Conference of the Representatives of the Governments of the Member States, 1997f: 84). No other revisions were made to the Treaty text, and there was notably no mention of the goal of conflict prevention.

The question of solidarity in Union actions was given increased significance in the light of the introduction of new elements of flexibility (i.e. enhanced cooperation and constructive abstention) in the implementation of CFSP. It was agreed during the Irish Presidency that a clause to reinforce the general obligation of solidarity should be inserted in the Article on the general objectives of CFSP. The final draft agreed at the European Council in Amsterdam is as follows:[39]

Article J.1

1 The Union and its Member States shall define and implement a common foreign and security policy covering all areas of foreign and security policy, the objectives of which shall be:

- to safeguard the common values, fundamental interests, independence and *integrity* of the Union *in conformity with the principles of the United Nations Charter;*
- to strengthen the security of the Union and its Member States in all ways;
- to preserve the peace and strengthen the international security, in accordance with the principles of the United Nations Charter as well as the principles of the Helsinki Final Act and the objectives of the Paris Charter, *including those on external borders;*
- to promote international cooperation;
- to develop and consolidate democracy and the rule of law, and respect for human rights and fundamental freedoms.

2 The Member States shall support the Union's external and security policy actively and unreservedly in a spirit of loyalty and mutual solidarity.

The Member States shall work together to enhance and develop their mutual political solidarity. They shall refrain from any action which is contrary to the interests of the Union or likely to impair its effectiveness as a cohesive force in international relations.

The Council shall ensure that these principles are complied with.

Determining major policy guidelines and clarifying policy instruments

By June 1996 it was already accepted that the policy guidelines for external action, and in particular the main aspects of joint actions, should be set by the European Council. In the following six months it was agreed that this should be made explicit in Article J.1.1. The Irish Presidency's draft text for such an amendment read:

> The Union and its Member States shall define and implement a common foreign and security policy, governed by the provisions of this Title and covering all areas of foreign and security policy. The European Council shall define the principles of and general and strategic guidelines for the common foreign and security policy.

Article J.1 was comprehensively revised shortly thereafter in order to clearly identify the instruments of CFSP, and in March 1997 in the Addendum to the Dublin text (Conference of the Representatives of the Governments of the Member States, 1997b) the following and ultimately final text was agreed:[40]

> *Article J.2 (former J.1(3))*
> The Union shall pursue the objectives *set out in Article J.1* by:
> - *defining the principles of and general guidelines for the common foreign and security policy;*
> - *defining common strategies;*
> - *adopting joint actions;*
> - *adopting common positions;*
> - *and strengthening* systematic cooperation between Member States in the conduct of policy.

The policy instruments introduced in this Article were later explained in Articles J.3 to J.5. Article J.3 contains new text defining the Union's common strategies:

> 2 *The European Council shall decide on common strategies to be implemented by the Union in areas where the Member States have important interests in common.*
>
> *Common strategies shall set out their objectives, duration and the means to be made available by the Union and the Member States.*
>
> 3 *... The Council shall recommend common strategies to the European Council and shall implement them, in particular by adopting joint actions and common positions.*

Article J.4 (former J.3) contains the following new definition of joint actions adopted by the Council:

> 1 *...Joint actions shall address specific situations where operational action by the Union is deemed to be required. They shall lay down their objectives, scope, the means to be made available to the Union, if necessary their duration, and the conditions for their implementation.*

Article J.5 (former J.2(2)) introduces a new definition of the Union's common positions. These *shall define the approach of the Union to a particular matter of a geographical or thematic nature.*

Both common positions and joint actions explicitly commit the member states in the positions they adopt and in the conduct of their activity.

A *new policy planning and early warning unit*

At the beginning of the IGC it was agreed that the existing modes of preparation of CFSP decisions often resulted in a policy of reacting to events rather than anticipating them, and were inadequate in promoting a common view of the member states and the Commission. One popular option to remedy these shortcomings was to establish a facility for analysis, conception and forward planning. This idea had received wide support from various states, institutions and the Reflection Group in the previous year.

In June 1996, one of the outstanding issues related to the relationship of the proposed facility with the existing system. It raised the question of whether the facility should be placed under the responsibility of: a political figure with some degree of autonomy in implementing the CFSP (Ms/Mr CFSP); the joint authority of the Presidency and the Commission; or the Secretary-General of the Council.

The French delegation was notably one of the strongest supporters of the first option, arguing that a Ms/Mr CFSP within the existing structures would have the advantage of creating a synergy between them and preventing a dichotomy between the functions of analysis and administrative management.

In June 1996, the Italian Presidency declared that there was some support for placing the facility in the Council Secretariat and called for further study into the role of the High Representative for CFSP (Ms/Mr CFSP) and into the possibility of combining the post with that of Secretary-General of the Council. One month later, as a result of the Cork ministerial meeting of 5–7 July, the Irish Presidency drew up a draft text indicating the remaining options: 'A policy planning and early warning capability shall be established in the General Secretariat of the Council under the responsibility of the [Secretary-General of the Council] [Secretary-General for CFSP] [CFSP High Representative] with a remit to. . .'

During the remaining four months of the Irish Presidency, France apparently dropped its insistence on the post of High Representative of CFSP in the face of widespread opposition eventually joined by Germany.[41] Consequently, the draft text prepared for the Dublin Council in December 1996 was able to settle the question. The provisions for the establishment of the facility were spelled out in a Declaration to the Final Act of the Treaty (Conference of the Representatives of the Governments of the Member States, 1996i: 71). The first draft of this underwent little substantial change until it was finally agreed at Amsterdam in the following form:

Declaration to the Final Act on the establishment of a policy planning and early warning unit

The Conference agrees that:

1 A policy planning and early warning unit shall be established in the General Secretariat of the Council under the responsibility of its Secretary-General. Appropriate cooperation shall be established with the Commission in order to ensure full coherence with the Union's external economic and development policies.

2 The tasks of the unit shall include the following:

  (a) monitoring and analysing developments in areas relevant to CFSP;
  (b) providing assessments of the Union's foreign and security policy interests and identifying areas where the CFSP could focus in future;
  (c) providing timely assessments and early warning of events or situations which may have significant repercussions for the Union's foreign and security policy, including potential political crisis;
  (d) producing, at the request of either the Council or the Presidency or on its own initiative, argued policy options papers to be presented under the responsibility of the Presidency as a contribution to policy formulation in the Council, and which may contain analyses, recommendations and strategies for the CFSP.

3 The unit shall consist of personnel drawn from the General Secretariat, the Member States, the Commission and the WEU.

4 Any Member State or the Commission may make suggestions to the unit for work to be undertaken.

5 Member States and the Commission shall assist the policy planning process by providing, to the fullest extent possible, relevant information, including confidential information.

This text envisages a significantly stronger planning cell than some states, such as the UK, had originally supported. For example, the proposal for such a planning capability suggested by the UK in July 1996 called for 'a modest strengthening of the Council Secretariat to enhance the capacity for planning and analysis in CFSP' (Conference of the Representatives of the Governments of the Member States, 1996f). It would have five or six secondees from member states' foreign ministries, a secondee from the Commission and a contact point in the WEU. Member states and the Commission would provide information on an informal basis through their secondees, but there should be no formal requirement to supply confidential information to the Council Secretariat.

On the other hand, earlier texts by the Italian Presidency indicated that there was support for a more robust planning capability. These texts mentioned that extra staff from the General Secretariat of the Council and the WEU should be included in the cell and stressed that the facility would require permanent, *systematic* access to confidential information from the member states and the Commission. With regard to this key issue of the provision of information, the final text has been slightly strengthened from that presented at Dublin since the earlier draft left it up to the member states to decide which *relevant*, and not necessarily confidential, information they should provide the planning capability.

While the final text establishes a mandate for the planning unit which implies that it could play a highly influential role in shaping the CFSP and ensuring that its policies are coherent with the Union's external economic and development policies, whether or not the unit will realize this potential will depend entirely on the cooperation of the member states. For it to be effective, the unit will require substantial resources in terms of highly qualified personnel with expertise in political and intelligence analysis, development, economics and environmental matters as well as able managers. It will also rely heavily on information from member states and will need to develop efficient mechanisms for processing public information and analysis. Indeed, precisely because of its limited access to information from member states, it will need to develop innovative approaches to incorporating information from non-state actors which might be particularly valuable for its early warning function.

Ways of relaxing the unanimity requirement

The introduction of 'constructive abstention' from European Council decisions requiring unanimity, except those with military or defence implications, had widespread support at an early stage in the negotiations. It remained to be determined whether or not such an abstention required political and financial solidarity (Conference of the Representatives of the Governments of the Member States, 1996a: 2). While the first draft text on abstention was agreed in July 1996, the issue of financial contributions from the member states concerned remained unresolved.

In the draft text of the new Article J.8a, prepared for the Dublin summit, there was no mention of obligatory financial contributions, however, and a provision limiting the number of constructive abstentions was added. Article J.8a provided for states to qualify their abstentions by making a formal explanatory declaration. Where members of the Council qualifying their abstentions in this way represented more than 25 weighted votes, the decision would not be adopted. This was later agreed at Amsterdam and is stated in the new Article J.13.[42]

The option of constructive abstention was not, however, the only one to relax the unanimity requirement. Many states favoured the extension of majority voting for decisions of the Council, excluding the security and defence field, such as was already included in Article J.3 of the TEU. After three months of negotiations, there were two remaining options under consideration:

1 the application of majority voting for the determining of joint action by the Council within guidelines set by the European Council

2 the systematic application of majority voting for measures in implementation of a joint action (excluding the security and defence field).

In either case the extension of qualified majority voting might be made easier by allowing a state to oppose majority voting on the grounds of 'essential national interest' invoked at the European Council level (in the spirit of the so-called 1966 Luxembourg compromise).

By December 1996, the issue of extending majority voting had still not been resolved. Nevertheless, the compromise text drafted by the Irish Presidency suggested that the first option alluded to above had the most support. A new Article J.8a allowed for decisions to implement measures for an approved joint action to be adopted by the Council acting by a qualified majority. These decisions could, however, be subject to a veto by a member state for stated reasons of national policy. In these cases, a further provision enables a qualified majority to delay the vote by referring the issue to the European Council for decision by unanimity. These provisions were ultimately agreed in Amsterdam in Article J.13.2 of the final text.

Noel Dorr (1996), the Irish representative to the IGC who chaired meetings of the conference for the duration of Ireland's Presidency, was nevertheless optimistic that implementation measures of an approved joint action would be decided by a qualified majority as a rule rather than an exception. While this intention was supported by the widespread reference to the veto as an 'emergency brake', many believed that this provision would not change the status quo and would result in implementing decisions being effectively those reached by consensus.

According to the compromise agreement reached in Amsterdam (and which is detailed in the new Article J.13), the decision-making arrangements are related to the type of CFSP instruments concerned. When the European Council adopts principles, guidelines and common strategies the rule is unanimity with the possibility of constructive abstention. When the Council adopts joint actions, common positions or implementing decisions on the basis of previously agreed common strategies, joint actions or common positions, the rule is qualified majority except when a state objects, citing important reasons of national policy. This compromise, proposed by the French, both preserves national interests and paves the way for more systematic resort to qualified majority.

The role of the European Parliament

The evolution of the debate on the role of the Parliament in decision making was evidence of the growing consensus that there should be no change in the distribution of powers between the institutions. Article J.7 of the TEU established that the Parliament shall be consulted by the Presidency on the basic choices of CFSP, that it shall be regularly informed by the Council and the Commission about the development of CFSP, and that its views shall be taken into consideration by the Presidency. In addition, the Parliament could ask questions of the Council and make recommendations to it and the TEU provided that 'it shall hold an annual debate on progress in implementing the CFSP.'

At the outset of the negotiations, the Italian Presidency reported that two options to enhance the Parliament's role had been advanced:

1 to provide information (especially within the competent committees) more systematically
2 to consult the Parliament on joint actions in individual cases (with a time limit set for the Parliament's opinion).

By July 1996 the Presidency had repeatedly indicated declining support for further involvement of the Parliament. The Irish Presidency claimed that there was consensus that there should be no Treaty changes while it may be envisaged to 'improve the provision of information to the Parliament' and 'possibly consult the Parliament on important policy papers of a general nature' (Conference of the Representatives of the Governments of the Member States, 1996e: 10). Even these weak provisions eventually fell. In December 1996, references to such improvements were removed altogether and the final text agreed in Amsterdam was altered only in name: Article J.7 became Article J.11.

Nevertheless, significant advances for the European Parliament were achieved in the field of financial scrutiny of the CFSP at a later stage in the negotiations. These were contained in an inter-institutional agreement between the European Parliament, the Council and the European Commission on provisions regarding financing of the Common Foreign and Security Policy (Conference of the Representatives of the Governments of the Member States, 1997f: 95–6) which was finally agreed at a meeting of the IGC representatives on 26–8 May 1997. Whereas the Parliament's role was previously limited to agreeing an overall figure for the CFSP budget, it is now entitled to further consultation and information and is able to agree the distribution of funds between six budget lines relating to CFSP expenditure. These are: observation and organization of elections and participation in democratic transition processes; EU envoys; prevention of conflicts and peace and security processes; financial assistance to disarmament processes; contributions to international conferences; and urgent actions.

With regard to the Parliament's consultation, the agreement obliges the Presidency to consult the Parliament on the main aspects and basic choices of CFSP on a yearly basis, and inform the Parliament on the implementation of CFSP on a more regular basis. The Council is required to communicate detailed estimates of the costs of all its decisions in the field of CFSP and the Commission is to provide the Parliament with financial forecasts on a quarterly basis.

Which body should be principally responsible for implementing CFSP?

The TEU gives the Presidency of the Council responsibility for the implementation of common measures and of representing the Union towards the outside world. The options outlined at the beginning of the IGC for strengthening the body responsible for implementing CFSP included:

1 Strengthening the Presidency by: extending the duration of the term of office; establishing a separate external Presidency of a longer duration to deal with all external relations of the CFSP; increasing the powers of the Presidency by delegating powers from the Council to increase the Presidency's role in the organization of work.
2 Introducing a Presidency/Commission arrangement which would have joint responsibility for implementing the CFSP but would not affect the allocation of institutional responsibilities.
3 Designation of a Ms/Mr CFSP who could be either an independent political figure or the Secretary-General of the Council.
4 Creation of a sort of 'executive Council' along the lines of the US National Security Council, which would be composed of the Troika, Ms/Mr CFSP, the Commission, and possibly a representative of the WEU.
5 Augmenting the role of the Troika to reinforce continuity in CFSP operation, together with a system of special envoys to carry out specific missions.
6 Creating a standing body of CFSP alternates to monitor CFSP implementation and deal with issues of day-to-day management.
7 Increasing the frequency of Political Committee meetings and/or creating a standing body of political directors' deputies to deal with day-to-day management.

These options were significantly narrowed down by July 1996 when the Irish Presidency documented more precise proposals for improving the Political Committee's capacity to deal with day-to-day events. It also presented three alternative options which provided for a strengthened role for the Secretary-General of the Council, the CFSP High Representative and a special envoy respectively. It noted that there was also wide support for maintaining the status quo with regard to the composition of the Troika.

Five months later, in December 1996, the Irish Presidency was able to draw up draft text on those proposals that received widespread support. One amendment to Article J.5 provided for the Presidency to be assisted by the Secretary-General of the Council, who would be given an enhanced standing and visibility in foreign policy (Conference of the Representatives of the Governments of the Member States, 1996i: 69). By May 1997 this draft had been modified, clarifying that the Secretary-General of the Council 'shall exercise the function of High Representative for CFSP'. The draft of J.5 stated that the Commission should be fully associated with the tasks of the Presidency, relating both to the representation of the Union's

CFSP and to the implementation of common measures. It also enabled the Council to appoint a special representative with a mandate in relation to particular policy issues. A new Troika resulted from these provisions, consisting of the Presidency, the High Representative and the next Presidency, plus the Commission. These provisions were finally adopted at Amsterdam albeit under a new name: Article 8.

Regarding the role of the Secretary-General of the Council, the Irish Presidency produced a new Article J.8b on this matter for the Dublin European Council (1996i: 70). This was only slightly modified before it was agreed at Amsterdam as a new Article J.16 which read as follows (Conference of the Representatives of the Governments of the Member States, 1997e: 108):

> *The Secretary-General of the Council, High Representative for the common foreign and security policy, shall assist the Council in matters coming within the scope of the common foreign and security policy, in particular through contributing to the formulation, preparation and implementation of policy decisions, and, when appropriate and acting on behalf of the Council at the request of the Presidency, through conducting political dialogue with third parties.*

The role of the Political Committee remains the same although it is now described under Article J.15 (formerly J.8(5)). As before, the Political Committee

> shall monitor the international situation in the areas covered by CFSP and contribute to the definition of policies by delivering opinions to the Council at the request of the Council or on its own initiative. It shall also monitor the implementation of agreed policies, without prejudice to the responsibility of the Presidency and the Commission.

A new Declaration to the Final Act (1997e: 107), however, augments this role in so far that:

> *Member States shall ensure that the Political Committee . . . is able to meet at any time, in the event of international crisis or other urgent matters, at very short notice at Political Director or deputy level.*

It remains to be seen to what extent the Political Committee will cooperate with, or duplicate, the proposed early warning and planning unit in fulfilling its role.

How should CFSP be financed?

It was agreed at an early stage in the negotiations that expenditure on the use of military means should at all times be charged to member states. Outstanding issues related to the conditions under which other CFSP expenditure would not be charged to the Community budget. During the course of

1996 it was repeatedly reported that the operational expenditure of CFSP would be charged to the Community budget provided that: it is possible to resort to financing by the member states in some cases; the budget procedure allows the Council to have the final say in budgetary decisions; and financing out of the Community budget complies with the financial perspective.

A further contentious issue related to the definition of CFSP expenditure as compulsory, which would effectively prevent the European Parliament from scrutinizing the CFSP budget. During 1997, the European Parliament proposed that this issue be resolved through the negotiation on an inter-institutional agreement between the Parliament, the Council and the Commission on CFSP financing.[43] Indeed, in the closing stages of the negotiations the Parliament's representatives implied that the Parliament was unlikely to give its approval for the new Treaty unless the inter-institutional agreement was concluded at Amsterdam. Such an agreement was reached and Article J.18 (former J.11) was adapted accordingly. Article J.18 stated that operational expenditure

> shall also be charged to the budget of the European Communities, except for such expenditure arising from operations having military or defence implications, and cases where the Council acting unanimously decides otherwise.

It also established that member states who had constructively abstained from a CFSP decision (under Article J.13.1) shall not be obliged to contribute to the financing thereof.

The negotiation on security and defence

The Union's objectives in security and defence

In April 1996, the conference of representatives published a note on the question of reforming Article J.4 of the TEU (Conference of the Representatives of the Governments of the Member States, 1996b). At this stage, the conference was only concerned with the degree to which common defence should become an objective of the Union. Article J.4.1 of the TEU established that the CFSP shall include all security questions including the 'eventual framing' of a common defence policy, which may lead to a common defence. In particular, the phrase 'eventual framing' of a common defence policy had been brought into question. After three months of negotiations, at the European Council in Florence, the Italian Presidency reported (Conference of the Representatives of the Governments of the Member States, 1996d: 46) that there was support for including 'framing of a common defence policy' in the CFSP, which would involve dropping the word 'eventual' from Article J.4 and replacing the 'possibility' of a common defence with the 'objective' of a common defence.

Other amendments had also been suggested during the first three months of negotiations. The first, which was introduced by Sweden and Finland and received support from most delegations, included the Petersberg missions of the WEU (peace maintenance, crisis management and humanitarian aid) as the content of EU policy on security and defence. The second, which was introduced by Greece, made the maintenance of territorial integrity and of common external frontiers an additional CFSP objective. A third option was to insert a solidarity clause into Article J.4 which would not constitute a commitment to an alliance. The last two options received little support.

The draft and heavily bracketed text, drawn up by the Irish Presidency after the Florence European Council in June 1996, indicated that consensus had been established on the inclusion of the Petersberg tasks in Article J.4.1, although the wording over the future development of common defence in the Union was not yet agreed. The Presidency also commented that there was some support for the insertion of a statement of the European Council's competence to set guidelines, including for the WEU, in Article J.4.1 and for some reference to be made to the principles of the UN Charter in inserting the objectives of the Petersberg tasks.

Some of these suggestions were later clarified and strengthened in amendments submitted jointly by Germany, France, Italy, Spain, Belgium and Luxembourg, with support of the Dutch Presidency (hence the name 'six plus one' coalition).[44] These amendments collectively attempted to expand upon the goal of a common defence policy. They clarified that 'The common defence policy includes the establishment of ground rules, goals and means in the field of defence' and stated that 'The Petersberg Tasks . . . are the first expression of a common security and defence policy. Armaments policy is a integral part of the common defence policy.' This attempt to expand upon the goal of a common defence policy was, however, ultimately unsuccessful in the face of strong opposition from the UK, Denmark, Ireland, Finland, Sweden and Austria. The final agreed text, therefore, was unchanged from that drafted for the Dublin summit in December 1996, except for an added reference to cooperation in the field of armaments.

The reference to armaments policy was a compromise between the proposals of the Franco-German coalition and those states which favoured the status quo. The new paragraph in Article J.7.4 simply states that:

> *The progressive framing of a common defence shall be supported, as appropriate, by cooperation between Member States in the field of armaments.*

This language is weak in comparison with earlier drafts, and maintains the national, non-Community nature of armaments policy. It would allow for cross-border mergers between defence firms, a development which is being increasingly forced by industry rationalization, although not for a common export policy to be established, other than through the CFSP instruments outlined elsewhere (Articles 2 to 5) in the Treaty.

Relationship with the WEU

Relations between the EU and the WEU were one of the most controversial areas in the negotiations.[45] One view, supported by the UK and many of the neutral states, was that the status quo should be maintained. The other view, supported by France, Germany and others, was that the Union's authority over the WEU should be spelled out ('the EU *instructs* the WEU') along with a timetable for eventual integration of the WEU into the EU. Indeed, in March 1997, Germany, France, Italy, Spain, Belgium and Luxembourg (with support of the Dutch Presidency) elaborated on these proposals in a draft protocol to be annexed to the TEU detailing a three-phase procedure and timetable for the integration of the WEU into the EU.[46] In accordance with these proposals, the European Council would decide general guidelines for the formulation of practical rules by the Council and the WEU, and would govern the transition process for their integration.

Although strongly favoured by the states which submitted them, all of the above proposals were ultimately blocked by the UK, Denmark and the neutral states in the final negotiations in Amsterdam. The final text, therefore, remains largely unchanged from that suggested at the Dublin European Council, although, as the result of a British compromise proposal, Article J.7.1(2) now refers to '*closer institutional relations with the WEU with a view to the possibility of the integration of the WEU into the Union*' and a protocol annexed to Article J.7 provides for '*arrangements for enhanced cooperation*' (between the EU and the WEU) within a year from the entry into force of the Treaty.[47]

The integration of the WEU into the Union will, nevertheless, be extremely difficult. It is subject to a unanimous recommendation by the European Council which is to be adopted by the member states 'in accordance with their respective constitutional requirements'.

The same procedure could govern the possible framing of a common defence policy within the EU, and therefore creates an opportunity for non-IGC-based reviews of this Article of the Treaty, although an IGC review is in any case planned by Article J.7.5.

The subtle compromise, brokered in Amsterdam, also reinforces the reference to NATO's role of providing for common defence in Article J.7.1(3), and the protocol on Article J.7 mentions the need to respect 'the obligations of certain Member States, which see their common defence realized in NATO, under the North Atlantic Treaty'. The Irish Presidency also formulated amendments, creating a second paragraph for Article J.4.2, to clarify that all member states could participate in actions involving the WEU, regardless of the status of their membership in that organization. Ultimately, however, this was not deemed necessary and the conference was able to agree a text which was essentially the same as that presented by the Irish Presidency in December 1996. The final draft of this subparagraph of Article J.7.2 reads:

When the Union avails itself of the WEU to elaborate and implement decisions of the Union on the tasks referred to in paragraph 1, second subparagraph, all Member States of the Union shall be entitled to participate fully in the tasks in question. The Council, in agreement with the institutions of the WEU, shall adopt the necessary practical arrangements. *These arrangements shall allow all Member States contributing to the tasks in question to participate fully and equally in planning and decision-taking in the WEU.*

Finally, the Irish Presidency reported that some states argued for an optional protocol, setting out the mutual defence commitment which applies to full WEU members, to be annexed to the Treaty. Unsurprisingly, this suggestion was not supported by those states who were not full members of the WEU and those who did not support the goal of WEU–EU integration. Therefore no such additional protocol was adopted.

Conclusions

There are some clear outcomes of the IGC negotiations, although whether or not these translate to a stronger CFSP remains to be seen. Amsterdam agreed both new institutions and mechanisms: a strengthened Secretary-General acting as a High Representative, special envoys, a policy planning and early warning unit, a mechanism for crisis management, and some introduction of qualified majority voting in the decision-making process. These innovations serve to make the web of European institutional interaction more dense, to embed certain aspects of military activity within it, and to encourage common reflection on Europe's place and role in the world. However, institutions alone do not change policies and it appears that there has been little spillover from the dynamics of EMU to the political dimension.

The European Union continues to oscillate between the French–German conception of a powerful Europe and the acceptance of US predominance in the post Cold War world order, and demonstrates parallel tensions between integrationists and intergovernmentalists. It remains a strange political animal where foreign policy decision making is more often than not dispersed and difficult to pin down. The exception to this is when big powers share common objectives. On an *ad hoc* basis they may, therefore, act in concert, establishing directorates like the Contact Group which influence events without furthering interstate integration or involving the smaller countries.

Nevertheless the Union will have a more efficient decision-making mechanism and its policies will probably be more visible, although subject to strong American influence and limited democratic control, both by the European Parliament and national parliaments. Big states and the Presidency are likely to benefit most from Amsterdam in so far as they will be given improved means to exercise leadership through managed coalition building. The same is true for the WEU where the notion of 'pilot nation' has been introduced at the operational level.[48]

With regard to military affairs, the Amsterdam Treaty has not weakened the WEU. The organization remains central to the elaboration of a common defence policy, while the prospects of its integration into the Union are distant (it would require a unanimous decision by the European Council with national ratifications or a new IGC). Prime Minister Tony Blair successfully defended the strategic interests of British bipartisan foreign policy by blocking significant changes to Article J.4 of the Maastricht Treaty. Consequently, the WEU maintains its privileged position with respect to the Union in so far as it has a legal personality.

Moreover, the UK strengthened the Treaty references to NATO, mentioning that NATO provides for the common defence of '*some Member States*'. This wording allows neutral states and France to keep their independent positions while codifying the subordination of the European defence identity to the Atlantic Alliance. Moreover, it appears that NATO will come to play a larger role in the EU, given the overlap and similarity of the combined joint task forces (CJTFs) concept within NATO and the Petersberg tasks within the EU/WEU. In sum, the interdependence between NATO and the EU is stronger than ever and could lead in the foreseeable future to direct bilateral relationships between the two organizations. This contrasts with the unclear future relationship between the WEU and the European security and defence identity (ESDI). France remains outside NATO's military structure after it lost its two battles over the Southern Command and NATO's enlargement at the Atlantic Madrid summit (July 1997). In addition, the role of the Deputy SACEUR in the activation of CJTF is still not settled and there is no prospect for any European caucus within NATO. Moreover, if the WEU is to play the role of a European subgroup of NATO, it may directly challenge the European Council which is theoretically empowered to decide guidelines for the Union's common defence policy.

For these reasons CFSP is likely to remain limited to some non-vital sectors of cooperation or 'low intensity' crisis management in nearby regions. For the foreseeable future the Union will remain largely a civilian power under the security umbrella of the US.

Notes

1 This section is mainly based on Istituto Affari Internazionali (1996) and Parlement Européen (n.d.a; n.d.b; n.d.c).

2 Benelux countries will be frequently quoted together because of their release of joint memoranda during the whole negotiation, although some differences will be noted about defence issues. We refer here to the Benelux memorandum of March 1996.

3 See especially the results of the French–German Foreign Ministers Seminar (1996).

4 He would be a German.

5 See also hereafter the section about the WEU's contribution to the IGC and the section about the negotiation on defence issues.

6 This word, often used by Jean Monnet, is preferred to 'supranational' which relates more to institutions being over the member states which does not apply to the second pillar anyway.

7 In Maastricht, a WEU declaration has been introduced in the Treaty (Declaration 30) but there had been no direct opinion by the WEU before the 1991 IGC.

8 Article 30(5) of the SEA.

9 Article C of the TEU.

10 Article J.5 of the TEU. Comments in Cameron (1997).

11 For an overview and analysis of this Commission's proposal, see Remacle (1991).

12 We will not mention further proposals regarding pure Community matters like common commercial policy, where the Commission has promoted especially the extension of Article 113 of the TEC to services and intellectual property and the clarification of the procedure in order to strengthen its role in international negotiations.

13 Sustainable Development Committee of the United Nations, negotiations on the European Energy Charter, International Labour Organization, Food and Agriculture Organization (European Commission, 1995a: par. 140; 1996a: par. 26).

14 European Commission (1996a: par. 31). The paralysing effect of the unanimity voting is especially criticized in two cases: when it limits the scope of sanctions, although these could be decided by majority voting (a direct reference to the failure to decide financial sanctions against Haiti because of unanimity voting is made in European Commission, 1995a: par. 131–2), and for the adoption of joint actions under Article J.3 of the TEU (1995a: par. 151–4).

15 An inter-institutional agreement between the Council, the Parliament and the Commission is proposed as the best solution (European Commission, 1995a: par. 157–8).

16 For comments by the Commission's representatives on CFSP, see e.g. Santer (1995), Bonino (1995) and Burghardt (1995).

17 Resolutions on the implementation of CFSP from November 1993 until December 1994 (*Official Journal* C151, 19 June 1995); from January until December 1995 (*Official Journal* C261, 9 September 1996); from January until December 1996 (Doc. A4-0193/97, Brussels, 28 May 1997).

18 Parlement Européen (n.d.a; n.d.b; n.d.c).

19 Resolutions on 17 May 1995 (*Official Journal* C151, 19 June 1995); on 13 March 1996 (*Official Journal* C96, 1 April 1996); on 16 January 1997 (Doc. B4-0040/97); on 13 March 1997 (Doc. B4-0266/97).

20 The Bourlanges–Martin Report is quoted as Document B4-0102/95. Resolution on 17 May 1995 as previously cited (*Official Journal* C151, 19 June 1995).

21 Resolution on 17 May 1995, par. 3 as previously cited (*Official Journal* C151, 19 June 1995). Among the provisions which did not survive the amendments of MEPs, one can note the proposal to appoint one Commissioner in charge of CFSP and another in charge of defence who would be at the same time Secretary-General of the WEU.

22 Doc. A4-0162/97, 14 May 1997, par. 6.

23 See hereafter.

24 *Declaration on the Role of Western European Union and on its Relations with the European Union and the Atlantic Alliance*, par. 8.

25 The Rome Declaration of the Atlantic summit in November 1991 speaks about ESDI as a reality within NATO not automatically linked to the WEU.

26 For a reminder of these decisions, see Jopp (1997) and Deighton (1997).

27 See Assembly of the Western European Union, Documents 1495 (De Puig Report), 16 November 1995, par. 123–53; 1458 (Aguiar Report), 16 May 1995, par. 136–58; 1486 (Hunt Report), 6 November 1995, par. 109–21; 1564 (Antretter-Squarcialupi Report), 9 May 1997, par. 151–6 and the Recommendation Project.

28 This term was already used for qualifying the impact of the 1984 WEU revitalization on Danish and Irish positions within the Dooge Committee about the inclusion of security in EPC competences: see Thune (1985).

29 This is Declaration 2 annexed to the Amsterdam Treaty (*Declaration of Western European Union on the Role of Western European Union and its Relations with the European Union and with the Atlantic Alliance*).

30 See the reference to the 'six plus one' coalition in the following description of the negotiation.

31 For example, the new Prodi government in Italy is more Europeanist than the Berlusconi government. In contrast, the return of the Gaullists in France strengthened the nationalist approach to foreign policy. In the neutral countries, social democrats remain reluctant to give up neutrality while conservative parties favour application to NATO.

32 For an application to foreign policy see e.g. Petersen (1977).

33 This is the broadest definition of civil society cited in Chilton (1995).

34 Some development, conflict prevention and peace NGOs argue that the EU should play a leading role (which is not effectively dictated by the US) in peacekeeping, conflict management and post-conflict reconstruction through the improved operationalization of the WEU. However, they are often reluctant to strengthen the defence identity of the Union more generally. Paradoxically perhaps, the reluctance of states such as the UK to cede a greater role in common defence to the EU, for fear that it might undermine the pre-eminence of NATO, ultimately resulted in a Treaty which realizes many of the goals of these peace movements.

35 Common position of 2 June 1997 defined by the Council on the basis of Article J.2 of the Treaty on European Union, concerning conflict prevention and resolution in Africa (*Official Journal* L153, 11 June 1997).

36 Moreover, the Council commits the Union 'to use the various instruments available coherently to promote effective conflict prevention and resolution ... including with regard to development cooperation and the support for human rights, democracy, the rule of law and good governance'. The Council also recognized 'that the availability of arms in quantities exceeding needs for self-defence may be a factor contributing to situations of instability' while it remains the prerogative of member states to practise restraint with regard to arms exports and to strengthen their efforts to combat illicit trafficking of arms.

37 See note 46 for references on the proposals to introduce flexibility in the second pillar.

38 Amendment in italics.

39 Conference of the Representatives of the Governments of the Member States (1997e). Amendments are in italics.

40 Conference of the Representatives of the Governments of the Member States (1997e). Amendments are in italics.

41 On the German position, see Reimund Seidelmann's contribution in Chapter 7.

42 This Article covers provisions on voting which appear in former Articles J.3(2), J.4(3) and J.8(2) second subparagraph. It is quoted from Conference of the Representatives of the Governments of the Member States (1997e: 106).

43 See the earlier discussion of the role of the European Parliament.

44 *Joint Proposals on the Relationship between the EU and the WEU, Document on Article J.4 to the Treaty on European Union*, quoted from *Agence Europe* (1997a: 4–5).

45 For a full discussion of the options initially under consideration, see earlier.

46 *Joint Proposals on the Relationship between the EU and the WEU, Document on Article J.4 to the Treaty on European Union*, quoted from *Agence Europe* (1997a: 4–5).

47 A Declaration also invites the Council 'to seek the early adoption of appropriate arrangements for the security clearance of the personnel of the General Secretariat of the Council'.

48 This was introduced in the communiqué of the Paris meeting of the WEU Council in May 1997.

6   France and the European Project: Internal and External Issues

Yves Boyer

Not since the beginning of the European project have domestic issues weighed so heavily on France's attitudes regarding the development of the European Union. In the past, the EU's objectives were debated in relation to their positive economic or industrial impact. Now they encompass qualitative developments which are felt by a large, although disparate, segment of the French public opinion to be potentially undermining France's identity. Accordingly, *nolens volens*, the EU construction now stands, more than ever, at the crossroads of external and internal problems confronting the French.

Such a turn of events occurs at a time when the country is experiencing social and political difficulties. It is, indeed, going through a profound crisis seldom appreciated by foreign observers. Its persistence may thus dramatically affect Paris's will, ambition and objectives concerning European integration. It also largely explains why French leaders are focusing their objectives, particularly where the Common Foreign and Security Policy (CFSP) is concerned, around mechanisms aimed at building the European Union as a 'power'. Their goal is *l'Europe puissance*. It is probably one of the most appealing ways to present the objective of greater integration within the EU to the French people, moulded by 1,000 years of proud history, and to make them endorse the idea of relinquishing part of their sovereignty.

The internal situation in France

The domestic situation in France is worrying[1] and could dramatically affect French attitudes and intentions concerning the European project. For many years already, France has been in a difficult state that can be likened to a psychological 'depression'. Symptoms of this crisis are numerous. Control of the National Assembly has, for example, changed hands in five straight elections in the last sixteen years. These past elections, and particularly those held in May–June 1997, also revealed the existence of a strong extreme right.

It became France's third largest political party, in voter numbers, a phenomenon out of proportion with what exists elsewhere in Europe.[2]

In fact, the country is full of potential and strength. It has probably never been wealthier. However, it suffers grave malfunctions and has the feeling of being deadlocked. The French have collectively lost a vision of their future. Neither ideologies, nor political projects, including the EU project, seem able to capture and mobilize their energy. Such a situation has not arrived overnight. It has various origins, particularly the unsatisfactory relationship between on the one hand the citizens, and on the other the politicians and the class of upper-level civil servants. A gap is widening dangerously between the French people and their political and administrative elite.

This situation is probably of greater consequence for France than for any other West European country in so far as a long historical tradition gives the state a leading role in practically all domains of activity, from industry to culture,[3] in addition to its traditional role in domestic, foreign and defence affairs. In order to carry out its diverse missions, the state has relied on a hierarchical civil service whose tradition of centralization goes back to Colbert, one of the most pre-eminent ministers of King Louis XIV at the end of the seventeenth century. The organization of the civil service was successively improved by Napoleon, then by the Third Republic (created after the defeat by Prussia in 1870–1) and by the Fifth Republic, under the guidance of Charles de Gaulle.

Upper-level civil servants are recruited by competitions open to two schools. One of these schools, well known outside France, is the Ecole Nationale d'Administration (ENA) which was created in 1945. The other, to a certain extent more prestigious, is the Ecole polytechnique (known as 'l'X') which was created in 1794. Each young high civil servant, at the age of around 23–4, leaves ENA or l'X ranked according to academic performance. At ENA, the five or six best graduates, from an average group of 40–5 persons, choose to enter the highest levels of the French administration called *les grands Corps de l'Etat* which include the Inspection des Finances, the Cour des Comptes (the accounting office) and the Conseil d'Etat (the Supreme Court for administrative acts). At l'X the 20–5 best, from around 200 persons, choose the Corps des Mines (known under the abbreviation of X-Mines), the Corps des Télécomunications (X-Télécom) and the Corps des Ponts et Chaussés (civil engineering, X-Ponts). While all graduates from ENA and l'X are almost certain to occupy the most important places in the administration or in the private sectors in which the state is more or less involved (banks, industries, etc.), the most powerful will remain in the Inspection des Finances and the X-Mines who, for the most part, control the French industrial, banking and administrative system, additionally maintaining close relations with politicians. They are able to work in almost every sector and, when they choose to go back to their *corps*, the state automatically guarantees that they will receive a salary related to their respective seniority in the *corps*.

These types of privileges are now seen by a huge segment of the French population as similar, to a certain extent, to those attributed in the old France to the Fermier Général. The Fermier Général was a kind of governor who was charged by the king to collect taxes. The position was 'bought' by interested persons who would collect taxes, some of which it was agreed would be for their own personal use. This powerful person was an illustration of the idea of feudality and anti-democratic practice. Such a system has given and continues to yield moments of glory and great achievement as most of these people are very talented. However, the system is becoming dysfunctional. It has resulted in producing a kind of caste with its own mechanisms of control, its own network of influence, allowing for excesses contrary to the normal practice of democracy.[4] The most striking example characterizing the dysfunction in the state of things has been the management of a key French bank, the Crédit Lyonnais, by an *inspecteur des finances* whose eccentric management, according to various estimates, cost each taxpaying French citizen in the mid 1990s an additional 4,500 FF. The state-owned bank had to be bailed out. The head of the bank was, of course, dismissed, but without giving any justification for past behaviour, and he returned to the Inspection des Finances to await his retirement.

To a large extent this caste, known in France as the *technostructure*, has seized power and has gradually deprived political leaders and members of Parliament of much of their role. Jacques Chirac's campaign during the May 1995 presidential election was aimed at downsizing the weight, power and influence of the *technostructure*. In reality, nothing has changed. If one examines the cabinet members that surrounded the head of state, former Prime Minister Alain Juppé, and the government ministers ousted after the May/June 1997 elections, there were more members of the *technostructure* than ever. This phenomenon is repeated in the Jospin government which came into power in June 1997. The political parties have also been largely monopolized by the *technostructure*. The Prime Minister Lionel Jospin, his successor at the head of the Socialist Party François Hollande, the former RPR leader Alain Juppé and his successor Phillipe Seguin, as well as most leaders of the UDF, are graduates from ENA. As already mentioned, the world of business is also largely in the hands of the *polytechniciens* or the *inspecteurs des finances*. This 'consanguinity' between interchangeable people has led to dysfunction in the political system, in business and in the industrial world in France. Misuse of power, confiscation of power (the plurality of offices being a by-product of the current malfunction),[5] misuse of company or state assets, and misappropriation of corporate funds by the French ruling elite have reached a point where violations of the law exceed the number of cases before the courts (Abescat, 1996). This state of dysfunction and corruption coincides with the aggravation over other problems which bear down on the French.

One of these problems is unemployment, which in the 1990s stabilized to a little more than 12 per cent of the active population. Nothing indicates a rapid improvement in the current trend. This factor provokes fears in the future for a large segment of the population, aggravating the feeling of uneasiness felt by many people, particularly the young. They fear becoming part of the growing number of social outcasts (*les exclus*) if deprived of their jobs.

The second issue stems from the previous one and is related to the economic policy followed by French authorities, left and right, since the early 1990s. This policy is perceived as sheer deflation, which has been personified by the chairman of the Bank of France, Jean-Claude Trichet. It has been justified by the necessity to reduce growing public deficit, particularly to conform to the Maastricht criteria regarding the move toward a single currency. In a negative manner, it has also been depicted by some of its opponents as yielding to the diktat of the Bundesbank and of financial markets. Heavy taxes, amounting in 1997 to about 55 per cent of the French GNP (a record among OECD countries), add to the effects of the deflationary policy of the *franc fort*.

Hopes were raised that the President elected in 1995 could follow a different policy, as suggested by some heavyweight supporters of Jacques Chirac like the Chairman of the National Assembly, Philippe Seguin. In a televised speech in October 1995, Chirac ended speculation about *l'autre politique* ('the other policy'). The line largely inspired by Jean-Claude Trichet prevailed. It later heavily influenced the choices made in the autumn of 1997 by Jospin's Socialist government.

The policy of the *franc fort* and heavy taxation, combined with the effects of the growing globalization of the economy, have translated into a high social cost (unemployment, redundancies, etc.) attributed, rightly or wrongly, to the *technostructure*, to the European Commission, and to the European Union. The overall result is a growing doubt and scepticism about the benefit of the European construction as it is pursued. Accordingly the IGC could not be presented, as was the Maastricht Treaty, as a gateway to a brilliant future, and it therefore never became a widely discussed topic.

The accumulation of a sense of immobility, of anxiety about an uncertain future, epitomized by the high unemployment rate, by the unresolved problems linked to immigration, the growing political and business scandals, the increasing distance between the so-called elite and the French people (*pays réel* versus *pays légal*), have produced an explosive cocktail in a country where 'fever eruptions' have been frequent in history. The current complex and very volatile situation has led to a proliferation of analyses oscillating between drawing a parallel between the current situation and that prevailing in France in the years 1785–7, and emphasizing the potential implosion of the society when some of its members, disappointed and disillusioned by the way the country has been ruled for many years, abstain from participating in democratic life. Here lies the central issue: democracy has to be fully restored in France. As pointed out by the Prime Minister, Lionel Jospin (1997b), 'the French people have the need to regain self confidence . . . in their public institutions . . . in political life.' In a humorous vein, the newspaper *Le Monde* in July 1996 published an editorial aimed at reminding the head of state of the request sent to Louis XVI by some of his subjects in the spring of 1789 in order to compel those in power to abide by the law. This text perfectly describes the present situation prevailing in France (Rollat, 1996). More seriously, analyses from qualified and moderate observers emphasize the dramatic mood of the French. One editor of a major newspaper, *Ouest France*,[6] wrote in July 1996, that

> many leaders, and not only political leaders, are wondering if this country is going to experience a severe crisis in comparison with which last [1995] December's strikes would only be a light fever? They are wondering if, in the next few months, the country will undergo a crisis similar to ones we have known in our history due to this profound, almost revolutionary turmoil. Among the many reproaches the French address (to the 'ruling class') is its incompetence. The incompetence of the employers who run their enterprises badly, leading to redundancies . . . incompetence of those responsible for the school system which fails to prepare the young for acquiring a job, incompetence of those responsible for state-owned firms. (Duquesne, 1996)

This dramatic perception was still present a year later in mid 1997, when Denis Tillinac (1997), a close friend of President Chirac, explaining the reasons for the defeat of the right coalition at the legislative election in June 1997, wrote that 'France is a bomb, the match is burning and the scissors to cut it are long overdue.' As an echo, a similar view was expressed by a left-wing intellectual: 'the country is exasperated and the society is rumbling' (Cohen-Seat, 1997).

In this brief description of France's difficulties, Brussels, that is to say the European Union, not only appears no longer capable of providing positive solutions but, in the opinion of some, actually exacerbates France's internal crisis. In these circumstances, one can understand that EU reforms have been far from highly debated outside political circles.

French approach to EU transformation

In the months before the IGC started, French views on it were seldom heard (*CREST Monography*, 1996). A heavy internal agenda at the time resulted in very little open debate about the IGC among French political leaders. This attitude should not, however, be attributed to any kind of disinterest. It was a by-product of the prevailing political situation with the upcoming presidential campaign and the perceived aggravation of the political, economic and societal difficulties in France.

Gradually, however, a few themes emerged, indicating French objectives particularly aimed at CFSP and institutional reforms. As previously mentioned, France pursued a policy aimed broadly at a gradually built *l'Europe puissance*. This is probably what constitutes the bedrock of French ideas about Europe: deepening the European construction in order to build the EU up as a power, possessing various means, including military forces, to assert and defend its interests and to make its voice heard and respected on the world stage. There is clearly a strong consensus on that objective. Jacques Delors developed this idea (Vernet, 1994), as well as former President Valéry Giscard d'Estaing. As a matter of principle, France thus resists any drift away from the motives and rationale which have been fundamental to the European integration process since its beginning. It objects to the dilution of the EU into a kind of free market zone with *à la carte* obligations and 'opting out' possibilities as the former Conservative government in the UK sought, a policy that presumably the Labour government of Tony Blair will continue. For the French, the European construction is far more than a free market agreement. It is, above all, a political project whose objective is the creation of an unprecedented historical union between countries which have been at war so many times in the past and which are now confronted with many challenges requiring common, integrated and unified policies, particularly in defence and foreign affairs. It is, in the words of the Foreign Affairs minister Hubert Védrine (1997a), 'the most innovative regional integration enterprise ever seen in history'. Thus, the French maintained their opposition to a European Union being only a free market zone, which the British are suspected to favour. Addressing French ambassadors gathered in Paris in August 1997, both President Chirac and his Socialist Foreign Affairs Minister Hubert Védrine reiterated their commitment to that objective.[7] The practical translation into deeds of this goal is the development of the EU in two 'circles'. The outer circle would be open to new members agreeing on basic common policies, and the inner would contain more integrated countries (*le cercle des solidarités renforcées*) (Juppé, 1995). In preparation for the IGC, the French acknowledged that the past enlargement of the EU to fifteen members has brought together countries which are less united in their aspirations than the initial six signatories of the Rome Treaty. According to Hubert Védrine (1997b), Foreign Affairs Minister: 'the European Union is more unwieldy with fifteen members than it was with twelve, which means that we have to break new grounds'. It was recognized that the process of enlargement to include Eastern and Central Europe would probably reinforce centrifugal forces within the EU. Accordingly, the 1997 IGC was devoted to defining mechanisms aimed at allowing countries such as Germany and France to pursue their objective of 'reinforced cooperation' (de Charrette, 1996). This essential objective was the subject of a common letter sent to all members of the EU by President Chirac and Chancellor Kohl on 7 December 1995, advocating the development within the Union of 'enhanced solidarity' (*solidarités renforcées*). France and Germany called for new flexibility in the functioning of the Union to allow members to deepen their cooperation without risking a veto from reluctant partners. If such a proposal should be rebuffed, hints were being made – bearing in mind Britain's attitude – that enhanced cooperation would go ahead if necessary outside the EU.[8] This debate reflected the implicit feeling that the future of the EU lay in the development of concentric circles defining different types of integration and commitment. In an EU of 25–6 members, one will probably see the development of a core of about five to seven countries, including France and Germany, committed to progress towards building *l'Europe puissance*.

In addition to this fundamental issue, an agreed position was reached after intense discussion by Bonn and Paris on the type of institutional reform needed by the EU. It was decided that the European Council should be the highest body for action and decision in the field of the EU's foreign and defence policy. The holder of a new position, the *Haut Représentant* (High Representative) advocated by France, would have the task of representing the Union in relation to the Presidency and with a mandate from the Council, particularly when 'enhanced cooperation' necessitated common action. Regarding the transformation of the decision-making process of the EU, various topics have had to be addressed during the IGC. First, the weighting of the votes has been discussed. At present a qualified majority is obtained by the equivalent of 58 per cent of the European population; at twelve, the percentage was 63 per cent. In an enlarged Union, it would fall to the equivalent of less than 50 per cent. It appeared necessary to correct this imbalance by increasing the weight of the most populated countries of the EU. Secondly, to respect the principle of subsidiary, it was decided that national parliaments ought to be associated with the decision-making process, a goal proposed by the Irish Presidency at the EU's Dublin summit in December 1996. Lastly, the number of Commissioners was to be reduced to ten. At the same time, when institutional issues were debated within the IGC, a key issue emerging as the crucial stake in the development of the EU as *l'Europe puissance* was that of currency.

Towards a common currency

The euro serves various purposes. In addition to its sheer economic and financial impact, it is seen by observers as bringing strategic transformation to Europe itself between those countries 'in' and those 'out' of the single currency system (Vernet, 1997). It represents 'the ending stage of the economic union and the first step of the political union' (Boissonat, 1997). It was portrayed by the former Juppé government as an instrument of 'political unity',[9] as a political endeavour. As stated by a former Foreign Affairs Minister, Hervé de Charrette (1997), 'today there is a worldwide currency, the dollar, and a few regional currencies . . . Tomorrow there will be two worldwide currencies, the dollar and the euro.' Declarations by the Jospin government have been in the same vein. For M. Jospin (1997b), 'the euro will give Europe the possibility to restore its monetary sovereignty.' The European Affairs Minister, Pierre Moscovici (1997), emphasized this goal, pointing out that the euro will allow Europe to be 'a power able to weight with its currency against the dominant currency and the dominant power. The dollar and the United States.' Indeed, even for foreign observers, the euro may become a key currency rival to the US dollar on exchange markets with a positive influence on the stability of the international monetary system (*Le Monde*, 1997). A former member of the Bank of France monetary policy council and a respected commentator on monetary issues in France, Jean Boissonat (1997), added: 'we are developing the euro partly in order to question the privileged position of the dollar in the sense that, due to the status of their currency, the United States is the only country in the world which does not pay for the consequences of an undervalued currency, high interest rates.'

One has to mention that, for their part, the German authorities expressed almost the same views on the fundamental consequences of the euro. Klaus Kinkel emphasized, for example, that the euro 'was a question of destiny for Europe' (*Financial Times*, 1997a). As usual, British commentators were quick to point out expected disagreements between France and Germany at this stage of the negotiations on the euro:

> the Germans want the planned Stability Pact to discipline the budget deficits of national governments by rules that are fixed and automatic; the French (and others) want rules that allow for political judgment. For the Germans, monetary stability is an absolute priority; but the French want something like an economic government for Europe which would promote stability and growth. (Davidson, 1996)

Speaking of Franco-German relations, Karl Lamers (1997), member of the Bundestag and CDU/CSU spokesman for foreign affairs, noted, referring to the Stability Pact agreed at the EU's summit in Dublin, that 'the struggle about the Stability Pact has revealed once more that interdependence between France and Germany is ineluctable.' In fact, peripheral to the preparation of the Amsterdam summit of July 1997, there had been intense Franco-German discussions about the euro. After reiterating its total support for the single currency, the Jospin government fought hard at Amsterdam for an agreement on including the monetary discipline required for the euro in the framework of broader considerations, particularly linked to employment, stating 'our economies cannot grow and satisfy our people's demands if we base our approach solely on stability and monetary concerns' (Jospin, 1997a).

If money comprises one part of state sovereignty, the other is defence. On that front as well, Paris made proposals directed at developing *l'Europe puissance*.

The evolution of the European security framework and its influence on French positions at the IGC

Tensions and contradictions within the Western world make the awaited adjustments in the European security architecture a slow and complicated process which was debated at the IGC with regard to EU foreign and security policy.

One has first to be aware that since the early 1990s, major Western

European nations such as the Federal Republic of Germany, the United Kingdom and France have reduced their defence budgets, but at the same time have been trying to maintain many of the former missions assigned to their forces. In the meantime, as economic depressions were translated into cuts in defence budgets, new perceptions of risks and vulnerabilities led to a reassessment of the role of military forces in international relations. More disturbing in the long term, cuts, when they apply to procurement, may have an indirect consequence on high-tech civilian industries in Western Europe since military R&D effort largely supports those industries. This pattern of evolution may prove to be very worrying in the medium term. It reduces significantly the active forces immediately available for military operations, which could result in the potential development of the European Union's Common Foreign and Security Policy (CFSP) becoming an empty shell if it cannot be backed by significant and potent military forces.

Secondly, for a certain period, the security institutions created during the Cold War continue to play a role before radical transformations. They take account of the new balance of power, risks and responsibility between the US and the EU that will lead to a new security landscape in Europe. A time will then arrive when a simplification will be necessary because current institutions may end up by contradicting each other and may no longer reflect the actual balance of power within the Western Alliance.

The potential development of a genuine European pillar within NATO may profoundly transform the Alliance in ways that are not yet totally assessed. When France announced at the North Atlantic Council of 5 December 1995 that she would join part of the military integrated structure, her move was also aimed at modifying the internal balance of NATO. As pointed out by the then French Defence Minister, Charles Millon (1996), 'we intend to incite a change . . . Nato's renovation has already begun but is still incomplete.'

This was seen from Paris as a means to implement decisions reached at NATO's Brussels summit of January 1994, regarding the European security and defence initiative (ESDI). Later, in a speech at a NATO Ministerial Council in February 1997, the French Foreign Affairs Minister Hervé de Charrette, recalled the French vision of a renovated Alliance, based on a renewed and genuine partnership between the US and Europe in which 'Europe, if it wants to become a major actor in the next century on the international scene, should accept responsibilities and with them the burden of being powerful. America, if it wants to remain engaged in Europe, should not forget the meaning of collective action and the discipline of multilateral cooperation.' For Paris, the implementation of the decisions reached at NATO's Brussels summit of January 1994 regarding ESDI have to be transformed into actual concrete measures. In this process, three points were emphasized by Paris:

1 NATO's command structure would have to be transformed to take into account new military and geopolitical realities. France will certainly

play an active role in this transformation and looks forward to Europeans taking charge of regional commands (Isnard, 1996) since there are actually fewer European NATO commanders at the level of regional commands now than when France left the integrated command in 1966.

2 The adaptation of the political and military decision-making process of the Alliance has to be achieved. For Paris there is a need to increase the role of the sixteen defence and foreign affairs ministers who need to consult more frequently at the level of the North Atlantic Council (NAC). At the same time, the Military Committee should be called upon to play a greater role in providing the NAC with military advice.

3 The definition of mechanisms allowing the Europeans to use NATO's assets for joint military operations should be worked out. These operations are those envisaged in the WEU's Petersberg Declaration. Within a renovated Alliance, the European contribution to defence should become more visible and more efficient at both the political and the operational level (Millon, 1996). That means that the 'Europeanization' of the Alliance should be 'effective not only at the outset of an operation but during peacetime as well. It should be translated not only during the operations but also at the level of planning, preparation and decision making at the political-military level' (Millon, 1996). In this domain, although progress has been made regarding the future tasks assigned to a Deputy SACEUR (Chirac, 1996), a sensitive issue remains the Europeanization of NATO's regional commands. The inability of the US to accept a shift of responsibility led French authorities, in July 1997, to stop any move towards the integrated structure of the Alliance. Within a renovated Alliance, the European Union's contribution to defence should be made through WEU. The development of a defence component of the EU is, indeed, at a very early stage but is absolutely needed, for 'Europe shall put an end to its impotence. It shall assert itself as a key player on the world stage, of a multipolar world that we have to develop in finishing to erase Yalta' (Chirac, 1996).

French views regarding the WEU have to be understood in the framework of providing the European Union with a defence component of its own. Enhancing the role of WEU presupposes reaching four objectives:

1 Reinforcing WEU's operational planning cell, to give it the capacity to plan, from the outset until the end, military operations launched by WEU.

2 Developing a comprehensive military space policy to provide Europe with an independent reconnaissance capability, a *sine qua non* for strategic autonomy. The cooperation developed between France and Germany and probably in conjunction with Spain and Italy should meet the objective of creating a European space intelligence system.

3 Giving coherence to the different multinational forces already existing among West Europeans: Eurocorps, EUROMARFOR, EUROFOR,

EAFG. France will offer proposals for better articulating these forces with WEU.

4 Continuing to integrate European efforts to build a European defence industrial base.

At a ministerial meeting in Rome in the framework of the IGC, France and Germany, backed by Belgium, Luxembourg, Italy and Spain, proposed a protocol to the Maastricht Treaty that would incorporate the WEU in the framework of the EU. The idea underlying such a proposal was the development of the EU's responsibility in the field of defence to avoid being fully dependent on NATO and the United States. Different stages of the process were suggested, the last step being around 2010 with a total fusion between the two organizations (Lemaître, 1997).[10] This proposal was met by a fierce counterattack from the UK Foreign Secretary, who stated that the proposal 'risked undercutting the alliance and provoking Russia' (*Financial Times*, 1997a). This traditional British opposition is based as usual on London's determination not to undertake actions that could affect the US military presence in Europe and the central role the US plays in NATO.

The mixed results of the IGC

The results of the Amsterdam summit were in large part seen as disappointing. Former French President Valéry Giscard d'Estaing (1997) evoked 'Amsterdam's failure'. The influential Chairman of the National Assembly's Foreign Affairs Committee, Jack Lang (1997), called the accord 'a rump treaty' that he would not ratify since 'the path chosen in Amsterdam is not the right one, neither in its vision nor in its method. By patching up and adding a coat of glossy paint, we have merely plugged the leaks of a ship without a skipper, a course or an engine.'

In practice, the government acknowledged the shortcomings of the Treaty. Unresolved issues were seen to require another round of discussion, particularly on institutional reforms: 'the results of Amsterdam are inadequate; we have not built Europe for forty years in order to agree to it being dissolved in a vast jumble, to the detriment of its current and future members. The forthcoming enlargement must be preceded by a genuine institutional reform' (Védrine, 1997b).

However, in effect, the Treaty did bring a few positive responses to issues raised by Paris regarding institutional reforms and CFSP. First, regarding the euro, in addition to the already agreed Stability Pact, Paris was able to convince the other participants and particularly the Germans, who were eager to satisfy the social demand placed on them in terms of jobs, to accept that the Stability Pact be made part of a dynamic package incorporating measures on growth, jobs and social progress. In that perspective it was agreed that a special EU summit on employment and growth would be held in Paris in the autumn of 1997. Secondly, it was agreed, as Paris requested, that a high-ranking European public figure with responsibility for dealing with common foreign and security problems be appointed. And thirdly, the principle of enhanced cooperation through a qualified majority was accepted.

However, the summit left wide open the question of transforming the decision-making process of the EU to efficiently accommodate its enlargement. Through its inability to move forwards on the defence issue, it also left open the question of the final shape of the Union where concentric circles with a fully integrated 'little Europe' at the center would coexist with a wider Union inspired by the British approach. Nothing can be more illustrative of these different perspectives than reading reports made by President Chirac and Prime Minister Tony Blair of the Amsterdam summit's conclusions on defence. The British Prime Minister declared: 'getting Europe's voice heard more clearly in the world will not be achieved through merging the EU and WEU or developing an unrealistic common defence policy. Instead, we argued for, and won, the explicit recognition, written for the first time, that NATO is the foundation of our and other allies' common defence' (Blair, 1997). President Chirac stated that 'we have made considerable progress regarding European defence in moving the EU and the WEU closer' (Chirac and Jospin, 1997).

Conclusion

In a way, such diverging views reflect ambiguities that have always been part of the EU building process. It may be the price for further steadfast integration. It, however, remains disappointing considering the very meagre results of the Amsterdam Treaty regarding CFSP. Accordingly, in the current French internal context, EU deadlock on CFSP may reinforce the views of those who, in France, ranging from the left to the extreme-right, observe that, really, there is definitely no political will from France's EU partners to build '*l' Europe puissance*'. Such lack of ambition may have profound impact on France's European policy. It could weary the staunchest supporters of the European ideal, opening the scene to a more nationalistic attitude vis à vis Europe. The failure to precisely build this '*Europe puissance*' will be seen by the pro-European as a nightmare. It may, indeed, mean the triumph of a European construction around German aspirations for quietness, non-intervention and international 'isolationism' and British hopes of a free market zone (Lesourne, 1988). If episodes such as the lack of will illustrated during the Albanian turmoil of 1997, or the crisis with Iraq in early 1998, when the absence of any British will to build, as chair country of the EU, a political consensus among Europeans, preferring to 'slavishly follow the United States' according to the leader of the Socialist group at the National Assembly, Jean-Marc Ayrault, the French will be part of an explosive contradiction. On one hand being part of the euro zone, France will integrate more than ever its economic and monetary policy; on the other hand this integration will not be balanced by a more cohesive foreign and security policy. In the end, the greatest beneficiary of the European construction may be the United States. Thus will resound the echo of an old French saying meaning that, too often in its history, France has worked for the benefit of others, which is expressed in French as '*travailler pour le roi de Prusse*'.

Notes

1 Among many press comments on the present situation see *Le Monde* (1996).

2 At the first round of the legislative elections on 25 May 1997 the Front National (extreme right) had 15.06 per cent of the votes, the Socialist Party (PS) 23.84 per cent, the Gaullists (RPR) 15.48 per cent and the liberals (UDF) 14.43 per cent.

3 France is one of the very few democratic countries having a ministry for culture.

4 On 11 May 1997, in the midst of the electoral campaign, a group of 103 personalities, mainly judges, wrote an open letter to the President asking for renewed practice of democratic life in France, highlighting the necessity to avoid concentration of power in the hands of the very few. A similar letter was again sent to the President as well as to the Prime Minister on 16 July 1997.

5 As an example among so many, Alain Juppé, a former Prime Minister, in office between June 1994 and June 1997, has been at the same time Chairman of the RPR movement, Mayor of Bordeaux, Chairman of the Bordeaux greater area, etc. This phenomenon of accumulation of responsibilities is widespread in most political parties at the National Assembly. When arriving in power in June 1997, the Socialist government made a commitment to limit the plurality of offices.

6 *Ouest France* has an average circulation of 800,000 copies each day, against about 400,000 for *Le Monde* or *Le Figaro*.

7 Conférence des ambassadeurs, Paris, 27–29 August 1997.

8 On that issue, see declarations made by Michel Barnier, then Minister for European Affairs, press conference, Paris, 12 February 1997.

9 Michel Barnier, press conference, Cairo, 16 February 1997.

10 In order to show agreement on that matter, Lamberto Dini and Hervé de Charrette, Foreign Affairs Ministers of Italy and France, published in *Le Monde* and *La Stampa* an article on that topic (Dini and de Charrette, 1997).

7 The Security Policy of a United Germany

Reimund Seidelmann

The problem and the basic characteristics of German security policy

In contrast to other countries, Germany's role in Europe has often been disputed. While some political elites in Europe raise concern about the 'true' character of German foreign policy because of its historical past as well as increased power after unification, others define Germany as the new leader of Europe. Both views seem understandable in psychological terms, but ignore nearly five decades of FRG's foreign performance.[1] Furthermore they overlook the basic concept of FRG's security policy: the broad domestic and foreign consensus it has generated since 1949, as well as the remarkable record in continuously achieving its desired ends.

Willy Brandt's introduction to FRG's first[2] *Whitebook for Security of the FRG and the Situation of the Bundeswehr* summarizes the political essence of both the old FRG's and the new united Germany's security policy:

> Peace is not a donation. In the world, in which we live, the will for peace is not enough. Our children can only enter a better world, if we are ready and able to preserve peace. Therefore, security policy is an essential part of our peace policy – a basis of our foreign and domestic policy.[3]

Although defining security as an essential part of peace, or linking peace with security policies, became détente's trademark and the major source of foreign policy initiatives, the above statement characterizes FRG's security and foreign policy from 1949 to the present.[4] It is most likely to continue into the foreseeable future. It reflects both the realistic pursuit of interests as well as the idealistic perspective for a better world which guides, shapes, and plagues German policies and political discourse. At the same time it indicates the basic paradox of FRG's security policies, which not only follow the strategy of deterrence – to prevent war by preparing for war – but go far beyond, as they build up and maintain Europe's strongest, most modern, and in many aspects best conventional armed forces, only to use these policies as a political tool. While the key data for FRG's military capacity from the 1970s[5] until today (Table 7.1) show both the absolute and relative importance in and for European NATO, WEU, Eurocorps, and the future EU defence dimension, the Bundeswehr's historical record from 1956–97 shows, in contrast to the French and British, no participation in any war, hostile military operation, or military intervention. This does not mean that

TABLE 7.1   *Key data on FRG's military capability*

Defence budget	
1996, in absolute terms and NATO criteria[1]	60 billion DM
(Investive spending 24.4%)[2]	
(1985, in absolute terms and NATO criteria	59 billion DM)
1996, in % of defence budgets of NATO Europe	22%
1996, in % of GDP	1.6%
(1980–4, average	3.4%)
Manpower	
1996, military personnel[3]	347,300
(Planning for 2000	338,000)
(1985, military personnel	495,000)
(1990, military personnel after unification[4]	550,000)
After mobilization (1996 planning)	680,000
1996, civilian personnel	150,000
(Planning for 2000	137,000)

[1]NATO criteria include more than the narrow defence budget, which was for 1996 48.2 billion DM and will be for 1997 between 45.0 and 46.0 billion DM or between 10% and 11% of the federal budget.

[2]Spending for R&D (6.4%), military equipment (12.6%), military infrastructure (4.7%), and other investments (0.7%). Planning (Bundeswehrplan 1997) forecasts an increase up to 30% until the year 2000.

[3]Present arms control treaties allow a maximum of 370,000.

[4]These figures include Bundeswehr and those parts of the Nationale Volksarmee (NVA) of the GDR, which had not been dissolved but had been integrated into the Bundeswehr. Both CSE and the 2+4 Treaty demanded quick and far-reaching cuts, which were implemented in the following years.

the FRG does not seek or use power politics. Instead, it means that as a fundamental change to German foreign policies of the past, the FRG now pursues a 'soft' power politics[6] which relies on economic and diplomatic instruments built on cooperative patterns of consensus building as well as multinational and supranational approaches.[7]

Based on the idea that German foreign and security policy has to be explained by both a realistic and an idealistic approach, three basic denominators dominate the analysis: political history, political geography, and democratic norms and principles.

The historical factor

From a historical perspective, German foreign and security policy results from three learning processes.

The first, a regularly revitalized and commemorated process, is the debate about the dynamics, causes, and political guilt of German fascism. The new democratic beginning[8] of 1945 and 1949 asked for a foreign policy to re-establish sovereignty, create democratic credibility, and compensate for the Third Reich's policy of military aggression, holocaust, and repression. The answer was a foreign policy of cooperation, restraint, and a demilitarization[9] oriented primarily to Western, and in particular US, standards, patterns, and interests. When the Adenauer government introduced remilitarization in the mid 1950s, it translated these ideas into three basic guidelines for German security policy which are still valid. The first was the unconditional integration of German armed forces into NATO[10] which included not only the transfer of security and defence sovereignty, but also the explicit control of Germany's military capability by its allies. The second was the explicit quantitative and qualitative restraints on manpower and armaments, in particular in regard to the renunciation of the production and possession of nuclear forces[11] and the early integration of the Bundeswehr into arms control and confidence-building measures (CBMs). Lastly, there was the elaborate package of measures to ensure democratic control of and in the armed forces,[12] a non-aggressive military, and numerous civil rights in the armed forces.[13] Together these measures set high standards for democratic armed forces and represent, even today, a model for other European armies.

The second learning process was related to the Soviet threat which dominated German foreign, security, and defence policies for nearly 40 years. In terms of military logic it meant first to deter a Soviet military capability – trained, organized, and equipped for quick and decisive offensives primarily against FRG's territory. Secondly, it meant to accept the risk, in case deterrence failed, of vital damage to the FRG.[14] Such damage could result from a conventional war which, in the worst case, could trigger a quasi-automatic escalation of nuclear warfare on and against German territory[15] – a war which most probably would not end immediately. Thirdly, in terms of a political logic, it implied that US security guarantees played a vital and irreplaceable[16] role for the FRG. Furthermore, the decoupling, eroding, or endangering of these guarantees became the prime trauma of any German defence planner.

Thus détente and the CSCE/OSCE policy[17] promise to reduce the risk of military confrontation, to introduce common security thinking, and to establish long-term interests in political-economic cooperation was regarded as a first step to solve these military dilemmas and as a means to reduce dependency on the US. So when the East–West conflict diminished, ending the fundamental military threat to Germany and the dependency on US guarantees, new opportunities also emerged. One important aspect was Germany's chance to extend its influence eastwards by widening and deepening détente's political, economic, and cultural cooperation with Eastern Europe.[18] If one introduces the politically questionable concept of 'winning the East–West conflict', Germany should be considered one of the winners: it rid itself of the risks and costs of the Soviet military threat and dependency on the US; it became unified for a very low price;[19] and it acquired large and undisputed political and economic influence in Eastern Europe, including Russia.[20] Looking back, these major advantages and overall changes to the German situation affirm German views on the necessity and rationality of détente as well as the principle that even vital military confrontations can be controlled, reduced, and overcome if political will is available.

The third learning process relates to the lessons from early and consequent military integration. Like economic integration, this fundamental political innovation which Adenauer introduced to German policies has developed into a sacrosanct credo of German European policies, because of both institutional settings and political orientations towards Western Europe. The real cause of Germany's addiction to integration is integration's indisputable political, economic, and military advantages. In sum, the transfer, or loss, of national sovereignty added considerable and cumulative net advantages to the general status and power of Germany, as well as to its vital economic and security interests. From the German viewpoint, Adenauer's plan to use integration as a political strategy to regain sovereignty without a national focus, but in relation to the EU and NATO, proved successful. The FRG developed from an occupied country into EU's, NATO's, and OSCE's central European player. The German economic success and its considerable degree of security, even during the most confrontational periods of the East–West conflict, would have been unthinkable without EU and NATO integration. In sum, the past proves and the future promises that Germany's policies of integration will remain highly cost-effective and risk-free, and allow for a widely accepted increase in Germany's soft power – in other words, allowing Germany to develop into a basically cooperative regional superpower. Thus, the reason for Germany's support of Maastricht, CFSP,[21] WEU, Eurocorps, and CEAM (see later) lies in the historical lesson that Germany benefits from integration and in decades of experience in military integration as well as in Adenauer's still-valid understanding of national sovereignty – a sovereignty not understood in its traditional way[22] but as participation in, influence on, and benefit from a greater European supra- or superstate.[23] Such a conviction constituted the German starting point to support an extended economic integration into security and foreign policy, Maastricht's CFSP project,[24] a merging of the WEU and EU, and the development of a stronger security identity for the EU during the IGC. Believing in the idea of integration, Germany has employed tactics demanding integration as a political price for continued EMU support. This integration has the potential to improve Germany's power position in strategic terms, on the basis of the core group of Europe,[25] and allows Germany to play the role of the new European 'unifier'.[26] Thus, Germany will continue to support the build-up of the effective security identity of the EU[27] in future IGCs.

One hypothesis is that democratic Germany's new beginning in foreign, security, and defence policies was predominantly produced by objective necessities, without reflecting true political will. In contrast, the idea of historical learning implies that Germany's policies in these areas resulted from objective necessities and an explicit willingness, by both the public and the elite, to avoid the mistakes of the Weimar Republic and thereby develop a truly democratic foreign, security, and defence policy.[28] While the objective conditions have changed, the willingness has not only survived, but constitutes one of the fundamentals of German policies. Idealistic in nature, it has nevertheless created a new reality.

Political geography

To understand German foreign and security policies, one has to understand both German history and political geography. Although developments like economic globalization and global military power projection have reduced the relevance of political geography, this concept has shaped German foreign and security policy in three aspects.

The first aspect is related to alliance building. As Adenauer[29] had already pointed out, Germany's special historical situation in the late 1940s and early 1950s demanded and offered the pursuit of two politically different, yet complementary, options. The first option has been, and remains, close cooperation with the US.[30] This 'Atlantic' option was determined by both general political reasons and specific security reasons.[31] At the same time it has been supported by the US benevolent partnership policy towards the FRG, from the late 1940s assistance in the rebuilding of political, economic, and cultural life to the US support for the unification process.[32] The second option, which also remains, is the European option supporting the European integration process including a special German–French partnership.[33] By pursuing two options simultaneously, Germany satisfied both US and Western European interests in controlling, influencing and cooperating with the re-emerging power, thereby allowing FRG to optimize its own interests. Germany was able to benefit from both Atlantic and Western European relations and occasionally even play one option against the other.[34]

Preserving and further developing the Atlantic and Western European options, Willy Brandt's *neue Ostpolitik* also alluded to history[35] and political geography, while adding a third option, Eastern Europe and the Soviet Union, to Germany's alliance and cooperation network. Brandt's *Ostpolitik* was first related to Atlantic and European politics[36] and secondly a supplement to, although no substitute for, the existing options. Consequently, Germany's new geopolitics or Europolitics constituted an optimal, cohesive, and comprehensive concept, making Germany a central European player during détente. As mentioned above, the end of the East–West conflict reconfirmed rather than challenged this three-option concept. With the phrase 'partnership in leadership', the Atlantic option made Germany a prime partner of the US in Europe. The Maastricht concept and EU widening[37] further improved Germany's influence in a more 'strengthened' EU. As the most important European economic and political partner for the Eastern and Central European states[38] and Russia, Germany recaptured its old role as a central European power.[39] Yet in contrast to the past, Germany's soft power approach, its cooperative, peaceful and democratic pattern, and its explicit political self-restraint secured widespread support and acceptance for Germany's role.

Again the careful balance between the Atlantic, European, and Eastern options constituted the old as well as the new basis for Germany's role in political geography. Therefore US–French disputes from de Gaulle onwards constituted a diplomatic problem for Germany (not wanting to alienate either the French or the US partner). However, in addition, this gave Germany an opportunity to act as mediator, placing itself as a true and reliable partner, explaining why Germany supports NATO expansion plus the new NATO–Russian partnership. This positions Germany as the trustworthy European partner of the US. While supporting the gradual establishment of a common foreign and security dimension in the EU, German priorities in political geography indicate a modernization of its Atlantic option, an improvement to its position within NATO and an emphasis of its relevance for Russia. In sum, this implies improving the European option, reconfirming its close cooperation with France and limiting its security dependence on the US.

The second aspect of Germany's political geography refers to military security. Owing to its political, economic, and military geography the FRG constituted the prime USSR target for any major war in Europe. If the Soviets were to wage war, victory over the FRG was an objective and subjective necessity for Soviet military planning, deployment, and training.[40] In combination with the numerical asymmetries in favour of the USSR,[41] the Soviet surprise attack option, the advantage of the Soviet second echelon in terms of military geography and the accepted notion[42] that such a conventional, chemical, and even tactical nuclear war would be fought primarily on FRG's territory[43] turned military geography into a prime concern for German security. Still, strengthening FRG's defence against a Soviet attack was in the interests not only of the FRG, but also of Western Europe.[44] In this way the permanent presence of French and NATO forces underlined FRG's unique situation in Western Europe and the relevance of military geography. Only by fully understanding the security situation, its severe risks and dilemmas, one can comprehend the relief that CSCE, CBMs,[45] the double-zero solution, CFE-I, and finally the end of the East–West conflict brought for the FRG.

Germany's military threat perception today concerns the current Russian military potential. Even in a politically worst case and highly improbable scenario, this is the only potential military threat for the coming years. Secondly, this so-called 'potential' threat is actually perceived as no major threat, either to Germany or to Central Europe.[46] A further reduction of Russian armed forces, continuous[47] arms control, and disarmament are defined not as a primary but more as a secondary political problem. Again, bearing in mind Germany's past experiences with the Soviet threat and its widened and deepened interests in Eastern Europe, Germany continues its traditional support for a common and cooperative pan-European security architecture to address this problem. Furthermore, it tried to harmonize

NATO enlargement with a special NATO–Russia arrangement based on political and military cooperation. In this context one should not overlook that within such a pan-European security architecture, composed of NATO, EU/WEU, OSCE, and a NATO–Russian Forum, Germany will constitute a central player in both military and political terms.

The third aspect of political geography refers to Germany's new and increasing engagement in peacekeeping. From a German viewpoint, participation in peacekeeping is primarily a political instrument to provide security. Peacekeeping through an integrated NATO force or as part of a multilateral WEU force continues along traditional German multinational and supranational lines, eases domestic legitimization and foreign acceptance, underlines Germany's willingness to share new responsibilities, and gives Germany a considerable degree of flexibility in choosing missions, troop numbers, and specific military roles. Owing to the developments in Yugoslavia, domestic consensus and bipartisan parliamentarian support[48] were built up much quicker than originally expected. German peacekeeping, on the other hand, will follow political priorities influenced by political geography. This means that active German participation in peacekeeping missions will give priority first to 'narrow' Europe, including Yugoslavia, the Balkans, and the Baltic Sea, secondly to greater Europe, such as Ukraine, and thirdly to out-of-Europe areas. German participation in traditional military intervention, even when legitimized by the UN as in the case of the Second Gulf War, will be (if any) a matter of long-term developments and occur only as part of NATO, EU/WEU, or Eurocorps action.

The normative factor

It was said at the beginning that German security policy is not only a matter of cost–risk–benefit analysis or the optimizing of interests. There is also the element of a strong idealistic basis which influences political action and dominates concept formation. This normative dimension has four main aspects.

The first aspect, outlined above, refers to history. Dealing with the history of the past demands a comprehension of the collapse of the Weimar Republic, the Third Reich, and the general lessons learned by the past world order of the European nation-states which proved unable to control, resolve, and prevent the disappearance of democratization, economic disaster, and two world wars. These developments resulted not from a lack of willingness,[49] but from the structural limitations of a nation-state organized on the basis of unlimited sovereignty. Referring to the realist debate[50] one can say that it was precisely the search for a better order (a peaceful order or an order capable of solving the security dilemma) which led to the desire for a transfer of sovereignty, particularly in the area of security and defence. This was conceived of as an integration which could transform Western Europe into a peaceful and democratic community. The political logic of Germany's foreign, security, and European policies have thereby taken this approach further, to benefit from it by widening, deepening, and modernizing this community. And this view, which has dominated Germany's security thinking since 1949, and is valid despite the lessons of Yugoslavia, adapts the European security architecture to new types of conflict. Moreover, it strengthens political and military supranationalism to deal with malevolent state actors.

The second aspect refers to Germany's understanding of democracy, which not only is an explicit part of its constitutional record of democratic norms and the way the German political system is organized, but has become part of its political culture as well. Putting aside the debate as to whether modern democracies *per se* are 'peace-loving' or not, German security policy, in particular its military dimension, is restrained by the democratic norms of the German Basic Law. Interpreted by the Supreme Court,[51] these laws define peace as a general objective of German policies, and restrict military activity to defensive purposes.[52] In broader terms, German federalism not only serves as an inbuilt inhibitor of military aggression, but has recently established and institutionalized direct participation of the German states in foreign and European affairs.[53]

The third aspect refers to Germany's political culture and general means of legitimizing politics. In terms of Germany's 'new' foreign and security policy this leads to ambivalent results. On the one hand, as an important part of the historical learning process, German political culture, which developed along civic lines, traditionally defines itself as anti-militaristic and maintains a deep and far-reaching scepticism about any form of military grandeur or nationalism. This demilitarization of national identity, the general political legitimization process, and the uncompromised NATOization of its military explain that for Germany, in contrast to countries like Britain and France, the establishment of an integrated or common European security, defence, and military policy, either in the framework of CFSP or parallel to it, poses no major political problem for its elites, its public, and its military. On the other hand, however, traditional self-restraint, politically necessary and legitimate in the past and a cost-effective means of conducting soft power politics, has created a pattern of comfortable passivity when it comes to active, military, global, and European governance and policing. In recent years, both governing elites and some opposition elites[54] have been searching for a new and more active role for German foreign, security, and European policies, which would combine 'common' power[55] with a special responsibility for promoting European integration.[56] The elites and the public do not believe that such a new role means additional burdens, re-emerging distrust in European countries suffering economic and political decline[57] of various degrees, and a new type of internationalist or global thinking.[58] Once again, it has to be underlined that in line with the continuity of German policies, this does not mean the establishment of a German unilateral leadership but rather a continuation of the integration-oriented cooperative pattern and a search for common advantage, as exemplified by German efforts in the establishment of the EMU.[59] While there is no long-term alternative to such an adaptation of Germany's role in Europe and beyond, it nevertheless means a new learning process with all the contradictions[60] and setbacks[61] that this implies. Thus, finding a balance between traditional norms and the necessity for a new responsible power politics will remain the main problem of Germany's new role in Europe. This will require the harmonization of German interests with common European and global ones, as well as linking effectively the normative dimension of peace, democracy, and community building with the realistic dimension of economic, political, and military interests, while using power as an instrument for the fulfilment of foreign and security policies.

Problems and perspectives for the next decade

In addition to this general problem, Germany's security policies face a number of specific problems. While Germany's concept of its security has not changed in principle, its general strategy and its military policy as well as the related armament policy are in a process of modernization which can be characterized by three developments.

First, the end of the East–West conflict which brought to an end the old Soviet military threat and allowed unification not only constituted the success of the concept of common and cooperative security but in addition led to cuts in Germany's armed forces of about 200,000 military personnel as well as a defence budget reduction from 3.4 to 1.6 per cent of GDP (see Table 7.1). While such developments reflect public opinion in a civic society and parliamentarians' unwillingness to spend more money for defence than absolutely necessary, the present defence budget does not allow armament modernization, maintaining a force of 350,000, and new missions like global peacekeeping at the same time. Given the necessity of modernization and the weight the Kohl government placed on participating in peacekeeping, this implies a choice between politically unattractive increases in defence budgets or the further reduction of the armed forces.[62] Domestic pressures resulting from unemployment, political protest against the ongoing modernization of the welfare state, the relation between capital and labour, and the tax system create further limitations.

Secondly, the revitalization of EU integration and especially of WEU[63] not only created a European option for military integration[64] but also allowed for a dominant German role in a Common European Armament Market (CEAM). However, Maastricht's perspective of a political union as a security union[65] constitutes for Germany both an opportunity and a dilemma. In any Europeanized version of integrated or common security policy, either in the European pillar of a reorganized NATO[66] or within an EU with a functioning CFSP and an integrated WEU, Germany will play a major or even a dominant role owing to its conventional military capacity and political leverage. For Germany, therefore, supporting revitalized integration in general implies continued support for CFSP, the widening and political/military upgrading of WEU/Eurocorps, and the CEAM project. On the other hand, such a Europeanization of Germany's security could damage not only Germany's special relations with the US but also its general strategy to pursue both Atlantic cooperation and European integration. In addition, consequent Europeanization not only would create additional political conflicts concerning military nuclear capacities, arms export policies, and military out-of-area operations with Germany's closest European partner, France, but would mean a considerable increase in Germany's burden for such a European common defence.[67] Germany's present solution to this dilemma has so far been the parallel approach, that is, supporting both NATO and CFSP–WEU–Eurocorps–CEAM and the strategy of interlocking institutions.[68] But given the many frictions, the overall costs, and the limited security capacity of the present European security architecture, it is an open question how long Germany can and will continue with such a policy.

Thirdly, the gradual globalization of the EU's as well as Germany's political interests has led to changes in Germany's foreign and security policies in terms of global responsibility as well. While most of the German public, and parts of its opposition parties, still prefer the comfort of the traditional policy of restraint, the Kohl government has gradually entered global politics, going beyond chequebook diplomacy. Initiatives in global diplomacy, the wish to establish Germany as a permanent member of the UN Security Council, and participation in peacekeeping missions[69] indicate the will towards a new and more global responsibility. While critical voices argue that this in general, and the build-up of global peacekeeping capacities in particular, might allow or even prepare for the return of global military power politics, its supporters point out that this globalization of German foreign policy follows and reconfirms the old patterns of German security policy. These include integrated instead of unilateral policies and strict qualitative limitations of the use of military capacities for peacekeeping only. Thus, German peacekeeping, which is clearly defined and restricted by a specific ruling of Germany's Supreme Court, not only is more of a sort of global policing than traditional military interventionism but additionally follows the old Adenauer formula, seeking participation in multilateral and supranational military organizations in order to improve political status and influence. But while Adenauer's policy of restricted[70] remilitarization was based on a clear cost–risk–benefit calculation, the present globalization of Germany's foreign policy has not come up with a clearly defined formula when it comes to the question of whether such globalization should be pursued unilaterally or as an integrated part of CFSP.[71] Nor has it been decided whether Germany should follow the French or British model or develop a new kind of benevolent global policing.

Germany's current armament programme (Table 7.2) reflects these new developments and their dilemmas.

Germany's pursuit of three objectives – for example, modernizing its

TABLE 7.2   *Major German armament programmes until the year* 2000

Priorities
   C3-I
   Transport capacities[1]
   Logistics
Major programmes
   Franco–German satellite programme
   Tiger and NH-90 helicopter (Army[2])
   Armoured howitzer 2000 (Army[3])
   Eurofighter EF 2000 (Air Force[4])
   Future transport aircraft (FTA) (Air Force[5])
   Frigate 124 and submarine U 212 (Navy[6])

---

[1]With special reference to long-range power projection.
[2]The German Crises Reaction Forces will receive 112 Tiger helicopters until the year 2001.
[3]The German Crises Reaction Forces will receive from 1998 onward a total of 185 howitzers.
[4]Current planning foresees 180 aircraft.
[5]Current planning foresees 75 aircraft to be introduced after 2008.
[6]Current planning foresees 3–4 frigate 124 to be introduced after 2002 and 4 submarines U 212 to be introduced after 2002.

crisis reaction forces or the cornerstone of its conventional strength in terms of firepower and mobility, establishing an independent European satellite reconnaissance capacity, and creating means and infrastructures for global power projection – implies not only maintaining but increasing its status and power in NATO's and EU–WEU–Eurocorps's military hierarchy. However, it also necessitates involvement in missions like peacekeeping and potentially peacemaking, which inevitably will create costly financial, military, and political burdens and side-effects for which both Germany's political elite and its public are not yet prepared. In addition, increased involvement will contradict its traditional benevolent self-image in foreign affairs with the rising costs required for such an engagement. These consist of increasing defence budgets or restricting global missions. The resulting problems include how to deal with malevolent state actors, how to coordinate these policies with the US, and how to create domestic acceptance and foreign consensus. Again, it is the author's view that Germany will try to follow its traditional line in security policy such as cooperative and common security, military integration, and the primacy of political-economic means, while continuing as one of the main European military and military-industrial players and increasing its global engagement in peace policing. It is an open question whether Germany can preserve its traditional security policies *vis-à-vis* a growing participation in global governance and a build-up of a common European security, defence, and armament policy. But there is no doubt that Germany seeks to maintain its major influence without aspiring to leadership in these developments. German governments will, therefore, exert such influence on the basis of growing self-assertiveness, albeit through their traditional cooperative pattern.

Integration of European security policies: why so difficult?

Finally, if one discusses the prospect of the Maastricht vision, that is to establish a 'true', effective, and common European security, defence, military, and arms industry community, Germany's role, power, and politics are relevant in three respects.

First, while Germany belongs to the strong supporters of integration in general and has no major problems in setting up a common defence, an integrated military capacity, and a CEAM, it will try to continue its three-option policy. This means that Germany will not and cannot support a decoupled European military capacity which antagonizes the US, but it will support ideas like a two-pillar NATO in which the European pillar is made up of a gradually widened EU/WEU/Eurocorps on the basis of the *Kerneuropa* model. While it is already difficult to reach consensus on common defence, and in particular on the establishment of a fully integrated European military capacity, such a combination of Atlanticism with Europeanism, now cautiously supported by the French, will further enhance Germany's political influence in Europe.

Secondly, any CFSP in general, and common defence in particular, will lead to the question of how to integrate or Europeanize French and British nuclear forces, harmonize conflicting arms export policies, and coordinate different patterns and traditions of military interventionism. Again, the differences between France and Britain on the one hand, and Germany on the other, are obvious and far-reaching. And the more German influence grows, the less the other two will be willing to give up the last symbols of their political-military status and perceived national pride.

Thirdly, in addition to such conflict potentials, the strong German position and capacity create conflicts of interests and power. Establishment of the CEAM will revitalize anxieties in France, Britain, and other member states that German defence industries[72] will penetrate their markets, take over their most valuable defence industries, and establish economic dominance, leverage, and dependencies. Even in the case of an extremely restrained German policy, the upgrading, widening, and deepening of Eurocorps will mean a continued and probably increasing major German influence, if not dominance, in this organization as well. A WEU, Eurocorps, and CEAM based on the *Kerneuropa* model reduces the non-members' perception of threat in psychological terms, but this does not necessarily mean a decrease or limitation of German influence. In terms of power politics, the integration of security, defence, military, and armament policy will repeat in principle the process of Maastricht and its basic dilemma. While issue logic advocates following integrationism, propagated and supported by Germany, power logic indicates that owing to Germany's position, strength, and growing influence, any further integration will result in a further increase of Germany's net power. In the view of Gaullist thinking, for example, the dilemma of Europe is that there is no feasible strategy to stop or counterbalance Germany's new power. Control through integration means increasing Germany's net advantage, and continuation of the status quo means precisely not being able to control Germany's power. Even the most restrained and cooperative German policies can only lessen and not overcome this dilemma.

Together with the comfort of the status quo and a US which reluctantly continues its traditional role in guaranteeing European security interests within Europe and beyond, the answer of traditional power politics *vis-à-vis* such a dilemma is to delay, postpone, or even block the establishment of an integrated security dimension for the EU. The close identification between national identity and national sovereignty in defence, military, and armament policies in countries like France and Britain will further exacerbate this hesitancy. Thus, the difficulties for such integration prospects lie not only in differences in specific aspects of security policy, but more in the German dilemma experienced by other European powers. Additionally, integration is affected by other different experiences, evaluations, and expectations with regard to the transfer of sovereignty between Germany and on the one hand the other integration-oriented countries like Italy and Benelux, and on the other hand those EU members that regard national sovereignty as more important than supranationalism. And as long as the present external threat situation continues, and as long as the US provides relatively reliable, efficient, and, from a European viewpoint, cheap security, the maximum level that integration-oriented policies can reach is a slow, gradual, and selective supranationalization of security policies following the *Kerneuropa* model. But, once again, Europe's difficulties in integrating security policies lie more in the traditional linkage of power, national identity, the military, and national sovereignty than in democratic Germany's ideas and performance.

Notes

This chapter presents results from the research project 'Security Policies of East Central European Nations and the Development of a New European Security Architecture' (1995–7) funded by Volkswagen Foundation. However, the author is fully responsible for everything presented here.

1 FRG's security policy differs in many aspects from GDR's security and defence policies, which actively participated in the military intervention against the CSSR and sought Soviet–GDR intervention against Poland.

2 In 1969 FRG's Defence Minister published a smaller and politically less important forerunner to the later 'big' *Whitebooks* published irregularly since 1970.

3 See Presse- und Informationsamt der Bundesregierung, *Weißbuch* 1970. Zur Sicherheit der Bundesrepublik Deutschland und zur Lage der Bundeswehr. Im Auftrag der Bundesregierung herausgegeben vom Bundesminister der Verteidigung, Bonn, 1970, p. III: 'Der Frieden wird niemandem geschenkt. In der Welt, in der wir leben, reicht auch der Wille zum Frieden allein nicht aus. Nur wenn wir bereit und in der Lage sind, für seine Bewahrung einzutreten, können unsere Kinder in eine besssere Welt hineinwachsen. So verstanden, ist Sicherheitspolitik ein wesentlicher Teil unserer Friedenspolitik – eine Grundlage unserer auswärtigen wie unserer inneren Politik.'

4 For general reference see Haftendorn (1986).

5 This evaluation is valid for the period after the early 1970s. It has to be remembered that, especially in the 1970s, the period of détente, numerous quality improvement and weapon modernization programmes transformed an armed force, which in the early 1960s constituted a supplement to allied forces in Europe, into one of the strongest, and most influential, military components of NATO.

6 For details see Seidelmann (1996a).

7 For a recent summary of different views on German foreign policy (Foreign Minister, CSU, SPD, Bündis 90/Die Grünen etc.) see *Politisches Lernen* (1996).

8 For example, the establishment of the FRG.

9 Konrad Adenauer designed remilitarization primarily as a strategy to regain political sovereignty.

10 Until today – and in contrast to many other NATO members – nearly all German armed forces are fully integrated.

11 Political proposals or warnings that Germany should or would acquire nuclear military capabilities have been unfounded and do not reflect political reality. Integration mechanisms, legal bindings, and broad political consensus rule out that Germany follows the French model and establishes a national nuclear force. This, however, does not rule out that Germany participates in a multi- or supranational nuclear capacity such as the MLF project of the 1960s or projects to integrate existing British and French nuclear forces into a common European defence in which the Germans would take part. But while Germany did not have its own independent nuclear force, German forces were prepared to deliver US nuclear warheads until their withdrawal in the late 1980s. However, sophisticated technical and military procedures prohibited any non-authorized or independent use. Similar restraints characterize FRG's non-proliferation policies as well: see Kelle and Müller (1996).

12 See for example the special powers of the Verteidigungsausschuß des Deutschen Bundestages and of the Wehrbeauftragten des Deutschen Bundestages.

13 See for example the rights for conscientious objectors.

14 It was expected that a conventional war of three to five days would destroy one-third of Germany's infrastructure, industries, and population.

15 Even if the political elites in Germany managed to successfully block or delay early first use of US nuclear weapons in the case of a massive conventional and/or chemical attack, and although there was common consensus from the end of the 1970s that the Bundeswehr together with its allies would have been able to successfully defeat the first Soviet echelon, both sides had to accept the notion that as soon as the second Soviet echelon arrived on the German battlefield, NATO would have faced the alternatives either to capitulate or to use nuclear weapons.

16 French offers since the early 1980s to extend its nuclear deterrence to Germany never developed into 'hard' security guarantees able to substitute for the US ones.

17 For a summary of German views on OSCE see ISFH (1996).

18 German support for EU, WEU, and NATO enlargement is not only the logical continuation of détente but a strategy of alliance building to further increase German power and influence in these organizations.

19 Economic and financial obligations of the 2 + 4 Treaty towards the USSR/Russia were comparably low and indirectly often beneficial for FRG's economy. If one defines German foreign policy as in principle for integration in general and the development of the EMU project as predominantly the extension of the German monetary model to the rest of EU Europe and beyond, Germany's willingness to accept the Maastricht project in order to gain EU's acceptance and support for unification can hardly be defined as a political price but more as linking the advantages of unification with increased German influence within the EU.

20 See Weidenfeld (1996).

21 For reference see Regelsberger et al. (1997).

22 In addition and in contrast to France and Britain, the FRG has successfully decoupled German national identity from military grandeur or national independence, which makes it difficult for German politicians for example to fully understand the role of the *force de frappe* or the Malvinas war.

23 Kreile (1996) rightly underlines views in the German public critical of EMU and Maastricht. This, however, is more of short-term than long-term relevance.

24 Today, Foreign Minister Genscher's unilateral decision to support independence for Croatia, which violated both the letter and the spirit of CFSP, is regarded as a major mistake.

25 As a matter of fact, the existing WEU, Eurocorps, and the networks of cooperation of arms industries are already following the idea of *Kerneuropa*, in which Germany plays a central role.

26 When Helmut Kohl announced his willingness to run again in the coming election (*Süddeutsche Zeitung*, 4 April 1997), he argued using his historical responsibility to continue European integration.

27 It has to be noted that Germany's support for security, defence, and armament integration is much stronger than for foreign policy.

28 While in the 1950s government and opposition deeply disagreed on the strategy, they consented on principles like non-aggressive or defensive, sufficient, integrated defence etc., which were already laid down in the Basic Law of 1949.

29 See Konrad Adenauer 'Es ist ein wahres Wort, daß die Geographie, besser ausgedrückt, daß die geographische Situation einer der wesentlichen Faktoren bei der geschichtlichen Entwicklung darstellt. Deutschland liegt im Herzen Europas . . . [Deutschlands] Schicksal [war] in jedem Fall auf Grund seiner geographischen Lage von größter Bedeutung für die Entwicklung Europas' (1967: 90).

30 For general reference Hanrieder (1995).

31 The political value of this option became obvious in the Berlin blockade at the end of the 1940s.

32 If one takes images and collective emotions into account, the early and strong US support for unification (which has to be considered as one of the most emotionally moving issues in recent German history), in contrast to French, British, and other European partners' hesitance, has had a strong and lasting impact on the German public and political elite.

33 Not only to control and develop bilateral partnership but to control and shape integration as well.

34 A typical case has been Germany's attempts to become involved in French decision making concerning the use of nuclear weapons from and on targets in Germany in particular and the extension of the French nuclear deterrent towards German territory. Without the Atlantic option, even the limited German–French cooperation would have been unthinkable. On the other hand, the ambivalent French deterrent guarantee reassured Germany about US nuclear guarantees. It was argued that in the case that the US did not realize their guarantees, even a limited French nuclear attack against targets in Germany or beyond would force the US into nuclear war.

35 Compare the *Ostpolitik* of Bismarck and the Republic of Weimar.

36 It was one of the reasons for the broad Western consensus and support of détente that Germany's initiatives were prepared and harmonized both within NATO and EPC.

37 Recent and ongoing EU widening brought and brings mostly such nations into the EU, which have close economic and political ties to Germany and whose membership was strongly supported by Germany.

38 In addition, one has to mention the development of the special German–Polish military cooperation.

39 It must be noted that while Germany was one of the prime net winners of the

end of the East–West conflict, France lost both relative power and the basic rationale for its European policies. Altogether this redefined the German–French alliance in favour of Germany.

40 Until the end of the East–West conflict, the Soviet Union's most modern, best trained, and most privileged troops were deployed in the GDR.

41 In contrast to many views during the 1970s, asymmetry does not mean superiority.

42 However, Germany was successful in preventing NATO from adopting strategies making the Rhine its most Eastern line of defence in the early 1960s.

43 Despite the obvious disadvantages such a strategy meant for the FRG, FRG governments never supported operative offensive designs. On the contrary and in order to support détente, the Bundeswehr's logistical system was reorganized in the early 1970s in a way which made even mid-range attacks towards the East militarily unfeasible.

44 It allowed, for example, France and Benelux countries to regard FRG as a cordon sanitaire and to keep smaller conventional troop numbers than they would have had to keep in the case of a neutral or weakly armed Germany.

45 CBMs not only had a political role; they had significant military relevance as well, for example, in preventing surprise attacks.

46 Including Poland.

47 There is major understanding that, owing to the break-up of the USSR in upcoming CFE-II negotiations, certain Russian interests have to be considered as legitimate.

48 Peacekeeping missions have to be approved by the German Parliament.

49 There were numerous well-intentioned activities from different political forces, nations, and social movements before both world wars.

50 A still typical example of US realism, its analytical and political limitations, can be found in Mearsheimer (1990).

51 The latest, most important example of the Supreme Court's role and policy of interpretation was the dispute between the government and the opposition as to whether German participation in peacekeeping is defensive and as such legal, or offensive and as such illegal. Here the Supreme Court, with special reference to the constitution's call for a global security order, ruled in favour of the government's interpretation and allowed peacekeeping, but set up clear restrictions such as its compatibility with the UN's global governance.

52 Again, it has to be underlined that the German constitution explicitly rules out national possession of nuclear weapons. In other words, political suggestions such as those put forward by US scholars in the 1980s to establish a German *force de frappe* are not only politically unfeasible but also unconstitutional.

53 Representatives of German states, for example, have become official members of Germany's delegations in OSCE and IGC negotiations.

54 Such as the SPD and the 'realists' in the Green Party.

55 See, for example, the CDU's concept of *Kerneuropa*, which has to be regarded primarily as a power formula to produce progress in integration.

56 In the German view, there are only two options for a future IGC: either there is no overall progress, with all its negative psychological and political effects, or there is a German-led initiative to introduce, harmonize, and implement progress in specific areas and issues.

57 See, for example, the outbreak of anti-Germanism in Britain during soccer games in 1996.

58 For example, major parts of the German political elites lack the necessary know-how for global diplomacy.

59 With all the typical public blaming but *de facto* support.

60 See, for example, Germany's unilateral decision to support Croatia's independence. While rightly accepting the principle of self-determination, it violated the

letter and spirit of CFSP, was politically counterproductive, and was a typical example of ill-fated unilateralism.

61 For example, the German public is not accustomed to dealing with human losses from peacekeeping activities.

62 Such further reductions would not be implemented unilaterally but within the framework of CFE-II negotiations. The SPD opposition discussed further reductions and introduced manpower figures around 250,000.

63 For further details see Lotter and Peters (1996).

64 See Seidelmann (1995).

65 See Tsakaloyannis (1996).

66 Today, Germany supports a reform agenda for NATO which consists of enlargement, special relations (plus treaty) with Russia, reorganization of military structure: 'It will reflect a new balance in the division of North America's and Europe's responsibilities and burdens' (Rühe, 1996).

67 For a more detailed calculation see Seidelmann (1997).

68 See Kinkel (1996).

69 Yugoslavia is a typical case of German peacekeeping politics. Germany's Bundeswehr not only participated in IFOR but contributes 3,000 troops to SFOR, which makes Germany the third largest contributor. It has to be underlined that Germany participates in SFOR not on a national basis but as an integrated part of NATO.

70 One has to remember that, in both qualitative and quantitative terms, the Bundeswehr developed into a major military player not in the 1950s but during the 1960s.

71 This, for example, would mean seeking a permanent seat in the Security Council for the EU and not its member states.

72 It had been the explicit objective of former Daimler-Benz Chairman Edzard Reuter to establish CEAM and to make Daimler-Benz its dominant player.

8 British Security Policy

Michael Clarke

Britain's security policy is presently under the microscope as a new government, the first Labour administration since 1979, settles into office, conducting its long-awaited defence review that sets the guidelines for British security policy from 1998 to well into the next century. Even to use the terminology of 'security policy' in this context is something of a departure for British policy makers. Though recent official *Statements on the Defence Estimates* – particularly in 1995 and 1996 – spoke of a British 'security policy', the concept remains something of an abstraction to the British government.[1] It is drawn from foreign policy and defence policy, which are the responsibility of two very different government departments that derive their respective ethos and political power from quite separate sources. Nevertheless, the notion that Britain should articulate a distinct security policy, as an amalgam of defence and foreign policy, has gained considerable currency over recent years as it has become evident how radically Britain's own international environment has changed.

For Britain is physically safer now than at any time in the history of a recognized British, or English, state – safer than it has been for at least 400 years. For the first time it cannot be threatened with invasion, and though it is quite possible to foresee Britain becoming involved in future wars, perhaps even major wars, it is not credible to suppose that the survival of the British state, or its territorial integrity, would be at issue. The only credible physical threat to the British homeland could be a ballistic missile attack, either from Russia now, or from other states in ten to fifteen years' time. Either scenario is difficult to envisage and does not form more than a very minor part of British security and defence planning. Britain may have many *interests* to defend, however, but in this respect has a growing measure of discretion over which interests to defend and how to do it.

In a literal sense, Britain has the choice to disengage from many of the crises that affect its other European partners. Britain does not (unlike France, Italy, Germany or Austria) suffer the direct ripple effects of refugees who are displaced in a crisis; its own national minorities are new Commonwealth rather than European; its trading patterns with the Central and Eastern European (CEE) states (unlike the USA, France and Germany) are not particularly vigorous and do not have the potential to hold sectors of domestic British society to ransom; British communications, service and leisure industries have grown strongly during the 1990s and not only account for the largest proportion of GDP – by far – but also provide a commercial mobility that many of Britain's partners do not have. Not least, there are no substantial British minorities abroad who could be the source of nationalist reaction or resentment, and Britain's own national identity and territorial integrity cannot be directly compromised by political collapse elsewhere in Europe. In reality, Britain does *not* adopt the isolationist – or neo-mercantilist – position that these facts might indicate; but the choice to do so still exists in greater measure than at any time in Britain's past. This, in itself, implies that Britain is in a position to make a major strategic reassessment of its international position. This, however, is easier said than done. The conceptual and empirical challenges in making a radical reassessment are considerable, and the British policy-making system is not well equipped to do so.

Britain is traditionally good at the specifics of policy but less good at formulating and expressing long-term objectives. Its skill at policy coordination within government frequently overcomes its need to develop policy coherence; coordinating complex domestic and multinational policies too often becomes an end in itself. In order to see how it is set to meet the challenges of such a new security environment, it is necessary to discuss the ways in which the British aversion to 'strategic visions' of the future nevertheless embodies some enduring assumptions and core values that Britain holds on to as it confronts the new century.

The core assumptions

British governments have long felt uncomfortable at the prospect of setting out any strategic vision of Britain's security, beyond simple platitudes.[2] Partly this arose out of the Cold War, where the strategic objective was simple, namely to make as much headway as possible in the perennial struggle with the Soviet bloc as a contribution toward the time – in the distant future – when the war might come to an end. Indeed, the ending of the Cold War on terms more favourable to the West than could ever have realistically been imagined has visited on Britain, more than most powers, the curse of having its wishes granted. The Cold War was good for Britain. It played to the country's strengths as a major military power at a time when it was no longer an economic pillar of the world community; it provided Britain with disproportionate influence within the Western alliance; it prolonged the country's status as a victor power of 1945; and it restricted Britain's European concerns to those parts of the continent – Scandinavia, Northern Europe and the Mediterranean – with which Britain was familiar and had some diplomatic acceptability. It is noticeable, for example, that British influence within the Western Alliance was at its greatest in those periods when the Cold War was at its most intense. During periods of détente British influence declined, since it was a less central player in *Östpolitik*, economic cooperation or the normalization of disputed borders. Though its diplomatic skills were generally well regarded, in periods of détente it had less to gain and more to lose in the process. When tension was higher, however, the United States was proportionately more grateful for so loyal an ally, and the diverse contributions which Britain made to the Atlantic Alliance and a tradition of diplomatic resolve tempered by experience made Britain a more central player during the darker days of the Cold War (Clarke, 1992a). None of this required a very extensive 'strategic vision'. The Cold War was a long-term – apparently inescapable – reality and the fighting of it was an essentially short-term tactical process in which Britain made the most of its available resources.

The British aversion to a strategic vision is also partly explained within the national political culture. Britain has been a status quo power in world politics since the end of the period of imperial expansion, having no overriding motives to overturn the existing order. British ministers and officials are frankly nervous at the prospect of articulating major blueprints for future security structures. Though Britain was undoubtedly one of the architects of the post-1945 restructuring of world security – which may be regarded as both visionary and successful – there can be no doubt that the vision was provided mainly by the United States and that Britain concurred with the concepts, sometimes against its better judgement, for the sake of solidarity and rapid reconstruction.

For British foreign and defence planners, the policy is in essence the *process*. As the process goes forward, core and secondary interests are recognized and safeguarded, but the characteristic British response to grand visions of a European future is to worry about the details, the financing and the staffing implications, and to insist that the participants address the practical issues before signing up to more ambitious schemes. British policy makers, for example, were traditionally sceptical at successive suggestions in the 1960s and 1970s that the Western European Union (WEU) could perform a more substantive role in European defence than it was bequeathed in 1955. In June 1984 when President Mitterrand used the Fontainebleau summit to try to revitalize the WEU, it provoked a British paper, *Europe – The Future*, which expressed exactly all the practical reservations the British felt to an explicitly political initiative (Sanders, 1990). For Britain, a revitalized WEU in this period seemed only to represent a challenge to the unity of NATO, the political and economic costs of which would far outweigh the benefits, and officials in Whitehall during these years were frankly derisive of what they saw as political initiatives towards greater European unity that were dressed up as military reorganizations. Though the tone of derision has changed, the substance of British concerns over the WEU has not. The new Labour government made it very clear in May 1997 that it saw the WEU as a practical adjunct to NATO, not a vehicle for a more visionary single European defence policy (*Financial Times*, 1997b). In a period when the status quo was in the interests of most – such as during the majority of the Cold War years – this approach can be regarded as pragmatic and helpful; it is useful to have at least one ally who keeps others' feet on the ground. In a period of rapid change, however – such as that which was clearly emerging in Europe from late 1984 – it is frequently regarded as pedantic obstructionism by those who worry that the Western world may be missing the tide of history.

From the early 1990s, therefore, British policy makers have constantly referred to the daunting uncertainties which all European foreign and defence ministers now face. NATO is poised on the brink of an enlargement which would change its character more radically than at any time since its foundation. The European Union is similarly set to expand and is in the process of major institutional reform – and if reform proves impossible it faces stagnation or even regression. The balance of immediate security threats to Europe is switching from an East–West axis to a North–South axis as Mediterranean issues preoccupy the security concerns of two or three of the major European powers. Finally, there is a significant danger of the development of a 'new Cold War' with Russia which – if it happens – will take very different forms to the old Cold War with the Soviet Union, involving widespread instability within and between the peripheral states of the Russian Federation.

In such circumstances, the British, unlike the French, are inherently sceptical over the viability of pan-European approaches to security. The Conference on Security and Cooperation in Europe (CSCE), in the British view, was always a useful forum, as the OSCE (Organization for Security and Cooperation in Europe) continues to be, and there are a number of genuine roles it might play: but the maintenance and enforcement of collective security is not among them.[3]

In this situation the British characteristically point out that all we have is diplomatic process and that it is far too early in the transition to the twenty-first century to pursue a single strategic vision of a European future. When optimistic ministers from partner countries articulate security constructs which could be achievable in the short term – pan-European, EU-centric, or regional collective security systems – if only several elements can be successfully juggled, the British approach is normally to point out that there are far more balls in the air than the juggler seems to be aware of, most of which are already perilously close to the floor.

Nevertheless, the British attachment to process over strategic vision is not devoid of core values or long-term thinking. Rather, as a status quo power, Britain is more acutely aware of that which should be preserved as the process goes forward rather than that which might be constructed. And if the British are characteristically vague over what might be constructed, they are very clear on what must be preserved in any future European security arrangements.

The first element to be preserved is the interest and involvement of the United States in European security issues (Baylis, 1984). For the British, US involvement in European security is a simple necessity which it would be both dangerous and impractical to forgo. The US provides a fund of tangible economic and military resources for which the Europeans cannot realistically substitute. It also brings to the Alliance the intangible but enormous value of its interest in European security: US political involvement in an issue normally brings about diplomatic movement for good or ill (Hurd, 1991: 15). This was demonstrated anew over the Bosnian crisis where three years of US vacillation gave way, in spring 1995, to a series of US-led initiatives that had the effect of driving a peace deal along which, 'for good or ill', certainly changed the context of the war in former Yugoslavia. At the end of the Stabilization Force (SFOR) mandate in June 1998 a US withdrawal from the multinational action would certainly have the effect of changing the basis for a settlement in former Yugoslavia yet again (Sharp, 1997). Above all, the US brings to European security the prospect – however distantly – of the employment of huge physical resources *in extremis*. Neither of the two world wars or the Cold War could have been won by the West without the employment of the resources of a superpower, and though contemporary American involvement in European security may appear sometimes quixotic, the British view of Europe is based on a bedrock belief that, if necessary, at some time in the future the United States would again be prepared to commit major military and economic resources to the defence of the Western powers should the need ever arise. The institutionalization through NATO and close bilateral relations of this enormous US potential in European security provides considerable reassurance that it will not be called upon.

The British fully accept that the relationship between the United States and Europe is in the process of rapid evolution and that US involvement in the particulars of European security has changed greatly over recent years.[4] There is a vigorous debate among the interested public over whether America has now in effect become a 'Pacific first' as opposed to an 'Atlantic first' power, but few disagree that the perceived intensity of US interests in European security is now less and that the degree of US involvement in European crises will vary considerably on a case-by-case basis (Heuser, 1996). The British approach, therefore, to the development of a European security and defence identity (ESDI) is balanced between the rationale that an ESDI will be necessary to compensate for the lack of American interest in certain crises and the realization that it is an essential pillar in creating a reformed transatlantic relationship precisely to *maintain* the institutionalization of American involvement in European security. British ministers and officials have moved a long way in their view of the future of a European security and defence identity since the debates of 1991 before the Maastricht summit on the reformed NATO force structure (June 1991) and the 'new strategic concept' (November 1991), but all subsequent authoritative statements have nevertheless been preceded by the assertion that the continued involvement of the United States in European security is a *sine qua non* of the process (Rifkind, 1995). This was as clear in the approach to the Amsterdam summit of 1997 as it was in the run-up to Maastricht in 1991.

A second core element in the British approach is the preservation, as far as possible, of the relationship between London and Washington. The so-called 'special relationship' between Britain and the United States certainly still preoccupies many British defence planners, and a majority of British politicians. Its existence is extremely difficult to verify in the 1990s, yet it is capable of making strange and sudden reappearances. It was a relationship uniquely appropriate to the circumstances of the Cold War. At the apex, it consisted of a genuine friendship between certain leaders – Churchill and Roosevelt, Macmillan and Kennedy, Callaghan and Carter, Thatcher and Reagan – which on occasion had discernible impacts on British policy and its standing in the world. At the practical base, it consisted of intelligence cooperation at a high level of detail, nuclear cooperation in both the deployment and testing of weapons, and the habits of cooperation and natural closeness born of experience between the three armed services – particularly the respective navies and air forces. Between the base and the apex of the relationship, however, it is impossible to discern any real substance to the special relationship and the vast majority of normal peacetime relations occur somewhere in this space (Clarke, 1990).

For that reason, the special relationship is very difficult to spot in the normal course of day-to-day international diplomacy. On the other hand, it has made surprising reappearances in times of armed conflict such as during the Falklands War, the Gulf War and in some of the operational details of the UNPROFOR, IFOR and SFOR deployments in former Yugoslavia. It is reasonable to suppose, though it is by no means inevitable,[5] that the substantive elements in the special relationship will decline in importance in the post Cold War environment, though it remains a major British interest to preserve as much substance in the relationship as possible.

The third core interest with which Britain approaches the future in European security matters is in the need to maintain room for political and military manoeuvre. In a changing European environment it has become abundantly clear since 1990 that only Britain and France at present possess the physical and political resources to engage in major external security operations. They are the only two European countries who can project significant amounts of military power and sustain them. The British Ministry of Defence, for example, normally aims to keep four battalions available at any given time for contingency operations, over and above other 'normal' commitments.[6] In a political sense, too, Britain has some natural room for maneouvre, being apart from the geographical centre of Europe, and having such a large measure of discretion over its involvement in future crises. Very few events that take place outside Europe, in the world that encompasses the 'new Commonwealth', have any domestic resonance within British society; British racial problems are created from within, not imported from the outside world, as is the case for some of Britain's European partners (Clarke, 1992b). Whether or not this leads Britain (and for different reasons, France) into a greater leadership role in European security questions, it is clear that British policy makers feel they have both the opportunity and the desire to retain some real flexibility in the way they may deploy their forces. Like France, Britain has a permanent seat on the UN Security Council, extant overseas dependent territories – some thirteen at present – and a number of important foreign policy commitments which demand freedom of action.

This core interest appeared in very tangible form in Britain's approach to the Intergovernmental Conference of 1996–7. The British approached all defence and security questions on the basis of strict intergovernmentalism: only this can guarantee sufficient freedom of manoeuvre to serve both external interests and the requirements of domestic unity, where both main political parties are neuralgic at the implications of increased federalism. As the previous Government's main memorandum of 1 March 1995 on European defence questions stated:

> The Government believes that the nation state should be the basic building block in constructing the kind of international order we wish to see; and that the nation state remains in particular the fundamental entity for co-operation in the field of defence . . . so the unshakeable conviction on which our approach to the development of a European defence policy will be based will be that the basis for European action in the defence and security field should be inter-governmental, based on co-operation between nation states.[7]

These core interests form a reasonably coherent whole and are mutually reinforcing. They are easier to safeguard in institutional debates – such as over the security architecture which Europe should adopt – than over policy debates in the face of real crises. They were easily defended, for example, in the British approach to the 1996–7 Intergovernmental Conference. On the other hand, all three interests have arguably been damaged by the course of the Bosnian crisis. Certainly, British policy makers would have been appalled in 1991 had they appreciated the level of British military involvement in the conflict, the limited scope for diplomatic or military manoeuvre, the damage the conflict has done to transatlantic relations and the risks to NATO unity that involvement has incurred. For this, if for no other reason, the British may be more wary of engaging in similar operations in the future, even though other pressures may lead them towards interventionism in regional and factional conflicts. The future of European security architecture, in the British view, will be determined by the way the Europeans, and the US, react to the next major series of European crises.

It is generally accepted that future crises will not concern wars of survival for Britain but rather 'wars of discretion' (Freedman, 1996). Britain will have the choice of the degree and level of involvement that is deemed appropriate, though there is no shortage of potential crises over which discretion will have to be exercised. Wars in Europe are certainly possible, not least on the periphery of the Russian Federation, but they will not necessarily involve Britain and the degree and type of engagement in such crises will be up to the government on a case-by-case basis. Britain can bring few economic or politically heavyweight resources to bear on crises in Central, Eastern or Southern Europe. Its strength lies in its military instrument and the military specialisms it can employ. Since the end of the Cold War, Britain has engaged, at its discretion, in high-intensity wars, as in the Gulf in 1990 to 1991, in civil conflicts, as over northern and southern Iraq, and in peacekeeping and peace support operations, as in Cyprus, former Yugoslavia, Angola, Rwanda, Mozambique, Cambodia, Western Sahara, Somalia, and Haiti.[8] In a sense, the British are not frightened of the prospects of European crises: they tend to take a neo-realist view that the present relaxation will prove an all too brief holiday since such crises will always be with us. The European conflicts that British policy makers tend to foresee include further crises in the Balkans, a Russian–Baltic crisis in the aftermath of NATO enlargement, smaller crises involving groups of the 3.8 million Hungarian minorities in non-Hungarian Europe, and persistent instability around the southern periphery of the Russian Federation – in particular in relation to Ukraine. Structural instability in the Mediterranean is also a likely contingency. Some of these potential crises are closer to home for Britain than others, and all of them, it could be argued, have a relevance to British security in Europe. But the outbreak of crises as such is not the prime worry of British planners who, after all, perceive that the country is fundamentally safe. Rather, the dangers and threats which British planners see arise from a collapse in the collective Western approach to security issues and in respect of the longer-term relationship between the West and Russia.

Britain has benefited more than most from collective security approaches in Western Europe. Its diplomacy was critical in founding NATO and it can be argued that Britain has benefited disproportionately from collective defence in Western Europe, paying a relatively modest military and economic price for a very robust allied defensive organization in the integrated military structure. This is not merely a security interest but an intensely felt foreign policy interest too, since Britain has gained in several ways from the intense economic interdependence of Western Europe, particularly over the last 30 years. For Britain, therefore, we may say that no European crises are uncontainable if the Western allies deal with them through a genuinely collective approach. But a comparatively minor and distant crisis could be debilitating for British interests if it sows disunity within the Western camp – as the Bosnian crisis has so nearly done. Indeed, such a crisis would undermine a principle which the British have nurtured for exactly half a century.

The second real danger which the British foresee in European security is that relations with the Russian Federation might enter a long-term spiral of decline. No less than Churchill in the 1940s or the Liberal leadership in 1907, the present British government regards businesslike and workable relations with Russia as the essential linchpin of a more constructive European policy. This is a key reason why Britain has worked hard over the last eighteen months to accommodate Russian demands on the revision of the CFE Treaty, and has been so muted in its reactions to Russian suppression of the guerrilla campaign in Chechnya. Relations with Russia may not be genuinely cordial and Britain has always been relaxed at the idea that they can be no more than cool and correct. The pattern of bilateral relations with Russia has never been very intense (though on particular issues they have often been very delicate), trade relations are thin by comparison with Russian trade relations with other major European countries, and the British have been generally less affected by periods of poor East–West relations than many other countries.

British governments never particularly minded that Russia was undemocratic; nor do they feel that the economic reform process in Russia is vital, except in so far as it is a key element in Russia's external behaviour. The view, rather, is that a good working relationship with Russia must be established in order to facilitate diplomacy in Central and Eastern Europe. This will be as much a requirement in the post Cold War world as it was during the Cold War itself. If the West fails to establish such a relationship on the basis of the Founding Act of 1997, then little else in Central and Eastern Europe will succeed or, if it does, will be secure.[9] In this circumstance, the West may need to fall back again on its collective defence assets, the United States and the centrality of NATO as an institutional linking mechanism. This, clearly, serves to reinforce the importance of NATO, the American connection and the Anglo-American relationship in British thinking, since the possibility of poor relations with Russia for perhaps a considerable period must now be taken seriously. Such a consideration also reinforces Britain's attachment to policy process rather than policy blueprints. The onset of a new Cold War is possible and only a concentration on process – preserving NATO, continuing to institutionalize the American commitment, fostering the Anglo-American relationship and maintaining diplomatic room for manoeuvre – will provide a sensible way forward with appropriate reassurance that we are not throwing out the baby with the bathwater.

Domestic elements of security policy

The underlying consensus

Public opinion in Britain is highly supportive both of a strong defence policy and of the employment of armed forces in a succession of wartime and peacetime operations. Though there has, on occasion, been notable public dissent in Britain over the war in Korea, the Suez crisis of 1956, and in the emergence of the anti-nuclear peace campaign in the 1960s and then again in the 1980s, these controversies were almost exclusively over particular policies of the government of the day – colluding with Israel, hosting US nuclear deployments in Britain, and so on – rather than the employment of the armed forces as such (Clarke, 1992b). Though the tolerance of the British public for casualties has not been severely tested since the Korean War, circumstantial evidence from a succession of post-colonial operations, from the Falklands War and from opinion poll data on the crisis in former Yugoslavia indicates that the British public do not object to casualties providing that they are not accidental or pointless (Crewe, 1985: 26–9).

If the British public has been generally stable in its support for a traditional security policy, the party political arena has shown more fluctuations than trends in public opinion, though since the end of the Cold War it has been, of necessity, bipartisan. There have been times in British political history when security questions have been matters of intense political bitterness, most notably in the late 1940s over the onset of the Cold War and the question of American leadership, and then again in the early 1960s and early 1980s on nuclear issues. A great deal of parliamentary heat has been generated over attitudes to the Russians, nuclear deterrence, and the perceived aggression of American leadership on all sides of the House of Commons. But with the exception of a relatively brief period from 1981 to 1985, when the Labour Party adopted an outright policy of nuclear disarmament, such debates, heated as they were, have been within, rather than between, the main political parties. Since 1945, the party leaderships have been at one in their adherence to NATO, the importance of the American connection, and their general attitude of wary scepticism toward the prospects of reform in the Soviet Union. Nor is there a discernible party political pattern in attitudes among the party leaders to the relationship with the United States. Leaders of the Labour Party are not generally less committed to the relationship with Washington than those in the Conservative Party. Rather, it has been a matter of circumstance and friendship at the apex of the special relationship described above. Harold Wilson as Labour leader was caught up in the period of the Vietnam War and clearly did not enjoy good personal relations with Lyndon Johnson. It seemed at the time – particularly in the light of Britain's withdrawal from east of Suez in 1967 – that the relationship with the United States was in decline. This impression may have been reinforced by the succeeding Conservative premiership of Edward Heath, who similarly did not enjoy good relations with President Nixon, and was also in office not only during the most delicate period of the Vietnam withdrawal but also in the post de Gaulle era when he was able to achieve one of his major political ambitions in negotiating British entry into the European Community in 1973. But this apparent trend was quite reversed by the Labour premiership of James Callaghan, who struck up a close friendship with President Carter at a time when 'interdependence' G7 summits had become fashionable in the mid 1970s, and reached new heights of cooperation under his Conservative successor in the Thatcher/Reagan relationship of the 1980s, which spanned for Britain the fighting of two important wars. Relations between President Clinton and the Conservative Prime Minister John Major were never close, though Major's government worked hard to bolster US-British relations as part of its independent stance on European issues; whereas the Labour Prime Minister, Tony Blair, committed to a more cooperative relationship with the European Union, struck up a positive rapport with the US President during 1997. Though the party political scene has fluctuated greatly since the 1940s and is characterized by greater volatility than ever before, the underlying bipartisan consistency – particularly on the relationship with the US and the importance of transatlantic dimensions in European security policy – is undeniable.

Attitudes to European security

Faced by the present uncertainties of the post Cold War era in European security, there is little party political debate on European security structures as such. It is an arcane and confusing subject which most politicians assume is best left to officials who, in the British case, have developed the process with some consistency. On the other hand, both main political parties have had major problems in their attitudes to European integration and it was further apparent, with the onset of the Intergovernmental Conference of March 1996 and the question of institutional reform in the three pillars of the European Union, that defence and security questions can easily be caught up in a vociferous debate between 'Eurosceptics' and 'Europhiles' within each of the two main political parties. Though the Labour Party in government has become less Eurosceptic, partly because of the large influx of new 'Blairite' members who are more pro European Union in their basic attitudes, the fact remains that there are significant areas of 'scepticism' within the governing party when particular questions are put. And for the Conservatives in opposition, the 'European issue' remains a fundamental source of disunity which many feel strikes at the heart of British conservatism and constitutional sovereignty. Only the third party, the Liberal Democrats, has no ideological problems on European Union issues, though it too has some disagreements over policy and tactics.

The previous British Conservative government became far more sceptical about the future of European integration after the last 1991 Intergovernmental Conference. In her famous speech in Bruges in 1987, the then Prime Minister Mrs Thatcher set out an approach to the European Community which stressed a particularly British interpretation of national sovereignty and which won increasing acceptance within subsequent Conservative administrations. The European ideal, in this version, was best envisaged through the centrality of the nation-state and via intense cooperation between states – not through integration that undermines them. This version of the European ideal also appealed to the emerging leaderships in the democratizing CEE states since they saw in this conception a way of being more politically integrated with Western Europe at a time when they also needed to build (or in some cases to cope with) a post-communist national consensus within their own countries, which were anyway incapable of achieving more functional economic integration with their Western neighbours. The 'Bruges vision' of Europe resolved their dilemma.

Moreover, on European defence issues – as opposed to matters of economic and social integration – both past and present governments can exploit a fair degree of bipartisan consensus where movement towards a common defence policy and 'eventually a common defence', as envisaged in the 1991 Maastricht wording, is hardly favoured by anyone on the British political scene. Successive governments have also taken some comfort from the fact that Britain cannot be so easily bypassed by the more *communautaire* members of the European Union on defence issues as it can on economic integration, monetary policy and social provision. Britain can be marginalized by a powerful Paris–Bonn axis on most EU matters (where such an axis genuinely exists) but not on defence questions, even where Paris and Bonn might be determined. The gradual and hesitant way in which the Eurocorps grew out of the Franco–German Brigade was a good example of how limited were the choices open to Paris and Bonn in a case such as this where Britain was unenthusiastic about the idea.

Nevertheless, where European security issues touch on the European Union – such as in questions over the most appropriate security architecture, the role of the Western European Union, or any prospect of 'European-only' defence cooperation – it becomes difficult to disentangle security questions from the intraparty debates over European integration. The Eurosceptics argue that British sovereignty is at stake; the Europhiles that British influence in the tide of history is the real issue. The result is that, at the political level, the rhetorical stakes are higher and even a strong Labour government with a landslide majority has comparatively little room for detailed manoeuvre on those aspects of European defence policy which seem to touch on Britain's relationship with the great 'European project'.

Western cooperation

If British defence officials have no clear sense of what the future of European security will be, and have to operate within a domestic political framework that provides uncertain political leadership, they nevertheless have a consistent view over how the process of decision making among the Western allies should be structured. NATO remains the cornerstone of all allied military cooperation, embodying the political and military virtues and having demonstrated in war, peace and now 'peace support' the invaluable habits of cooperation. The British do not feel that any further case need be made for NATO: its centrality to the picture is demonstrated by the history of European security since 1991 and the fact that it is presently the almost exclusive focus for security thinking among the non-member states who wish to join it through the Partnership for Peace (PfP) programme.

The British are, however, determinedly conservative on PfP issues. They were keen on the establishment of the North Atlantic Cooperation Council (NACC) as a way of forestalling East European demands for NATO membership, and have taken very much the same view of the PfP process and the Euro-Atlantic Partnership Council that has replaced the NACC. When it was first announced, at the Brussels summit of January 1994, the PfP initiative was welcomed in London as a way of reconciling a difference within NATO over enlargement and serving the same function as the NACC – to forestall precipitate membership. But within the year, the process had followed the logic and momentum of events: PfP had become the mechanism by which NATO *would* eventually enlarge to embrace new members, perhaps around the year 2000. London has gone along with this evolution somewhat reluctantly. Unlike Germany, Britain stands to lose more tangible advantages than it will gain intangible ones by such a process. An enlarged NATO may be a more diluted NATO: harder to manage internally, more difficult to maintain the transatlantic commitment to, less of a vehicle for British diplomacy and politically dominated (as opposed to merely influenced) by Germany. It will probably be a NATO less 'North European' in its orientation since the enlargement, in the event, only involves three of the four Visegrad countries in the first round. Above all, it risks alienating Russia in a way that might be irredeemable which, for the British, would be a general price higher than any localized benefits in Central and Eastern Europe, where British interests are comparatively slight (MccGwire, 1997).

Within the last three years, therefore, Britain's position on extended membership of NATO has been reversed. Up to 1993 British officials argued forcefully that extension was not possible. By 1995, they accepted that it was part of NATO policy. For the sake of collective solidarity in the Alliance, therefore, Britain goes along with the PfP process and states, logically enough, that all applications for membership will be judged on their merits and that Moscow will never be given the right of veto over NATO decision making. Nevertheless, the 1995 *Statement on the Defence Estimates*, in particular, went out of its way to establish the fact that PfP was a general partnership arrangement and should not be seen only as a mechanism to facilitate membership. We should not lose sight, in the current obsession with the membership issue, of the central purposes of PfP which are to improve relations between NATO and all other European states. As the defence White Paper pointed out in uncharacteristically direct terms:

> We place great value on the concept of partnership, for we seek a balance between partnership and membership in the development of the wider Europe we wish to see. But there is an unhelpful preoccupation with the latter, and in particular with membership of NATO and the European Union. Playing down the value of co-operation and playing up the significance of decisions on membership will risk re-creating the type of divide in Europe which we wish to avoid.[10]

This sentiment is echoed very faithfully in states such as Ukraine, Moldova or Belarus where it is understood quite clearly that membership for them is a very distant prospect.[11]

Britain is also more conservative than some of its European partners regarding the future of the WEU, for reasons not dissimilar to those behind British attitudes to PfP. Britain sees the WEU in strictly functional terms and resists moves to elevate it – for essentially political reasons – to a position that would undermine the cohesion that underpins NATO. Again, however, British planners are more relaxed on WEU questions than they appeared to be prior to 1992 since they consider that events have confirmed

NATO's practical competence and emphasized the WEU's limitations by comparison.

For these reasons the British government is opposed to any suggestion that the WEU should be formally merged into the European Union as a fourth pillar, and opposed the idea just as vigorously in May 1997 as it had done during the middle of 1991 when it was proposed by Italy. Rather, the WEU should concentrate on the further elaboration of the Petersberg missions articulated in 1992. The Maastricht Treaty left the WEU finely balanced between NATO and the EU. The British government accepts the logic that the WEU should be more explicitly adjacent to the EU, but regards as impractical the possibility of an integration between the two. It tends to emphasize the role of the WEU as a vehicle for NATO's greater 'Europeanization' rather than the mechanism by which the EU moves into the defence sphere.[12] It therefore argues for a greater specification of the distinctive tasks which the WEU should be capable of performing, and the British tried to use its Presidency of the organization during 1996 as an opportunity to make real progress in upgrading its operational capability (still very small) to the level where it may be capable of running perhaps one or at most two full divisions with attendant air and maritime assets, in operational circumstances.[13] Beyond that, the British approach to Western cooperation lies in two particular practical directions.

The first is to address the question of a more effective European military contribution to Western security by making the best of those European-only military assets which presently exist. British policy makers begin from the assumption that all effective defence planning must be task-based. It is pointless to define forces and political structures unless there is some clear exposition of the military tasks to be fulfilled. For the British, this helps to define the difference between the rationales of NATO and the WEU. NATO, say British officials, must still be capable of fighting a major strategic war as envisaged in the original Washington Treaty. In real terms, this requires NATO to have an ability to engage in high-tempo operations on more than one main front simultaneously for a prolonged length of time. Though it is extremely unlikely that NATO will be called upon to fulfil such a mission in the foreseeable future, the Alliance must nevertheless be maintained and sized upon this continuing requirement.

In the British view, any lesser operations which NATO forces engage in cannot be allowed to detract from the need to maintain such an overall capability. The WEU, on the other hand, is not required to fulfil such a collective defence mission (at least as long as the full membership of the WEU remains coincidental with that of NATO), even though the revised Brussels Treaty is written in somewhat stronger terms than that of the Washington Treaty. Nevertheless, the WEU is regarded by British officials as having more potential flexibility in its command and control arrangements and the missions for which it can be adapted. This dichotomy does not presuppose that NATO should be preserved for war and the WEU for operations short of war: no such simple distinctions will be possible, and the eventualities in which European military forces may be deployed will be so contingent on particular circumstances that judgements will have to be made on a case-by-case basis.

Though NATO may find itself performing nothing more than crisis management roles for the next two decades, London believes that it is important that its collective defence function is not compromised. For the British, therefore, the task is not to devise a new organization for the defence of Western Europe, but rather to develop arrangements whereby the growing multinationality of European forces can be most efficiently used and interoperability encouraged. A number of potentially important European multinational forces already exist such as the ACE Rapid Reaction Corps (ARRC) and within that the Multi-National Division (Central), the UK/Netherlands Amphibious Task Force, the Eurocorps, EUROFOR and EUROMARFOR, the German/Dutch Corps, the French–British Air Group agreed in November 1994, and the model provided by the Franco-British Rapid Reaction Force founded in early 1995 for operations in support of UNPROFOR in Bosnia. More such initiatives are likely in the future, if the IFOR and SFOR deployments are regarded as useful models of operations. British defence officials are generally relaxed about this pro-liferation of multinational European forces, since greater interoperability in these formations will increase the interoperability among all NATO forces, including those of the US. Then, too, officials stress that they see British self-defence almost entirely in a collective framework, pointing out that Britain devotes very few resources to the defence of the homeland itself. Rather, the British see the need for Europeans to be capable of pro-jecting significant military power quickly to particular areas to engage, if necessary, in high-intensity operations, and then withdraw. The chances that this can be achieved neatly by the members of only one European security arrangement are remote and *ad hoc* coalitions of the willing are almost certain to be required if European military assets are to be used at all.

The second thrust in the British approach is to move forward as far as practicable on the concept of combined joint task forces (CJTFs). For Britain CJTFs should provide 'separable but not separate elements of NATO's command structure for European-led missions', and, on this interpretation, represent a way of using NATO assets more efficiently for 'European-only' operations.[14] British military planners have generally taken the view that the first proper attempt to specify the concept was too much driven by SHAPE planning processes. The report *A Concept for a CJTF Headquarters* drawn up at SHAPE in March 1994 implied an exten-sive staff requirement of several thousand people. For the British, this was simply too big and implied a corps-level deployment that would probably be responsible to SACEUR. British officials argued for the specification of a CJTF structure that would allow for smaller operations at brigade or task group level, run from the most appropriate HQ according to its size and purpose (the new HQ for AFNORTHWEST at High Wycombe, for example, would suggest itself). The British also argue for a smaller structure for political reasons, precisely so that it would not exclude a role for the WEU and in order to agree with French reservations which – for different reasons – also attach to the SHAPE-based approach. For although the British view of the practicalities of CJTFs puts it nearer to France than the US, the accepted view in London is that CJTFs are not merely an initiative that NATO could usefully pursue, but rather an acid test of the Alliance's operational ability in the new European order. British officials point out that the next NATO operation is likely to be in effect a CJTF in any case – as its involvement in Bosnia has turned out to be in the event. There is no problem, they claim, in putting together either CJTF forces or even HQ assets once the specific context is known. NATO does this all the time both in exercises and in real operations. The problem lies in the *pre-designation of command* in situations which are hypothetical at the time of planning. NATO's Berlin ministerial meeting in June 1996 made some real progress on these issues and the British were satisfied that they had kept the role of the WEU down to pragmatic contributions that would reduce the perceived need of the EU to have a defence component outside the NATO frame-work; neither the Americans nor the Europeans would be able to conduct NATO military operations without the cooperation of the other.[15] Though the Berlin Declaration would still have to be tested in practice, from the British point of view it represented a very successful outcome.

Collective security and multilateral operations

The range of organizations through which European security is normally viewed includes the United Nations, the OSCE, NATO, the WEU and the EU. In 1990–2 it would be fair to say that the British were tempted to make clearer distinctions between the competence of these organizations for the different purposes of crisis management, crisis prevention, peacemaking or peace support operations than would now be the case. In the immediate aftermath of the Cold War, it seemed that only NATO and the WEU could have a practical role in the employment of forces for peacekeeping or peace enforcement, whilst the CSCE, as it then was, the UN and the EU would provide legitimacy, political backing, and possibly early warning of future crises. The course of the crisis in former Yugoslavia, however, has made such relatively simple distinctions impossible.

It is apparent now that 'crisis management' (as in the case of Macedonia) may require the deployment of armed forces no less than 'peace enforce-ment' and that it is, in reality, difficult to uphold the distinctions between peace support, peacemaking and peace enforcement, however distinct they are in theory. All three armed services in Britain have wrestled with these definitions as they have tried to articulate doctrines for peace support oper-ations. All three are still some way from finalized versions of a doctrine and the armed forces in general are a long way away from a joint and agreed doctrinal statement.[16] For the British, therefore, both the political and the operational definitions of crisis management activities are in the process of evolution, and to cope with this uncertainty there is a general acceptance that the future security structure in Europe will be one of 'variable geometry' where a different combination of organizations will be required according to the differential intensity of interests and level of engagement that each ally shows. This will be particularly the case for the US, and it may become normal to expect American involvement to wax and wane over time in the event of a protracted crisis. Whereas this would have been anathema to British officials even five years ago, they now approach the prospect with unaccustomed equanimity:[17] partly because it is a simple statement of the inevitable, but also because they feel the events of the last five years have demonstrated the continuing relevance of NATO to any variation in the geometry which requires the deployment of armed forces.

The key problem in the British view is not, therefore, the relationship between NATO and the WEU. This can be worked out in both theory and practice if the WEU sticks to the Petersberg tasks and remains outside the EU structure. The problems arise rather in relation to two weak points in the organizational geometry.

The first and most important weak spot arises in the relationship between the WEU and NATO on the one hand and the UN on the other. In principle, the British are in favour of the UN's use of regional organizations. In its July 1993 response to *The Agenda for Peace* the British government supported the view that regional organizations enjoyed unique advantages:

> they have an intimate knowledge of local conditions and can provide expert knowledge on background... We support the concept of a division of labour, with regional organisations taking a greater role in their own areas, particularly as regards peacemaking, while recognising at all times the primacy of the UN in situations relating to international peace and security. (White-Spunner, 1995: 37)

In practice, however, this is not so easy. While NATO and the WEU have both learned from the Bosnian crisis, it appears that NATO/WEU and the UN have failed to improve their relationship as a result of the lamentable record in the crisis. The virtually complete exclusion of the UN from the IFOR and SFOR operations is driven by a deep distrust of UN operating procedures within the US military establishment, and not a little by personal differences between the US negotiators of the Dayton Accords and the then UN Secretary-General. The broad institutional interface is clearly unsatisfactory, and this has translated to grave deficiencies in the civil/military interface in general. Though British, French, Netherlands, Nordic and Canadian troops in particular performed with some distinction in the UNPROFOR operation, their commanders have run up against UN restrictions which they found barely tolerable. The UN, NATO and the WEU are likely to be much more wary of entering into a symbiotic relationship in future crises as a result of the disagreements and confusion caused by this one. This issue returns with renewed relevance after the transfer of the first SFOR mandate to a new force in Bosnia from June 1998.[18] Though many can see what needs to be addressed to refine the relationship of the UN to regional organizations under Chapter 8 of the Charter, it is quite likely that appropriate action in this regard will not follow, leaving this part of the security arrangement fundamentally – and perennially – inadequate.

The second weak point in the variable geometry of European security concerns the relation between NATO and the WEU on the one hand and the EU on the other. The problem here is not that relations are demonstrably bad but that they are so far in a melting-pot whilst EU institutional reform and expansion is under way. Though the WEU is presently equidistant between NATO and the EU, and though it is likely to be brought much closer to the EU over the next two to three years, the fact remains that its relationship with NATO is easier to specify than that with the EU. It is not clear quite how EU political authority will be translated into military tasks that the WEU might be asked to perform: not because such specification is in itself difficult, but because the expanded membership of the EU includes countries which will probably not be full members of the WEU and therefore would not take part in a pre-organized military structure. For ambitious security architects in the new Europe, this is a genuine problem; for British officials it provides yet another pragmatic comfort. For it reinforces what the British believe to be the simple reality that only NATO will continue to provide an all-purpose integrated military structure. That which can be derived for the WEU will be essentially complementary and should, in any case, draw upon NATO assets in a dual-hatting arrangement. This was the thinking behind the primary British security proposal to the Amsterdam summit in June 1997: that a head of state and head of government summit of the WEU should meet back-to-back with the European Council, supported by the relevant staff work and greater liaison between the relative secretariats. This, it is said, would provide more coherence between the EU and the WEU, and invest WEU implementation with greater political authority.

Meanwhile, at the operational level, Britain expects to engage in more peacekeeping and peace support operations (PSOs) for the foreseeable future, and sees the fate of such initiatives – when undertaken in a European context – as more important to the future shape of European security than the arcane arguments over 'security architecture'. The political will to be engaged in multilateral operations is clearly present, driven both by a residual sense of Great Power status among key politicians and the more particular concerns of the Foreign and Commonwealth Office (FCO) that British influence should be exerted through the most appropriate instruments. Nor is the marginal cost of PSOs prohibitively expensive. In 1993 – a year of peak PSO spending – the cash cost to the government of military contributions to the UN over and above the normal assessed British contribution to the peacekeeping budget (which is in addition to the normal assessed contribution for UN activities in general) was just under $218 million. This was not set against the defence budget, but rather against that of the FCO which was able to lay it against the central contingency reserve

(White-Spunner, 1995: 38–9). The FCO has been constantly more enthusiastic than some other areas of government that British forces should be involved, where appropriate, in peace support operations; indeed, in 1994 the FCO received 22 separate requests from the United Nations for troop contributions to multinational operations. The military, though certainly wary about the problems of overstretch and the degradation of warfighting training that PSOs involve, are also willing to demonstrate their usefulness and relevance by deploying forces in multilateral operations. The general consensus is that Britain's comparative advantage lies in the deployment of specialist forces, and throughout the 1990s the Ministry of Defence has been able to record that some 25–30 operational deployments are normally undertaken in different parts of the world every year.

It should be noted, however, that the general British willingness to be involved in multilateral operations, coupled with the expertise of professional and specialized forces in such situations, has resulted in a considerable degree of 'mission creep', wherein operations which began on strictly humanitarian grounds developed into containment and peacemaking and during 1995 verged on peace enforcement, with the concomitant necessity of deploying more troops differently and more appropriately equipped. Given a willingness to be involved, and the inherent nature of crises in which PSOs are deemed appropriate, it is not obvious how such 'mission creep' can be avoided in the future, even if the lessons of Bosnia are well drawn (Clarke, 1995: 51–2).

Finally, Britain possesses comparatively rich resources with which to engage in multilateral peace support operations. British military thinking is still vehement and unanimous that it is necessary to prepare for war in order to have the capabilities to engage in operations short of war. This view is consistent with a long tradition in the post-colonial world where British forces were structured to fight a third world war but found themselves, in practice, doing everything but that. It is a moot point whether this assertion can be sustained when the demands of modern peace support operations are so much greater than the demands made by either post-colonial operations or UN operations in the pre-1989 period, and where involvement in European crises necessarily suggests deeper commitments to peace support as an act of enlightened self-interest for the European powers. Nevertheless, on a conservative estimate, Britain can almost certainly field at one month's notice a high-intensity intervention capability that could consist of one corps HQ, one armoured division consisting of two brigades, one air mobile brigade, two MLRS regiments, two fighter and three fighter ground attack squadrons, and one naval carrier task group, which could be deployed almost anywhere in the world, and certainly in or around the fringes of the European continent. For lesser operations, such as a major peacekeeping operation, Britain is capable of deploying at one month's notice a minimum of one brigade HQ plus signal squadron, one to two infantry battalions, one engineering regiment, one logistic battalion, transport helicopter support, two fighter and two fighter ground attack squadrons, plus a small naval task force. In the case of either contingency, specialist troops are also potentially available, up to one brigade each of airborne troops and marines (Duncan et al., 1995). For operations that require a bigger build-up, of course, much greater resources are potentially available, depending on the political will to incur the costs of deployment and the use of regular or territorial reserves. In 1993–4 the legislation concerning the call-up of reserves was altered to provide a more flexible structure, and Territorial Army elements have been integrated with regular regiments in order to bring their numbers up to strength before further deployments in Bosnia.

Conclusion

In looking at national approaches to European security after the Cold War it is difficult to resist the conclusion that Britain is a status quo power in a situation where the status quo is rapidly changing. This does not make it irrelevant to the issue: indeed, on defence questions Britain cannot be effectively sidelined by its European partners as it could be over questions of monetary integration. But it does mean that Britain's approach to the future of European security has some very singular characteristics and that it remains an open question how much the emerging situation in Europe will play to Britain's relative weaknesses rather than its strengths.

To summarize the material in this chapter, it is clear that British attitudes carry a large historical legacy with them: a traditional influence within NATO; a strong relationship with the United States which has facilitated a great deal of diplomatic influence at certain periods during the Cold War; a traditional dualism toward Europe, whereby collective approaches to defence are a *sine qua non* of British interests whereas collective approaches to social and economic development in Europe are not; and not least, a residual world role – backed by the United States – which lasted longer and declined more gradually than it might otherwise have done in the absence of the pressures of the Cold War.

Secondly, Britain views the future of European security as a process more than a blueprint. The pieces of the security jigsaw are too numerous and the picture we are aiming to construct too vague for the British to depart from their concentration on process. This faith in the efficacy of process stems partly from a relative satisfaction with previous security arrangements. The Cold War provided some predictability in international behaviour and the Western Alliance functioned as a most effective institution of collective defence. For the British, therefore, it would be most unwise to undermine institutions which have proved themselves, in favour of more vague institutional arrangements which are as yet quite unproven, or worse, have performed badly so far in post Cold War crises. Hence, a step-by-step process of change will allow us to evaluate the costs of what we may be giving up as against the gains of any new security structure.

Thirdly, the British are entirely pragmatic in their view of any given change to European security structures. Political structures such as the EU must recognize the importance of intergovernmentalism and the natural differences of interest which are bound to arise among a community of fifteen nations. And military organizations such as NATO and the WEU must remain firmly task-based in their approach so that military forces can be sized, equipped, and commanded in such a way that they perform specified roles which are themselves regarded as useful and not duplicative of military tasks already assigned somewhere else. The British are naturally sceptical of the use of military organizations to make purely political gestures. Though NATO was used many times throughout the Cold War to make expansive political gestures it never lost its essential military rationale, whereas organizations which now may claim a significant defence role such as the WEU and the EU have yet to establish an essential military rationale that would give real point to any political messages they intended to send.

In practical terms, therefore, British attitudes to European security over the next two to three years are fairly easy to predict. The British believe that NATO has proved itself as an integrated military structure, and that the WEU has a useful subsidiary role to play but has yet a very long way to go before it can be a competent and self-sustaining military structure capable of commanding significant military forces. Even if this were a desirable outcome, it is not likely to be achieved in the short or even the medium term. The result, for the British, is that they feel a general European consensus has been arrived at whereby NATO remains the keystone organization and allows its assets to be used by other organizations or command structures as required in a flexible way which will be developed in response to current and future crises and to the development of the concept of CJTFs. For the British, the war in former Yugoslavia has reawakened an awareness that British forces can have a valuable role to play in European peace support operations and that they will have to be at least partially restructured in order to play it efficiently. But if the Bosnia crisis has taught the British the importance of multinational peace support operations in Europe, it has also demonstrated for them the value of traditional coordination between national forces rather than the need for more integrated defence structures as such. The costs, the dangers, the professionalism and the political will, which are all part of deploying major forces in peace support operations, indicate for the British that they have an influential role to play at a national level rather than a destiny to help create politically integrated defence structures where such elements would be diluted and possibly ineffective in future crises. If Bosnia has indicated that the Europeans have an important military job to do in Europe, then it has also demonstrated that they should do it intergovernmentally.

For similar reasons, the British are extremely sceptical at the prospect that the European Union should move toward the eventual framing of a common defence policy. At root, British officials point to the logical consequences of a common European defence policy. Defence entails the symbolism of sovereignty, and the British ask the rhetorical question: 'Which European countries are prepared to give up their national control over defence and foreign policy?' In truth, countries such as Belgium and Luxembourg and perhaps even Italy would be prepared to do so, but it is inconceivable to officialdom in London that France, Germany or Spain would do so, and the British themselves certainly have no expectation of doing so in the foreseeable future.

This attitude leaves the British increasingly unsympathetic to any prospects of deepening European integration in the defence field. Instead, it leaves them suggesting or supporting a number of sensible and limited initiatives: the creation of a European centre for security analysis within the EU; an increase in the directive powers of the Secretary-General of the European Council; an improvement across the board in the staff work prior to European Council and WEU summit meetings; a back-to-back summit of the European Council with heads of state and heads of government of the WEU countries; and a determined attempt to coordinate more efficiently the command arrangements between the growing number of European military structures. This approach is entirely sensible and difficult to criticize on either ideological or practical grounds. It seems unlikely, however, that such gradualism will be enough to satisfy Britain's European partners whose views are frequently more expansive.

Notes

1 See HMSO (1996: 3; 1995b: 9). The 1998 *Statement* did not follow the usual format and was wrapped into the new government's defence review.

2 See, for example, the conclusions of over twenty years ago in the seminal work by William Wallace, *The Foreign Policy Process in Britain* (1975).

3 See the speech of the Defence Secretary on 'NATO' of 16 December 1993, in Centre for Defence Studies, *The Framework of United Kingdom Defence Policy*, London Defence Studies 30/31, December 1995, pp. 51–2.

4 See, for example, British views as expressed in Sharp (1990).

5 It is possible that if Western nations engage in a great deal more 'constabulary' action, then the military basis to the special relationship could be revitalized, since there are few Western nations, other than the USA itself, capable of projecting and maintaining specialist military forces in an expeditionary capacity.

6 Information from a personal interview, 2 March 1995. It was also observed that this guideline is now more honoured in the breach than the observance, but it still remains an aspiration of defence planners which indicates a certain sense of Britain's self-image.

7 Unpublished memorandum, 1 March 1995, *Memorandum on the United Kingdom Government's Approach to the Treatment of European Defence Issues at the 1996 Inter-Governmental Conference*. A version of this appeared as *A Partnership of Nations*, Cm 3181, 12 March 1996, and was paraphrased in HMSO (1996: 12–13).

8 Britain has made contributions to all these operations, though in some cases, such as Somalia and Haiti, token ones, more as an expression of Anglo–American solidarity.

9 See, for example, the arguments of Mandelbaum (1996).

10 See HMSO (1995a).

11 See, for example, Smeshko (1995). This view, however, did not stop the Ukrainian President hinting that his country might reverse its view on membership – somewhat to the alarm of NATO officials.

12 The best expression of these arguments, by an American, is to be found in Gordon (1997).

13 Personal interviews.

14 Memorandum cited previously, par. 30.

15 'NATO, CJTFs and IFOR', *Strategic Comments*, 2(5), June 1996.

16 The Army's doctrinal statement is *Wider Peacekeeping*, presently being incorporated into a joint *Peacekeeping and Peace Support* doctrine that will include questions of enforcement. The Royal Navy and the Royal Air Force deal with such questions in their general doctrinal publications: *The Fundamentals of British Maritime Doctrine*, BR 1806, London, HMSO, 1995; and *Airpower Doctrine*, AP 3000, 2nd edn, London, HMSO, 1993.

17 See for example, the statement by the then Foreign Secretary Douglas Hurd on 28 February 1995, when he said in a speech to the Deutsche Gesellschaft für Assenpolitik that we must be intensely practical about making the best use of WEU assets since we in Europe cannot 'expect direct American involvement in every crisis or operation in Europe or on the periphery'.

18 This possibility was first openly acknowledged at the end of January 1996. See Erlanger (1996).

9 Spanish Security Policy and the Mediterranean Question

Esther Barbé

There is a European dimension of security that cannot be forgotten, and this dimension is the Mediterranean one.

(F. Fernández Ordóñez, 1990)

Since the end of the Cold War, Spanish security policy has been dramatically transformed. This chapter analyses why and how much this policy has been transformed, focusing on two topics: the role played by Spain in European and security organizations during recent years, and the Spanish interest in linking European security and Mediterranean stability.

Spain: from newcomer to mainstreamer

Deeply rooted interests, values and identities have divided European Union countries, with regard to the Common Foreign and Security Policy (CFSP), into opposing groups, developing cleavages. Three cleavages can be identified (Barbé, 1997a). The first cleavage, concerning institutional matters, opposes federalists and intergovernmentalists. The second cleavage is related to security and defence, and opposes those who defend the priority of NATO, the Atlanticists, and those who pursue the existence of a strong organization of European security, the Europeanists. The third cleavage is a multiform one, based on the world views of the member states. These world views can give rise to diverse cleavages. Factors such as the size of the state, big versus small, or geographical location, North versus South, are a source of divergence when creating mechanisms and implementing policies. The fact is that the historical differences become increasingly important as the Union grows. In other words, the initial Club of Six has been joined by others who have brought with them a baggage of different expectations and a legacy of different histories (Wallace, 1993: 96).

Spain's position in each of these cleavages will enable formulation of the basic characteristics of Spanish policy in matters of CFSP and connected topics (WEU, NATO). From these characteristics one can determine the level of change or continuity in Spain's strategy in recent years. This chapter argues that Spain's position in the matter of European security and defence has undergone changes between the 1991 Intergovernmental Conference to reform the Community and the 1996–7 one. Like many other countries,

Spain has reformulated its positions to adapt to the present international system.

Since its entry into the EC in 1986, Spain has participated in the formulation and debate on European construction in relation to foreign, security and defence policy. Its attitude in this respect has been a very active one. In this sense, we can talk of Spanish activism in CFSP matters (Barbé, 1995: 114) with regard to current management (Presidencies of 1989 and 1995) as well as the development of the operational structures. In fact Spain, who might have been a latecomer at a certain stage, has now turned into a mainstreamer (Diedrichs and Wessels, 1996: 315). The mainstreamer role of Spain is assumed in this chapter, and on that basis we will deal with Spain's position in each of the above-mentioned cleavages.

Concerning the first cleavage, over the European integration model, Spain is part of the federalist group of countries. Spain, like Denmark and the United Kingdom, is not one of the founding members of the Community and is peripheral in geographic terms. Nevertheless, and unlike those two countries, Spain's entry into the Community was experienced as a 'historical solution' for Spanish democrats. Its membership in the EC was equivalent to the overcoming of Spain's isolation and Francoism.

Concerning the second cleavage, over the European defence model, Spain is part of the Europeanist group of countries. In line with Greece, Spain was in the 1980s a country characterized by its anti-Americanism. Spanish society did not share the historical experience of the Second World War. Owing to the USA–Spain agreements signed in 1953, and as an imperialist power in Latin America, the United States was identified not as a liberator from Nazism, but as the supporter of Franco. The fact is that Spain's entry into NATO caused a big split between the political forces of the country.

Concerning the third cleavage, diffuse and varied in nature, two important issues must be mentioned in the Spanish case. One is the impact of the North-South cleavage, and the other is the impact of historic and geographic factors that led Spain to have its own diplomatic agenda.

The North–South cleavage has made itself clear in the past few years, and particularly so since the enlargement to fifteen. Whereas the Southern countries, such as Spain, motivated by the risks deriving from destabilization in the Arab world, design a Mediterranean space for a European Union commitment, in the North, Germany and the Nordic countries are rediscovering the Baltic world.

As far as Spain's own agenda is concerned, it must be pointed out that it gives priority to two regions: the Mediterranean and Latin America. Attention must be directed to the fact that Spanish policy with respect to the Arab world picked up considerably after the end of the Cold War. We will see in this chapter that Europe's displacement towards the East owing to the end of the Cold War placed Spain in a peripheral position. This situation reinforced Spain's choice to make the Maghreb a priority on its agenda, particularly because it generates a risk zone for Spain's security. Unlike the Maghreb, Latin America constitutes a prestige area, not a risk zone, and the factor at stake is not security but values and identity (Barbé, 1996a: 128). Therefore, the Spanish agenda will link European security and the Mediterranean question.

A reluctant partner during the Cold War

Spain joined NATO in June 1982. Between 1982 and 1989, Spain participated actively in the European security structure of the Cold War period. In fact, Spain was already a base of the Western military system from 1953 through bilateral agreements with the United States (Viñas, 1981). Spain's security policy in the period 1982–9 was marked by certain special features. They will be briefly enumerated, bearing the internal conditioning factors in mind. The subject of security was a sensitive one for Spanish society in the first half of the 1980s. As Fernando Rodrigo (1995: 50) puts it, the controversy that surrounded Spain's entry into NATO aroused passions.

Spain entered NATO based on a proposal from the Conservative government of Calvo Sotelo. The Spanish Parliament was divided on the issue (186 votes in favour and 146 votes against). It was the first foreign policy matter to break the consensus reached by the political forces to overcome the transition from Francoism to democracy. Therefore, the NATO issue was very important during the next electoral campaign of October 1982. Many citizens gave their votes to the Socialists in the belief that the PSOE would take Spain out of the Alliance (Mesa, 1988: 173).

The attitude of Felipe González, who during the electoral campaign had promised to call a referendum to remove Spain from NATO, changed once in office. The referendum was delayed, but was held at last in March 1986, and González's campaign was in favour of staying in. The referendum on the Spanish relation to NATO finally took the form of a plebiscite on the figure of Felipe González. The question of the referendum was a complex one, since the Spaniards were asked if they agreed to stay on in NATO with three conditions that would 'facilitate' this stay: (1) Spain would continue in NATO without taking part in the integrated military structure; (2) Spain would prohibit the installation, storage or introduction of nuclear weapons in its territory; and (3) Spain would progressively reduce American military presence in the country. With these three conditions, González's government obtained a victory in favour of membership in NATO (52.5 per cent in favour, 39.8 per cent against, with an abstention of 40.6 per cent).

From this point on, González's government negotiated Spain's model of participation in NATO. The first condition of the referendum – not taking part in the integrated military structure – led to all kinds of interpretations. To what degree was the Spanish model going to copy the French one? However, Spain was in favour of being present in the Military Committee (MC), in the Defence Planning Committee (DPC) and in the Nuclear Planning Group (NPG). Therefore, the Spanish option was going to create a new model of 'reluctant' membership, different from the French one.

Creating this model took a long time. In 1986, Spain presented a first memorandum with some general points that constituted the basis for the development of Spanish participation in NATO (Rodrigo, 1995: 64). According to this memorandum, Spain would participate in every NATO organism and would adopt a military defence planning procedure similar to that of the allied countries; the Spanish forces would participate in military exercises, preferably in areas of strategic interest to Spain; Spanish forces would not be assigned to NATO integrated commands to carry out missions under their orders; and to the effect that Spanish forces, acting under Spanish command, would carry out joint missions with the allied forces, Spain would establish coordination agreements between its military authorities and the NATO integrated commands. Those coordination agreements were negotiated and signed between 1986 and 1992.

Because of the long period during which the Spanish model of participation in NATO remained undefined, together with the anti-Atlanticist rhetoric that persisted in Spanish society, Spain was considered a 'reluctant partner' (Snyder, 1988: 140), a 'free rider', 'semi-aligned' or a 'security consumer'.

The reduction of the American presence in Spain, one of the conditions of the NATO referendum, was a sensitive issue for Spanish public opinion. A successful agreement was reached in January 1988, leading to the withdrawal of USA F Wing 401 planes from Spain. Thus Spain normalized its relations with the United States, putting an end to the feeling of the lack of sovereignty (Spanish territory as an American base) linked to the Franco period.

Finally, Spain's entry into the WEU was a fundamental part of the Spanish model of European security. Owing to its European flavour, joining the WEU was a clear priority for the Spanish government. However, the aim of González's government clashed with the Spanish refusal to nuclearize the national territory. Because of this refusal some WEU members were reluctant to Spanish membership. Nevertheless, the initial reluctance of some WEU members was rapidly overcome by Spain's 'alignment'. The Spanish government expressed its full agreement with the main WEU guidelines (the Hague Platform, the Rome Declaration and the Treaty of Brussels), in spite of its nuclear dimension, as well as its willingness to participate in their implementation. This acceptance of a 'strategy of defence and effective deterrence based on an adequate mix of nuclear and conventional forces' made the Spanish accession to the WEU on 14 November 1988 possible (Cahen, 1989: 53).

'Spain is not different': the responsible partner

In short, Spain participated fully in the framework of European security in 1988. However, the Spanish security policy's homologation with that of its Western European allies took place because of the end of the Cold War.

Spain's participation in the Gulf War and its position during the Inter-governmental Conference in 1991 are the best examples of its adaptation to the 'new world'.

To start with, it must be pointed out that Western Europe's reorientation towards Eastern Europe after the fall of the Berlin Wall produced a 'periphery syndrome' in Spain. This 'syndrome' had two effects: first, Spain very decidedly advocated its own international objectives, particularly in the Maghreb; secondly, Spain made a pragmatic reorientation of its security policy, with the intention of participating in the hard core of the 'international Europe' (Barbé, 1994).

The Spanish position during the negotiation for the transformation of European Political Cooperation (EPC) into CFSP was based on two ideas: (1) a common foreign policy is a basic pillar of the political union and a counterpart of the enlargement process; and (2) European failure in the Gulf crisis can be explained by the lack of adequate tools to face the situation. Thus, Spain considered the creation of the CFSP fundamental for the process of European construction and was in favour of implementing new diplomatic and military mechanisms (Barbé, 1996b: 267). In this matter, the Spanish government had the support of public opinion in favour of developing a 'European identity' in the international system. Thus, the *Eurobarometer* of February 1991 indicated that 54 per cent of Spaniards were in favour of the CFSP, against 17 per cent who were opposed to the stated policy.

Spain's participation in the naval blockade organized by the WEU during the Gulf War was important in the domestic sphere. In fact Spain was participating for the first time in its recent history in a multinational fleet in wartime. The reaction of Spanish public opinion was positive; 48 per cent of Spaniards supported Spain's participation in the naval blockade as compared with 35.4 per cent against it. The Gulf experience showed that Spanish opinion was changing (Alonso Zaldívar and Ortega, 1992). This new situation facilitated Spain's homologation with the other European countries in the matter of security and defence. In effect, González's government approached the negotiations of the Intergovernmental Conference in 1991 having overcome two obstacles: mistrust of the allies and the reluctance of Spanish public opinion to accept the participation of the Spanish army in international operations.

In the reform process of the European Community, Spain was one of the promoters of the European defence identity. It defended, together with France and Germany, the inclusion of the terms 'common defence' and 'common defence policy' in the text of the Treaty as well as the incorporation of the WEU as 'an integral part of the process of European Union and in charge of implementing the security and defence policy' (Europe Documents, 1991). At the same time Spain supported the complementarity between WEU/EU and NATO, defending, for instance, the 'double-hat' system (Alonso Zaldívar, 1992: 23).

On the whole, it can be said that the disappearance of bipolarism 'facilitated' Spain's participation in the debate on European security. Since 1991 the Spanish government's discourse in the matter of defence organizations was pragmatic, looking for a way to fully participate in European security without having to modify its model of participation in NATO. In fact, the Spain–NATO coordination agreements made it possible for Spanish troops, in times of crisis or conflict, to enter into action as a part of the Alliance's operations outside Spanish territory, in accordance with the principle of reciprocity or preventive defence. The last agreements on Spain's role in NATO, coming into force in 1992, prepared the ground for practical decisions, such as the possible Spanish contribution to multinational forces.

Year 1995: three Presidencies at once

Spain's evolution in European security matters had been evident since the end of the Cold War. In effect, Spain was prudent when tackling the subject of European defence, supporting reinforcement of the WEU but always in complementarity with NATO. In fact, Spain implemented its model of participation in the Alliance in a pragmatic way. This led Spain, in 1995, to participate in the bombing of the Bosnian Serbs (eight Spanish F-18 fighter bombers operated out of the Aviano base). With respect to the Bosnian conflict, Spain placed a large number of soldiers (1,500) at the disposal of UNPROFOR who were later transferred to IFOR and SFOR. As regards WEU operations, Spain participated in patrolling the Adriatic and the Danube, as well as in tasks carried out in the city of Mostar under EU administration.

Thus, between mid 1992 (the beginning of the war in Bosnia) and mid 1995 (the start of Spain's Presidency of the EU and the WEU), Spain adopted an active policy in European security matters, going beyond participation in the conflict in the former Yugoslavia. In the field of operational capacity, mention must be made of Spain's incorporation in the Eurocorps in 1994. In the institutional sphere, it is worth mentioning the interest shown by Spain in strengthening the role of the WEU.

During the second semester of 1995, Spain took charge, for the first time since its entry into WEU, of the Presidency of the Council simultaneously with the Presidency of the European Union. The Spanish government insisted on underlining the positive value of this coincidence. It was the first time that both Presidencies had coincided since the EU–WEU harmonization process began after the signing of the Maastricht Treaty. Therefore Spain exercised, during the second semester of 1995, a triple Presidency: the EU, the WEU and the Reflection Group to prepare Maastricht 2.

The triple Presidency affected Spain's attitude throughout the period. In this regard, it must be pointed out that the Spanish government undertook a distinctly institutional function. In other words, González's government acted more as an arbiter than a party implicated in the coming conference.

This is obvious in all the documents inspired by the Spanish ministry, which, rather than reproducing specific points of view, list the problems and alternatives to be discussed at the conference, explaining and probing into the subject matter in detail.

Spain has approached Maastricht 2 with one idea in mind: the present reform constitutes one more stage in a process. In other words, it 'will not be the last stage of something that, by definition, is a long process' (Conferencia, 1995: 19). In this sense, Spanish documents consider that Maastricht 2 must be pragmatic, covering those reforms that are indispensable for making possible the next enlargement towards the East.

With respect to the CFSP, Spain considers that 'the reforms in this chapter will most probably have a limited reach, focusing, in the majority of cases, not so much on a modification of the Treaty as on provisions of a practical order' (1995: 42). In the matter of defence, Spain deals with the subject as an unresolved matter. Indeed, the Spanish documents recall that Maastricht 1 left some aspirations unsatisfied: specifically, the aspiration of the group of countries, Spain among others, that wished to provide the EU with a true defence dimension. Therefore the Spanish documents consider that Maastricht 2 is an ideal moment to advance the development of the European defence and security identity (EDSI) (1995).

Gradualist approach and intermediate options

The Spanish reflection on security and defence is fully developed in the report elaborated when acting as the Presidency of the WEU (Document, 1995). That report tackled in detail the future of the ESDI. It covered what the Spanish Presidency considered to be the feasible options as well as a minimum consensus to advance. This Document listed some premises on which there is consensus among the EU member states and how the WEU's contribution to revising the Treaty on European Union should be based. These premises are: the key objective is to make progress in constructing the ESDI; the point of view of each member state whose national security and defence is affected must be respected; whatever form the future institutional development of both organizations might take, the system which currently makes it possible for associated members of the WEU, observers and associated partners to participate in the construction of the ESDI must be maintained; the principle of national sovereignty should continue to govern relations between European countries as regards security and defence and, consequently, the decision-making process in such areas must continue to be based on the consensus rule as opposed to any other decision-making procedure based on majority voting in any form; and the possible participation of supranational bodies in the decision-making process must be restricted.

The Europeanist approach of the González government was manifest in this Document presented when acting as Presidency of the WEU

(Document, 1995). In this sense, it says that whatever else, a common defence policy should include a guarantee of mutual defence as an expression of solidarity between Europeans. In spite of this Europeanist approach, the Document established, in a pragmatic way, the premise that the Atlantic Alliance must remain a central element of European security and that relations with NATO should not be substantially changed, regardless of the institutional form which the EDSI might take in future. Decisions taken at the conference in this area should, therefore, also aim to strengthen common defence in the context of the Atlantic Alliance. Finally, the Document affirmed that the development of the ESDI should go hand in hand with a close relationship between Europe and its North American allies.

On the basis of the previous premises, the Document (1995) set out a list of three options: first, enhanced cooperation between an autonomous WEU and the EU; secondly, a range of intermediate options designed to bring about a convergence between the EU and the WEU; and finally, the possibility that the EU would itself assume the European defence role. To finish, the Spanish Document fully assumed the gradualist approach, affirming that the WEU's contribution to the conference might recommend a sequence of institutional steps, which might even be reflected in a proposed timetable for implementation. In other words, Spain was a part of the largest group of countries that, according to the Reflection Group Report, 'considers that establishing an EDSI consists of the gradual integration of the WEU in the EU' (Report, 1995: point 177).

This Spanish Document was elaborated by a Socialist government, replaced by a Conservative one in 1996. How much was Spanish policy with regard to European security and defence going to change? Throughout 1995 there was much evidence that the differences between PP and PSOE in these matters were on the decline. The approval by consensus in the Spanish Parliament of a report on the Spanish position regarding Maastricht 2 (Dictamen, 1995) is ample proof of the continuity between Socialist and Conservative governments in matters of European security and defence.

Low profile and continuity: Spain in Maastricht 2

The debate between the Spanish parliamentarians on the elaboration of the above-mentioned report made evident that security and defence are not conflictive issues anymore. The only political party raising difficulties about approving the text was Izquierda Unida (an electoral coalition dominated by the Communist Party), which was reluctant to accept NATO's role in European defence.

This parliamentarian report established the guidelines for Aznar's government during the conference as far as the second pillar is concerned. That report is based on the premise that Spanish national interest and European interest coincide in 'the creation of an operational defence instrument of the European Union, without endangering the cohesion of the Atlantic

Alliance' (Dictamen, 1995: 10). To achieve the stated objective, the report underlines that

> it is necessary to convert the WEU into the operational defence instrument of the EU. For this purpose, it would be convenient to have a plan of successive stages, or at least a clear orientation to enable going from the current status quo to a gradual integration of the WEU in the EU. . . In any case, it appears to be necessary to prepare the WEU to successfully take on tasks, such as crisis management, peace missions and the protection of European citizens. Finally, there is an asymmetry between the WEU and the EU that must be approached progressively with flexibility to guarantee coherence of the European project with collective security. It would be convenient to establish that membership of the EU is a requirement for the entry of new members in the WEU. (1995: 16)

With respect to this last point, which tends to favour convergence between the WEU and the EU in so far as their members are concerned, it must be noted that the report of the Spanish Parliament does not deal with the contrary case (membership of the EU and not of the WEU). This is illustrative of the Spanish will to avoid criticism from the neutral and Nordic countries. In other words, Spain has accepted 'variable geometry' in defence matters.

Since Aznar took office in May 1996, Spanish behaviour in the framework of the Intergovernmental Conference in matters of security and defence can be defined by two terms: low profile and continuity. The low profile of the Spanish government is due to the fact that the second pillar has not been a priority on the Spanish agenda. In fact, the present Conservative government has concentrated its efforts on the reform of the first pillar, in terms of institutional reform, and the third pillar, pledging for a European judicial space. Unlike the direct role played by Spain in 1991, together with France and Germany, to profile the Treaty in the defence aspects (Barbé, 1996b: 273), Spain played a discreet role in 1996–7. In this last conference Spain did not play a prominent role, holding meetings with France and Germany and elaborating joint communiqués. In short, the Spanish behaviour in matters of CFSP institutional reform has lost the activist profile it used to have in the past. In this sense Aznar's government is following the tendency already begun at the end of González's period (Barbé, 1997b: 26).

Continuity implies both losing prominence in matters of CFSP reform and keeping proposals for that reform. In this last sense, the Spanish approach in matters of security and defence, assumed by Aznar's government and supported by the Spanish Parliament, can be called a pragmatic Europeanism. In short, it means that Spain supports: a gradual approach with regard to integrating the WEU into the EU; the development of WEU and CJTF operational capacities; taking decisions by consensus in defence matters, but accepting reinforced cooperation case by case, among those member states ready to undertake military actions; all the countries should show political and financial solidarity for the military actions undertaken by a limited group of member states; and NATO must have a central role in European security and the European pillar of NATO should be strengthened. Because of the nature of the Spanish model in NATO, an open question remains with regard to the future role of Spain in the Alliance.

The end of the Spanish model in NATO

When Javier Solana, Spanish Foreign Affairs Minister, was elected in December 1995 to head the General Secretariat of NATO, a large part of the Spanish press already took for granted that the post had a counterpart: Spain's full incorporation in NATO. González denied it. However, much evidence during 1995 showed that the Spanish model of participation in NATO had to be reviewed. In the first place, Spain was fully participating in NATO's collective security operations in Bosnia although the country did not participate in the military command structure. In the second place, Spain wanted to reduce defence costs. Therefore, the Spanish interest in avoiding a duplication of efforts (WEU, NATO) was expressed by Javier Solana (1995: 7). Finally, Spain was afraid of the admission of new members into NATO. In fact, Spain lobbied for the reform of the military structure to be carried out prior to the enlargement.

Spain's complete integration into the reformed structure of NATO was not mentioned by either PP or PSOE during the 1996 election campaign. On the contrary, the electoral programme of both parties pointed out that they would not review the Spanish model of participation in NATO if they won the elections. The Conservatives pointed to the 1986 referendum to justify the status quo position.

However, once the elections were over, both parties supported the same position: the 1986 referendum referred only to Cold War NATO structure; therefore that referendum would not impede Spanish integration into the new NATO structure to be adopted in 1997. PP and PSOE shared this approach. King Juan Carlos visited NATO headquarters on 26 April 1996. His speech was 'inspired' in common by the Socialist acting government and PP advisers. The King's speech pointed out some issues of the Spanish agenda concerning NATO: NATO reform should permit full military integration of every member, Spain included; Spain favoured the emergence of an EDSI; disappearance of the NATO command in Gibraltar; and NATO's contribution to stability in the Mediterranean.

The will of the main Spanish political forces to put an end to the Spanish model in NATO, decided by the 1986 referendum, was a clear fact even before Aznar's government took office at the beginning of May 1996. The Spanish conditions for complete military integration into the reformed NATO were defined by the Conservative government in Parliament (Diario, 1996: 213): first, the structure should be different from the existing one; secondly, the Spanish statute in NATO should fulfil Spanish interests; and thirdly, a visible EDSI should be developed. What are those Spanish interests? In September 1996 Solana visited Madrid, acting as Secretary-General of NATO. On that occasion the Conservative government explained clearly the interests that should be fulfilled to have Spain fully integrated in NATO: the abolition of NATO command in Gibraltar (Gibmed) headed by a British general; the creation of a new multinational command covering the Spanish territory and headed by a Spanish general; and the control by the Spanish army of the western Mediterranean, including the Gibraltar area (*Nouvelles Atlantiques*, 1996a: 2).

The Spanish Parliament adopted in November 1996 a resolution supporting the government decision to start the process of full participation in the new NATO command structure. The parliamentarians advised the Spanish government to pay attention to five issues during the NATO reform process. Three of them are usually present on the Spanish agenda: a new and flexible NATO military structure; command responsibilities for Spain concerning the Mediterranean and Atlantic areas; and visibility of EDSI. In addition, the Spanish resolution pointed out that Spain is favourable to the enlargement eastwards and supports NATO negotiations with Russia.

Once the resolution was adopted, Spain communicated to NATO its will to fully participate in the new NATO structure. In return, the Atlantic Council (Brussels, 10–11 December 1995) decided to hold a summit in Madrid in July 1997. This summit was the opportunity to adopt the new NATO structure, to start enlargement negotiations with Eastern countries and to sign an agreement with Russia.

The Spanish commitment to a new NATO, clearer than the French one, was agreed by Socialists and Conservatives. However, beyond the NATO issue, the Conservative government has tried to portray itself as a good ally of the United States. In this sense, the new Spanish policy regarding Cuba's regime serves as an illustration. Therefore, many reasons justify the election of Madrid to celebrate in 1997 the most important meeting of NATO since the end of the Cold War. At the same time, the United States has supported Spanish demands in order to create a subregional command covering the Spanish territory. In this sense, General Joulwan (SACEUR) supported in April 1997 Spanish demands to have the Canary Islands included in the Spanish command. The scope of the Spanish command, confronting Spanish and Portuguese interests, is the main obstacle in an ongoing process: the complete integration of Spain in NATO.

Linkage between European security and Mediterranean stability

The fall of the Berlin Wall and the vigorous renewal of *Mitteleuropa* (German unification, Eastern perspective) revived in Spain, as we have seen, the feeling of being on the periphery of Europe. Therefore, the Spanish government insisted that the southern frontiers should not be forgotten. This is not the first time Spain has faced this dilemma, as for years it has insisted on balancing the Eastern and Southern dimensions of the European Community.

Since the end of the Cold War the main worries of Spanish security policy have been first the political union of the Twelve, supporting the development of a European security and defence identity, and secondly the southern frontier of Europe. Indeed, Spanish policy has tried for years to link those dimensions. To be more exact, Felipe González, in an interview granted to *Le Monde* at the height of the Gulf crisis, said: 'I think, like François Mitterrand, that the construction of Europe cannot be attained without first trying to resolve the explosive problems that are building up in North Africa with respect to demography, development, religion and the standard of living' (Entretien, 1990). Events in Kuwait enhanced the two aims of Spanish policy: strengthening the role of the Twelve in matters of creating a security and defence identity, and linking European security with Mediterranean stability.

The comprehensive approach to Mediterranean stability, tackling the economic, social, political and military dimensions of security, and its relation with European security was dealt with by Felipe González during the CSCE summit in Paris in November 1990. In other words, Spain was going to formulate a policy based on the close relationship between security in Europe and stability and progress in the Mediterranean region. The Spanish–Italian proposal to convene a CSCM, presented during a CSCE meeting in Majorca in September 1990, is the first clear step by Spanish diplomacy to create a Euro-Mediterranean scheme regarding security in a comprehensive way (Barbé, 1991).

In the last resort the comprehensive approach of the Euro-Mediterranean scheme has been re-created for obvious financial reasons in the framework of the European Union. The Euro-Mediterranean Conference in Barcelona, held in November 1995, is the most important product of this Spanish lobbying in favour of balancing the Eastern and Southern dimensions of Europe in the post Cold War era (Barbé, 1996c). The Barcelona process has involved every aspect of security (economic, social, political, military), but it has taken the clearest step towards a Euro-Mediterranean economic area (free trade agreements) (Marks, 1996). Prior to the Barcelona conference, Spain urged the equalization of external aid between Eastern Europe and the Mediterranean countries. Consequently, the European Council in Cannes (June 1995) changed the previous disparity in resource distribution between the South and the East (one to five): for the period 1996 to 2000 it increased the resources for the South by 22 per cent as compared with 8 per cent rise for the East.

Apart from the economic relations, Spain has tried to impel political dialogue between European member states and southern Mediterranean countries, supporting in every forum (CFSP, WEU and NATO) the linkage between European security and Mediterranean stability. As a result, this idea has been adopted by all the organizations dealing with European security: the communiqué of the European Council of Essen (1994); CFSP documents; the Petersberg Declaration of the WEU (1992); the NATO Declaration of the Atlantic Council of Brussels (1994).

The idea of balancing the Eastern and Southern dimensions of Europe has also been present in the traditional dimension of security. Spain, therefore, proposed to its allies in the WEU and NATO the creation of a network of relations with southern Mediterranean countries similar to that already existing with Eastern Europeans. A case in point was the proposal of the Spanish Minister of Defence during a NATO meeting in Seville, in September 1994, to create a partnership with Mediterranean countries similar to the Partnership for Peace (PfP).

In short, Spain has been very active in establishing the current dialogues between European security organizations and southern Mediterranean countries. The WEU began in 1992 to have meetings with some of these countries. At present, there is a dialogue process between WEU and Egypt, the Maghreb countries not including Libya, and Israel. WEU's aim is not so much to stress the creation of a multilateral Mediterranean security framework, but rather to establish exchanges with each of the countries concerned, while at the same time making military activities in the Mediterranean more transparent (Faria and Vasconcelos, 1996: 22). After the above-mentioned meeting in Seville, NATO envisaged in February 1995 an exploratory dialogue with Mediterranean countries: Mauritania, Morocco, Tunisia, Egypt, Israel and Jordan. This dialogue has little future. In fact, NATO does not want to duplicate the political dialogue created by the Barcelona process (*Nouvelles Atlantiques*, 1996b: 2).

In both cases, the WEU and NATO dialogues with Mediterranean countries, we are far from the network of cooperation existing between WEU/NATO and Eastern countries (WEU Partnership, Partnership for Peace, NACC). This is not surprising because the main problem between Spain or the other Europeans and the southern Mediterranean countries is the lack of confidence, the existence of negative perceptions between North and South. In this sense the participation of Spain along with Portugal, France and Italy in EUROFOR and EUROMARFOR produces suspicion in northern Africa. What is the aim of these Southern European forces assigned to NATO? Intervention on the southern shore of the Mediterranean (Faria and Vasconcelos, 1996: 11)?

Aznar's government is following the same policy as the previous government. As a result, Spain keeps improving military relations with its Mediterranean allies: Spain and Italy will form a new amphibian brigade to participate in EUROFOR and EUROMARFOR to start working by mid 1997. At the same time, the Spanish government keeps on supporting in diplomatic terms the linkage between Mediterranean stability and European security. In this sense, King Juan Carlos's speech during his visit to NATO headquarters in April 1996 stressed the idea that southern Mediterranean countries should be treated by the Alliance like potential allies.

Conclusion

Spain is a normal country in matters of European security organization. First of all, the Spanish model in NATO is over. In addition, security is no longer the conflictual issue between the domestic political forces that it used to be. The idea of normality is a simple one but is the main conclusion of the present chapter. In matters of security and defence, Spain has joined the mainstream, behaving in a pragmatic way during the current negotiation processes (NATO reform, Maastricht 2) and defending its national interests (pro-Mediterranean lobby) like any other European country.

III SECURITY ISSUES OF THE EUROPEAN UNION

10 Security Issues Emanating from the Mediterranean Basin

G. *Pinar Tank*

The end of the Cold War has been influential in defining the changes in the relationship between Europe and its southern neighbours. Prior to 1990, the geostrategic value of the Mediterranean region stemmed from its potential ability to influence the balance of power between the former Soviet Union and the United States. Owing to the dynamics of the Cold War, the period following decolonization, which should have resulted in the diminished importance of the South, instead ensured its continued importance.[1] However, as the centre–periphery relationship based on superpower competition for regional dominance is no longer relevant, the geostrategic value of this region is thrown into question, indicating that regional threats may not demand immediate attention. The disappearance of the system of patronage is reflected not only in the loss of strategic weight by the countries of the South but also in the appearance of new regional actors.

In recent years, the steadily growing problems of the South have been put on the sidelines and emphasis has instead been placed on the process of European integration. Rising Eurocentrism, focusing on the integration of the former Eastern bloc into the family of Europe, has meant a declining interest in the problems of the Mediterranean. The interest in Eastern and Central Europe stems from its greater facility to assimilate culturally with the West, while providing potential new markets for European investment with more predictable political risks. Meanwhile the declining quality of life in the South has heralded the arrival of what Boutros-Ghali (1996) has referred to as the new Iron Curtain on a North–South basis. This will invariably result in political fallout, certain to give rise to international instability if not addressed in a timely and thorough manner.

The purpose of this chapter is to outline the challenges before Europe deriving from the Mediterranean Basin. Emphasis will obviously be placed upon the rise of fundamentalism from this region – regarded by many as the new Western threat filling the void left by the disintegration of communist ideology. The chapter begins with an analysis of the rise of fundamentalism and its basis of support. It then continues with an examination of regional actors of particular geostrategic importance. These have been identified by theorists as 'pivotal states' (Chase et al., 1996) owing to their ability to affect overall stability in the region, and include Algeria, Egypt and Turkey. The effects of regional instability for European security are evaluated regarding both hard and soft security challenges. Finally, a short overview is given of European Union efforts to date at responding to these potential threats with preventive measures.

Images of Islamic fundamentalism

The Iranian revolution of 1978–9 brought the term 'fundamentalism' into the public limelight through the overthrow of the Shah of Iran by the mullahs' revolution with the Ayatollah Khomeini at the helm. Incidents such as the 1979 occupation of the United States' embassy in Tehran and Anwar Sadat's assassination in 1981 by militant Islamic fundamentalists gave rise to increasing fears of the spreading Islamic 'threat'. Perceptions of Iran's willingness to export revolution throughout the Middle East strengthened these apprehensions. Airline hijackings and hostage-taking by militant Islamist groups such as the Islamic Liberation Organization, Jihad, Iranian-backed Hezbollah, and Lebanese Islamic Jihad served only to confirm these suspicions throughout the 1970s and 1980s. The evolving media definition of Islamic revivalism was reduced to 'the facile equation: Islam = fundamentalism = terrorism and extremism' (Esposito, 1994: 20). The 1990s present a new challenge as there is an increasing awareness of the nuances within Islam, spanning the spectrum from the gradual process of Islamization at a grassroots level, through social work and political activity, to the more marginalized militant variety.

There is a need for a more thorough examination of the presuppositions made on behalf of the Islamic movement if effective policies are to be generated. First, it is necessary to determine its origins; and secondly, before making the assumption that it is basically opposed to the Western model of pluralism and democracy, various strands of the Islamist movement must be examined to achieve a representative picture. Without a thorough analysis of this growing trend, the European Union will be incapable of responding to the needs of its southern periphery.

The search for cultural identity and the rise of fundamentalism

Although it was the 1970s that rather spectacularly brought public attention to the Islamic movement, it was not merely an extension of the Iranian revolution. The political, social and cultural disappointments following the wars of independence culminated in this period, focusing attention on the steadily strengthening movement of Islamic opposition. It is difficult to assess to what extent the Islamic awakening is, in fact, a delayed response to the cultural colonialism of the Arab world or whether it merely serves as a means for mobilizing popular protest against the social, political and economic difficulties confronting the South.

In the wake of decolonization, particularly in North Africa, nationalist movements led by the intelligentsia established systems of government that proved over time to be economically unstable and corrupt, so lacking in the political legitimacy essential to their survival. The newly established regimes were a disappointment to those who had fought in the wars of independence to free themselves of the colonial influence. The new rulers did not seek to replace the systems of cultural and political hegemony established by the colonizers. In fact, in many cases, the national elites that came to power were harsher than their predecessors, attacking institutions and values that they regarded as regressive in the race towards modernization. Examples of this abound. From the closing down of the religious university, Zitouna, in Tunisia[2] to the banning of the fez by Ataturk in Turkey and Nasser in Egypt, many elements of traditional culture were abandoned in the name of progress. The outcome of this second colonization by national elites was a sense of inferiority and alienation experienced by great sectors of society, particularly among students and middle-class professionals whose access to the fruits of labour depended on their ability to assimilate the culture of colonization. In Algeria, those educated in the French language had access but not those whose previous studies had been in Arabic. This resulted in the exclusion and consequent embitterment of many, some of whom chose to continue their education further east in Egypt or Syria. This was also the impetus behind the search for an authentic identity that did not express itself in the language and symbols of the West.

Other factors that served to undermine the nationalist movement in North Africa included the Arab defeat by Israel in the 1967 War as well as the turbulent events occurring in Europe at the end of the 1960s. The Israeli victory discredited the secular nationalist and socialist agendas and encouraged a turn towards the more conservative Islamist movement. One year later, the 1968 riots in Paris led to the questioning of the certitude of Western values and systems with the resultant re-evaluation of the Islamic alternative. The cumulative effect of the alienation felt by parts of Arab society, the increasing social and political problems they faced, and the lack of a functional alternative meant that a new way had to be discovered. The bias toward Western modes of development had proven to be politically inappropriate and socially destructive. The nationalist experiment provided a learning process for many future Islamist leaders such as al-Banna of the Muslim Brotherhood in Egypt, Ghannouchi of En Nahda in Tunisia, and Madani of the Algerian Islamic Salvation Front (FIS).

As indicated above, the base of the movement was not simply derived from the poor and dispossessed, although they were also an essential element in the growing support for the Islamists. University graduates and lower-middle-class to middle-class professionals formed a great portion of the movement. The university graduates that joined were not necessarily from the religious universities but often from the faculties of science, law and medicine where the Arabic language had predominance. As an example, of the FIS candidates in the 1990 municipal and 1991 parliamentary elections, 76 per cent held postgraduate degrees (Esposito, 1994: 21). Similar statistics are to be found within the ranks of the Muslim Brotherhood in Egypt. Once again, it must be stated that it is difficult to assess to what extent the idea of an anti-Western Islamic identity grew out of the social and political problems and to what extent the need preceded its mobilization behind common concerns. The Islamist movement rallied behind the banner of re-establishing a true Arab identity as the socialism of the nationalist movements had failed them in both theory and practice.

However, scholars such as Halliday (1996) have argued that focusing on an oppressed cultural identity is misleading as its primary function is an attempt at building a unified Islamic image to mobilize support against governments who have been inadequate in addressing the needs of post-colonial states. It cannot be denied that the prevailing poverty and social ills are conducive in mobilizing support from the population, some of whom support the Islamists, not out of a particularly strong belief in their cause but as a symbol of protest toward the regimes in power. Militancy within these groups is subsequently fuelled by the lack of proper channels and means for expressing discontent.

Most importantly, it must be noted that while there are common elements throughout the region finding expression in Islamic revivalism, it is not, by far, a monolithic threat. There has been a propensity to assume that Islamic fundamentalism would be capable of sweeping aside national differences and forming a unified front of opposition to the West. However, not only does the term 'fundamentalist' provide an inadequate description of a state but it also does not determine whether or not it is anti-Western or militant.[3] The differences found within Islamic revivalism indicate that it does not at all form a homogeneous challenge.

In the Mediterranean Basin, there can be found greater commonalties among countries who have all shared in the colonial experience. However, national characteristics still remain an important factor determining the nature of their Islamist opposition. Among these variable characteristics are history (the length of colonial rule or protectorate status), politics (the response of national elites to fundamentalist movements) and economics (the arrival and effects of modernization). The strength and militancy of the Islamist movement is affected by these national characteristics.

Along political lines, there are also national differences that have had their effect on the strength of the present Islamic challenge. Primarily, this is focused on how national elites have responded to the demands for political pluralism and democracy with its subsequent effects on political legitimacy. In Algeria, the demands for political pluralism were not able to keep up the pace of economic change, while in Tunisia pluralism was guaranteed by the constitution of June 1959 but retracted soon after (Burgat, 1994: 146). Consequently, Tunisia remained under single-party rule for 25 years.

Morocco has made a cursory effort at political pluralism, having adopted three constitutions over the last twenty years, each allowing for the expression of opposition. However, they have all been problematic, the first and the second failing in less than two years, and the third requiring five years to activate its legislative provisions (1994: 147). Morocco has had greater fortune under the leadership of a charismatic monarchy which has bestowed upon it greater legitimacy. In Egypt the Muslim Brotherhood had established itself as an opposition group by 1928, but it has been only recently that the government has allowed them entry into the cultural sphere if not the political (with the view in mind of lending support to moderate Islamists over militants). Additionally, in the area of foreign policy, governments have reacted differently to events such as Khomeini's revolution, the question of Palestine, and the mujahedeen struggle in Afghanistan. Their foreign policy standpoints, developed during the Cold War, depended on the patronage they were receiving.[4]

Similarly, in the economic domain, the growth of Islamic movements varied from one country to the next, dependent often on the declining standard of living. Tunisia and Morocco experienced the effects of economic decline with its resultant rise in the popularity of the Islamists first in the 1970s. Algeria was protected by its oil revenues but was soon affected by the recession of the 1980s owing to the drop in oil prices and the value of the dollar. Egypt similarly suffered in the 1980s with the rate of annual growth falling to below 2 per cent in 1989–90, so changing Egypt's position from one of the World Bank's designated lower-middle income countries to lower income (Ajami, 1995: 85). This lay the groundwork for the consolidation of power for al-Jama'a al-Islamiyya. Population growth in this region exacerbated the problems of already failing economies.

Differences are also apparent in the reformist tendencies found among various Islamist groups in the region. While the temptation on the part of the popular media has been to portray all fundamentalist movements as hostile in principle to Western ideas of pluralism and democracy, there are reformist elements within the movement. For example, the Tunisian ITM (now known as En Nahda) has, in a process from 1975–90, adopted reformist positions on subjects such as democracy and women that have been strong enough to render the expulsion of their original authors when first proposed. En Nahda, in 1981, adopted democratic principles and espoused the pluralism it had previously rejected (Burgat, 1994: 82). In Algeria, the reformist movement is represented by Abbassi Madani although, owing to the extremity of Algerian experience, the reformist movement does not have the same popularity within the FIS. The Egyptian Muslim Brotherhood are also advocates of the reformist approach.

All of the factors above are essential in the analysis of the existing fundamentalist movements, which are as varied in their methods and goals as the countries in which they were founded. It is therefore a considerable error to group them together as a unified movement with a common agenda. While common elements persist, none of the movements can adequately be divorced from the social, economic, and historical context from which they arise. This is also an important consideration for the EU in making policy for the southern Mediterranean region.

Pivotal states in the Mediterranean

While the previous section examined the causes behind the reassertion of an Islamic identity in the Mediterranean and the differences that are formative in the emerging Islamist challenge, this section will look closer at countries whose future direction will be decisive in determining the stability and ideological outlook of the entire region. These states have been referred to by Graham Fuller (1995) as 'radical leadership states' or 'pivotal states' (Chase et al., 1996). They are those regional actors that will be capable of playing a leading role in confronting the West with an alternative voice. In the category of pivotal states in the Mediterranean Basin, Egypt, Algeria, and Turkey are identified as fulfilling most of the essential requirements.[5] Their importance lies not only in their capacity to affect the region from which they stem, but equally in their impact on international stability. Their internal problems include overpopulation, economic crises, ethnic conflicts and environmental deterioration which has the potential to affect international stability through spillover effects of migration, weapons proliferation, terrorism and trade disruptions, to name but a few.

Egypt

Egypt has historically assumed the role of regional leadership and fulfils the criteria of a radical leadership state. Its sheer size, population, and geostrategic position afford it this role. In the course of its history, it has been the focus of colonial attention and Great Power rivalries. Additionally, Egypt's location in an oil-rich region as well as its role in the Arab–Israeli peace process confirm its continuing prominence. The concern over Egypt's future is increased in the face of the rising tide of Islamic militancy evident in the 1996–7 bombings of tourist targets. According to Chase et al. (1996), the coming to power of an Islamic fundamentalist government would affect both regional and international stability in ways that may outweigh that of the Iranian revolution in 1979. The primary damage would be to the lengthy Arab–Israeli peace process. It would additionally provide encouragement in much the same way as the Iranian revolution did to other opposition groups in the region engaged in a struggle with secular politics. This would, in turn, affect the politics of oil world-wide as well as international financial markets.

The picture of the Islamic movement in Egypt is extremely complex. There are Islamic sympathizers to be found within the cadres of Hosni Mubarak's government and approved religious institutions like al-Azhar University. More extreme Islamic organizations include the Muslim

Brotherhood and al-Jama'a al-Islamiyya[6] as well as smaller groups such as al-Shawquoon and Tahreer Jihad. To many observers, the present troubles in Egypt took off in 1992 when the state declared war against al-Jama'a, the Islamic groups, an underground expression of political Islam in Egypt. However, the state had, early in the 1970s, encouraged the growth of the Islamic tendency to counterbalance the political left. With the diminishing threat from the left, the current government is struggling to stem the growth of Islamist resistance. If one is to understand the present nature of the Islamic challenge in Egypt, it is necessary to analyse the agenda of the two most important groups, the Muslim Brotherhood and al-Jama'a.

The major differences between the two lie in the region from which they originate, the al-Jama'a stemming primarily from the south of Egypt and the Muslim Brotherhood and other Islamist groups originating in the north (Fandy, 1994). This has been formative in defining their relationship to the government in Cairo and in deciding their agendas. The differences between the two are so fundamental as to make the possibility of a merger, like that of the Algerian FIS, highly unlikely. From its inception, the Muslim Brotherhood focused its attention on the international effort of liberation from Western domination, spreading its message across the region. However, this message is of greater relevance to the experiences of the north rather than the south which did not undergo the colonial experience and historically was not a region of great interest to central government. There has therefore been a lack of comparable development in the south. An effort at improving the economic climate was made through the economic liberalization (*infitah*) policies of Sadat but they have, in fact, had little impact. Thus, the agenda of the al-Jama'a is primarily one of regional dissatisfaction with a government it regards as unjust. It does not, unlike the northern groups, consider those in power in Egypt as un-Islamic. And also unlike the Muslim Brotherhood, which focuses its attention on international Middle Eastern questions, al-Jama'a addresses the poverty and grievances rising from the south.

The economic and political crises facing Egypt are not restricted to the southern regions and the growth of various Islamist groups is indicative of an increasing search for alternative solutions when the present ones seem to be failing. The economy is particularly suffering, with one-third of the population resigned to living in poverty (an increase from 20 to 25 per cent in 1990) while the chasm between the rich and the poor continues to widen. Unemployment is also on the rise with the 1994 figures at 1.5 to 2 million (Cassandra, 1995: 12). The government job creation plans over five years have targeted the creation of 400,000 jobs annually when actual figures indicate that 700,000 jobs are necessary to address unemployment and underemployment (1995: 12).

While outside observers optimistically note that the infrastructure of Egypt has improved under Mubarak (owing to large infusions of aid), this change has not been felt by ordinary Egyptians. For while macroeconomic performance has improved, microeconomic performance, which determines public assessment, has dropped severely. There have also been the additional pressures of population growth at a rate of 2 per cent per annum compared with an estimated GDP growth rate of 1 per cent for 1993–4, resulting in a negative per capita GDP.

The economic crisis has been worsened by the lack of faith in the Mubarak government. The growing tide of the young dispossessed are increasingly flocking to the ranks of extremist opposition groups in much the same way as occurred in both Iran and Algeria. Political participation, which could provide a vent for public dissatisfaction, has also been curtailed in the interest of 'stability'.

In response to the increasing popularity of Islamist parties, the Mubarak regime has wavered on its policies towards the Islamists. The government has opted to follow a policy of greater flexibility towards the inclusion of religion in cultural life. Although there has been some dialogue with the Islamists since the 1970s, particularly with the Muslim Brotherhood which is regarded as more approachable than al-Jama'a, the level of contact between the Muslim groups and the government fluctuates with the political climate. Mubarak, in a *Newsweek* interview in June 1995, denied that the government since 1992 has had any interest in a dialogue with the 'illegal Muslim Brothers and the so-called Islamic Groups'.

The regime's response to the Islamists has been met with reproach from both human rights groups and the Egyptian intellectual and political classes. Military courts, from which there is no appeal, passed 50 death sentences from the start of 1993 to April 1994, with several defendants tortured to sign confessions (Cassandra, 1995: 17).

Mubarak's legitimacy is further undermined by charges of corruption at high levels extending to his own family. Additionally, his decision to continue for a third term in office in 1993, thus breaking his promise to limit himself to two terms, and his refusal to designate a successor has raised questions about the legitimacy of his leadership.[7] Mubarak has been unable to provide Egypt with a visionary leadership to make the burden of economic austerity easier to bear, nor has he been able to generate political reform that would allow for an acceptable expression of discontent to emerge.

Egypt's role in the Middle East peace process   The internal difficulties faced by Egypt remain a factor relevant to its role in the Arab–Israeli peace process. Fundamentally, Egypt's national interest lies in the increase of internal security that would be a long-term result of the peace process. However, ironically its regional role in the Arab world has been enhanced by the difficulties confronted through the peace process. Historically, Egypt has been a leader on international issues in the Arab world. The relations between Israel and the Arab states have been to a great extent determined by the Egyptian position. Egypt has aspired to maintain this position by coordinating a common Arab policy toward Israel as evidenced in the December 1994 mini-summit with Saudi Arabia and Syria and the June 1996 summit of Arab leaders in Cairo.

The contest is one between historical rivals in the region. The peace process under Rabin/Peres diminished Egypt's mediator role between Israel and the Arab states. Israel has improved its economic position through its contacts, enhancing its potential to become an economic power in the Middle East, while Mubarak's regime is faced with economic crises that threaten its leadership role. The loss of public faith in Mubarak's regime is such that it could not weather the loss of regional influence without playing into the hands of the Islamists. However, normalization of relations between Israel and the Arab states is necessary as the failure to achieve an eventual peace would send an even clearer signal of encouragement to extremist groups in the region. The May 1996 election of Binyamin Netanyahu allowed Egypt the unique opportunity to once again ascertain its leading position in the Arab world while affirming the Arab commitment to peace.

Turkey

At a crossroads between North and South, East and West, Turkey is in a unique position to serve as a regional influence. It shares many common characteristics with Egypt. Like Egypt, it has had a history of empire and leadership although it did not undergo the former's colonial experience. Westernization was imported into Turkey by Kemal Ataturk in the 1920s through programmes which were replicated by Nasser in his efforts at creating a modern state. It has struggled like Egypt with internal difficulties brought on by civil unrest, both of an ethnic and, to a lesser degree, of a religious nature. The fundamentalist movement in Turkey has grown, for the most part, within the context of parliamentary democracy without the resort to militancy found among certain Egyptian groups. And finally, Turkey also faces the economic difficulties of a semi-industrialized economy where macroeconomic performance outstrips microeconomic.

Fundamentally, the challenges that Turkey faces are a result of an uncertainty of identity owing to a combination of its geographical position and the underlying doctrines that define the modern republic. Geographically stretching across the Dardenelles, its political centre, Ankara, is in the east while its business and historical centre, Istanbul, is located in the west. This duality is also expressed in the Turkish identity which alternately places its allegiances with Europe or the Middle East.

Turkey has struggled historically to find its place in the world. Its indefinite geographic position, neither fully in Europe nor in the Middle East, has been both a burden and an opportunity. Under the leadership of Ataturk, the modern state emerged from the remains of the Ottoman empire in 1923. Ataturk, aspiring to a seat for Turkey at the European table, enacted reforms to purge the country of its Islamic culture which he regarded as detrimental to its progress. These included the secularization of society through decisive measures such as the abolition of the Caliphate, the religious schools, the Ministries of Seriat (Islamic law) and Evkaf (pious foundations) one year after the foundation of the new republic (Ayata, 1996: 41). Ataturk also sought to sweep aside cultural Islam, from the removal of the Arabic alphabet, replacing it with the Latin, through to his insistence on adopting Western styles of dress. Most important in defining Turkey's secular status was the 1928 decision to remove the clause denoting Islam as the official religion of the Turkish state.[8]

His fervour in pursuing secularism was matched by his belief in the importance of a unitary nation-state that, owing to its early fragility, did not allow for the emergence of separate cultural identities. This was also a reaction to the attempts at creating an Armenian and a Kurdish state in Anatolia following World War I. The Turkish identity that Ataturk wished to forge was inclusive of all ethnic groups, provided they were able to condone the usurption of their own identities in the interest of state cohesion. The changes brought about by Ataturk were of a profound nature, overturning much of the traditional culture. His determination to develop Turkey into a modern European state involved the rejection of its Ottoman past with all its corollaries. Some of the internal difficulties that Turkey is currently undergoing find their root in this dramatic upheaval.

Redefining Turkey's strategic position   Turkey's geostrategic position has altered following the end of the Cold War. During the Cold War, it served as a firm NATO ally, and once again proved its allegiance to the West during the Gulf crisis in 1991. However, with the declining importance of NATO in the post Cold War era and the concomitant rise of global divisions based on religious and ethnic differences, Turkey has been repositioned in the Middle East (Huntington, 1993). This fact was further emphasized to a bitter Turkish population by the European Union's 1997 rejection, once again, of Turkey's application for membership. Additionally, persistent conflicts with Greece have forced the EU to take sides, further distancing Turkey from Europe.

Turkey has sought to remedy its relative loss of geopolitical power by taking a more active role in the newly independent Central Asian republics. Although it has taken an initiative in the region, from the Balkans to the Middle East and Central Asia, it will have to be able to resolve internal difficulties if it is to serve as a regional role model. Its most pressing concerns include the more than decade-long conflict in the south-east with Kurdish insurgents, its slow-growing economy and the rise of a fundamentalist Islamic movement.

The Kurdish question   The Kurdish nation is scattered from south-eastern Turkey into Syria, Iraq, Iran and parts of Armenia. Almost 20 per cent of Turkey's population is Kurdish.[9] Historically, the Kurdish people have rebelled against all their leaders – be they Turk, Arab or Persian. The present uprising has been the longest lasting and the bloodiest in Turkey's history, claiming 30,000 lives and costing US$84 billion (a conservative estimate). Although figures vary, it has been estimated to cost 40 per cent of Turkey's export revenues annually (quoted in Tunander, 1995: 417). The yearly migration of 400,000 peasants into Istanbul has also been greatly attributed to Kurds fleeing poverty and violence (Barham, 1997: 1).

In the mid 1980s, the PKK (Kurdistan Workers' Party), led by Abdullah Ocalan, stepped up its activity in Turkey ruthlessly with the aim of creating a Marxist-Leninist Kurdish state out of Iraq, Iran, Armenia, Syria and Turkey.[10] Initial victims were not Turks but Kurds, mostly villagers whose leaders would not support the PKK. As the campaign continued, government action to destroy the movement at its inception was equally harsh, placing the inhabitants of Kurdish villages between PKK terror on the one hand and state terror on the other. The resulting effect, as described by New Democracy Party leader Cem Boyner, has been the expansion of a 200 strong guerrilla army into a force of 10,000 (Tunander, 1995: 417). The costs incurred in human lives and drainage of the budget have been substantial, as well as the criticism of Turkey's human rights record which has been instrumental in delaying its integration into the European Union.[11]

There have been periodic ceasefires which have not lasted, and an end to the conflict does not seem likely in the forseeable future. The difficulty in resolving the conflict is intensified owing to the support the insurgents receive from Turkey's neighbours, Syria and Iraq, who have in the past used the conflict to achieve their own foreign policy objectives. Suggestions from foreign observers have included the establishment of an autonomous state in the region, but there is no guarantee that this would satisfy PKK demands. In an interview in Lebanon in 1993, Ocalan avowed that his interests lay in the destruction of the Turkish state, not in the establishment of an independent state. Additionally, an independent state would contradict the fundamental dictates of the Turkish state, and would be unlikely to be accepted by the majority, particularly in view of the methods undertaken by the PKK in securing their goal. Nonetheless, a body of opinion is gradually evolving that recognizes that the only means to achieve peace in the region will be through dialogue with moderate Kurdish leaders, accepting Turkey's human rights problem, assuring cultural autonomy, and developing a stronger economic structure.

Economic difficulties Economically, it is not only the south-eastern region that experiences difficulties. While the economy is on the upturn in the late 1990s, this is not always the perception of the majority of the population. After the generals yielded power to civilian government in the 1980s, the privatization of the statist economy began. The economy encouraged greater foreign investment, export–import controls were removed, and the lira was made freely convertible in 1989 (Church, 1992: 34). The transformation has resulted in accelerating export growth, with the share of exports in GNP increasing from 3 to 15 per cent from the start of the 1980s to the end. The share of manufactured exports has simultaneously increased from 36 per cent in 1980 to 80 per cent by the late 1980s (Önis, 1995: 66).

However, there is still a great deal of structural reform required to activate a lasting social transformation. Difficulties are present in the form of tax evasion, a failing social security system and the low productivity and deficits of state companies requiring substantial public sector borrowing. The economic problems faced by Turkey are representative of those faced by semi-industrialized economies. These include chronic inflation, a widening gap between the haves and have-nots, unemployment and underemployment, unequal distribution of wealth regionally, lack of sufficient funds to channel into education, manufacturing, research and development, and a difficult public enterprise sector (1995: 66).

The pauperization of certain portions of the population has been instrumental in mobilizing the demand for an alternative strategy. This is further strengthened by the diminished influence of ideology in the politics of the left. Thus, the final great challenge to Turkish internal stability is to be found in the form of the growing Islamist movement.

The Islamist movement in Turkey   National elections in December 1995 won by the religious Welfare Party (Refah Partisi, RP) by a little over 20 per cent of the vote resulted in the fear of an Islamist government taking power. In the ensuing confusion, deals were made between the Motherland Party (ANAP), led by Mesut Yilmaz, and Ciller's True Path Party (DYP) in an attempt to keep the Islamists out of power. However, in June 1996, after considerable tensions between herself and her previous political rival Yilmaz, Ciller announced that she would be willing to enter into a coalition with RP, if only to release herself from the coalition with ANAP and, more importantly, block the lodging of corruption charges against her by the Welfare Party. Thus the Welfare Party, whose political position was secured through the democratic process, had against all odds acceded to power. An examination of Turkey's gradual Islamization indicates the most salient factors in its rise to power.

Among the internal reasons held accountable for the rise of the Islamist movement in Turkey are the centre-right government's policies and government institutions, the effectiveness of Islamic parties in addressing the dissatisfaction of society in the face of ever increasing wealth differentials, and allegations of corruption. External factors, such as the increasing power of Muslim Middle Eastern oil producers and the threat of left-wing subversion directed from external sources, also play a part.

A step-by-step Islamization process has taken root particularly through the education system, and ironically through the support of the state. Religious schools have been instrumental in providing a suitable environment for the recruitment of fundamentalists. Recent governments have ridden the wave of Islamization in the effort to maintain their own power, as is evident in the budgetary increase in 1990 of 237 per cent given to the Directorate for Religious Affairs. This raised its budgetary allowance beyond those of nine full ministries, including Trade and Industry and the Interior (Robins, 1991: 40).

While the trends have provoked concern within the country, with parallels being drawn with either Algeria or Iran, the Islamic resurgence, with few exceptions, has not been marked by the violence associated with either of these two countries. Allowing the Islamists into mainstream democratic politics has been the route to moderation as coalition building has required compromise. The ultimate compromise was in their stepping down from power in 1997 through the 'gentle persuasion' of the military.[12]

It was hoped that, by cooperating with the moderate Islamists, Turkey would provide a model for other Arab states struggling with Islamist movements. However, the experiment was short-lived and therefore of limited value as an example. Nonetheless, the Islamist movement remains as a substantial element in the political landscape, and the manner in which the Islamists and other parties in Turkey adapt to one another will influence the Western outlook on the possible coexistence of fundamentalism with pluralism.

Algeria

Equally important to regional security is Algeria, caught in a relentless civil war between Islamic militants and the army. The conflict is increasingly polarizing civil society, adding to the risk of escalation. The cost of the struggle has been significant, with over 60,000 Algerians killed (from 1992 to 1997[13]) and over 100 foreigners. The present situation in Algeria does not bode well for the future despite a ceasefire agreed in September 1997 between the Islamic Salvation Front and the government which led to hopes that the road was open for a solution to the conflict.

Since independence was won in Algeria, power has alternated between the institution of the state as monopolized by the Front National de Libération (FLN) or the military. Immediately following the war, FLN leaders designated Algeria as a socialist state with the Front as the only legal political organization. Ben Bella was elected the first President and his autocratic leadership eventually led to a bloodless coup in 1965 by Boumedienne, then Minister of Defence. This brought about the rise to power of the army without any significant democratization. Additionally, socialism was incorporated into the Algerian constitution as the preferred political system in 1976. After Boumedienne, Benjedid was brought to power, following in his predecessor's footsteps but with looser political control. After his election to a third term of office in 1988, Benjedid was able to promote the passage of a new constitution, so allowing for a greater relaxation of the FLN's monopoly on political power. The democratic programme instigated by him was to legitimate the fundamentalist claims to power. Clashes in 1988 between protesters and government troops indicated that prevalent discontent was likely to translate into votes, given the opportunity. This was illustrated by the 1990 provincial and municipal elections in which the fundamentalist Islamic Salvation Front (FIS) won a substantial victory. They reaffirmed their success by winning the first round of balloting in December 1991, pointing them in the direction of a parliamentary victory. However, the military intervened, cancelling the election, suspending Parliament and removing Benjedid. Boudiaf, a founding father of the FLN living in self-exile in Morocco, was appointed to the helm of a High Commission of State but was assassinated only six months later amidst domestic chaos. Boudiaf's death further polarized the military and the Islamists, making reconciliation impossible. After a period of collective leadership by the High Council, Zeroual was appointed to the Presidency in 1994 and elected after an interim period. While Zeroual professionally stems from the army, he is in the 'conciliator' rather than the 'eradicator' faction within the army who recognizes that there can be no lasting solution to Algeria's problems based on military means alone (Mortimer, 1996).

Build-up to a civil war   The growing force of social unrest in Algeria over the past ten years has had the effect of strengthening the Islamic movement as an alternative. Several factors explain the build-up to the Algerian crisis. Among these are the political tradition in Algeria and the strength of the military, the declining standard of living, and the weak foundation on which the democratic experiment was tested in 1991.

The military perceives itself in its historical role as arbiter in Algerian politics, in much the same way as the Turkish army does in Turkey. It derives its legitimacy from the role it played in the war of independence (1954–62) which also conferred legitimacy upon the populist government, ensuring its stability until the 1980s. The military was content until the late 1980s to play its part from behind the scenes until it intervened in the October 1988 riots to reinstate order. Ironically, the army was in favour of multi-party democracy and a moderate Islamic party in 1990, considering it a 'safety valve' to ease social tensions, and so assisted Benjedid in passing reform programmes through the FLN convention that allowed for greater democratization (Mortimer, 1996: 21). However, what it did not expect, or accept, was that the Islamist party would win a parliamentary majority.

The political culture was also a factor that impeded democratization. Twenty-six years of single-party rule by the FLN made the public receptive to the promises of another populist party, the FIS, in the hopes that it would be able to fight corruption and declining living standards. This was a result of the growth of dissatisfaction in Algeria due to the deterioration of the economic situation in the 1980s, and the widening of the gap between the rich and poor. Corruption increased throughout this period as the middle classes slowly disappeared. Faced with a bleak future, with unemployment figures at 25 per cent among urban youth and school leavers (Spencer, 1993: 20), lacking faith in the government's ability to improve the economic situation, and feeling a sense of cultural alienation, the people responded to the Islamist movement's alternative of a morally just society. Finally, the greatest error in the passage from one-party to multi-party politics was the failure to define a civil pact (Mortimer, 1996) with the Islamist parties before the December 1991 election. This would have had the effect of assuring the protection of rights and values, ensuring the pluralism of Algerian society.

Agreement on a civil pact since the 1991 election has been attempted unsuccessfully by the state on several occasions. In mid 1993 the then ruling High State Committee (HCE) called for a national conference – the 'Platform for Democracy' – hoping thus to re-establish order. Another attempt was made by the Commission on National Dialogue established in October 1993. However, on both occasions, efforts failed owing to disagreements over the participation of the FIS, without whom any agreement would have been hollow. There was additionally the question of releasing the FIS leaders Madani and Bil-Haj which was one of the preconditions for FIS participation and was unacceptable to the army. Another government attempt in November 1996 to bring about peace was through a referendum increasing the powers of the Presidency and limiting political pluralism, so banning religious parties from taking power. This move was seen to contradict the conciliatory role that Zeroual had earlier appeared to adopt and served instead to condemn the more moderate elements within the FIS along with the Armed Islamic Group (GIA). Not distinguishing between the two makes dialogue on an anti-violence platform with more moderate elements impossible.

However, according to Robert Mortimer (1996), there is additionally a 'third force', representing a pluralist and secular Algeria, that has been unable to consolidate its power base sufficiently to form any real opposition to either the military-led government or the FIS. They have been able to initiate a platform for negotiation with the FIS through the January 1995 'Platform of Rome' agreement on the rejection of violence, support for democracy, open competitive elections and respect for human rights. It was a breakthrough for the secular opposition parties in their ability to take a first step and sit at the table with the banned FIS. However, the initiative was publicly berated as it supported the conclusion that there could be no constructive dialogue without the granting of some concessions to the FIS.

The October 1997 ceasefire: hope for the future?   The most hopeful sign in the six-year conflict came with the announcement in late September 1997 that the military wing of the Islamic Salvation Front was instructing its followers to abandon combat operations beginning on 1 October 1997. An impetus for the agreement was, among other things, the release on 15 July of Abassi Madani, after six years of imprisonment. However, his release and the recognition that the government was opting for an alternative approach to solving the conflict also prompted opposition from elements in the government opposed to all negotiation as well as from the more extremist Islamic groups. Although the announcement was made in October, the process was already under way in the preceding months. Opposition on both sides of the conflict ensured that the summer of 1997 was one of the bloodiest in the conflict, claiming the lives of hundreds of civilians.

Despite the moves towards negotiation on both sides, there is by no means any guarantee that this will provide a final resolution to the conflict. Had there been a willingness on the part of the army to negotiate with the FIS early in the process, the opportunity for a peaceful settlement would have been greatly increased. As it is, the offer comes too late in the conflict. For a start, the FIS no longer has any control over the hard-line GIA which has been responsible for the most extreme atrocities. In fact, not only have they no control, but since 1994 internecine battles among the militant groups have intensified. The GIA operates independently of the FIS military arm, the AIS, and has been criticized by the latter for its brutality. In response to this, the GIA leadership has declared war on the AIS. Opposition within the military government is also capable of exerting pressure on the government against negotiation. The Algerian state has already faced accusations of complicity in the political violence. While this may or may not be the case, the state can be held accountable for their lack of effort to stop the carnage. Both the forces of the military and the militant Islamists have the potential to incite more violence in Algeria which could put an end to these tentative first steps towards a resolution of the conflict.

Should the situation worsen, not only would the toll on human casualties be great but it would additionally endanger the stability of international oil and gas markets as well as the security of Mediterranean sea-lanes. The establishment of an anti-Western regime in Algeria would result in losses by Spain, France, and Italy of considerable investments. They would also be the first to feel the flood of middle-class, secular Algerian refugees. The regional consequences of Algeria's fundamentalists coming to power without the agreement of a civil pact would be significantly destabilizing. The 1979 revolution in Iran ignited the fear of the spread of radical Islam. However, Iran is neither an Arab state, nor Sunni (the majority following within Islam). While the Iranian revolution has certainly had an effect on the export of militant Islamist beliefs, an Algerian revolution would have a greater impact on the Sunni Arab world. It would provide impetus to the Egyptian movement, jeopardizing the Arab–Israeli peace process. However, it must be stated that the potential of universalist militant Islam should not be exaggerated, as the Arab world is renowned for its division along geographical, nationalistic, ethnic, cultural and religious lines.

The effect of regional instability on European security

Instability in the Mediterranean Basin has the potential of threatening European security. While this has been recognized by the states of Southern Europe in close proximity to this region, the nature of today's security dilemmas are such that they do not respect national borders. Challenges arising from this region can be categorized as either 'hard security' threats such as weapons proliferation and terrorism, or 'soft security' relating among other things to human rights and migration. Additionally, it is necessary to recognize the propensity for regional insecurity to result in spillover that is capable of affecting world order on a systemic level through its influence on the global economy.

Hard security threats such as proliferation, and more particularly terrorism, have been emphasized in the media. The end of the Cold War has resulted in a diminished importance for the region where previously, within the context of the East–West confrontation, the non-aligned movement held a respected position and political clout. The post Cold War environment has weakened the concept of alignment even if the issues of the North–South agenda remain important. This, in turn, has instigated the search for an alternative means to establish geopolitical weight, resulting, in some cases, in the build-up of conventional and unconventional arsenals. For the time being, despite much speculation on the consequences that the build-up of arms will have for European security, the motivation behind proliferation has been regional, increasing political leverage in South–South issues. While there have been calls for an 'Islamic bomb', this is unlikely to happen owing to the lack of solidarity among regional actors and the lack of a clearly defined threat.

Terrorist threats emanating from this region will have a more perceptible impact on European security owing to their high profile in the media. Western generalizations linking radical Islamic movements and political violence present an inaccurate picture of international terrorism. Only 8 per cent of all terrorist incidents are the product of militant Islamist organizations. However, one loses sight of this fact when this small proportion of incidents represents 30 per cent of the fatalities incurred. The reputation for violence stems from the lethality of religious groups who are willing to waive moral constraints in the interest of serving their God. The effects of terrorism emanating from the South are increasingly being felt in Europe through incidents such as the spate of bombings in Paris in the summer of 1995 by Algerian extremists angered by France's continued economic assistance to the regime in power. In addition to religiously motivated terrorism, Europe is also witnessing cross-border separatist terrorism as in the 1993 terror campaign by the PKK on several Turkish commercial and diplomatic centres in Germany and France.

There are several explanations for why European cities are increasingly being targeted. First, the tough security measures imposed by southern regimes do not allow for opposition groups to voice their dissent. While this is evidently not the case for the majority, there are a percentage who choose to adopt violent means to make known their opposition in the more open, and consequently, more vulnerable, cities of Europe. The existence of these small extremist groups within European countries also places a restriction on any form of intervention in the Muslim world without due consideration of its implications for a backlash in the form of terrorist incidents.

Equally challenging for Europe are the soft security issues of human rights and migration. In 1993 there were some 13 million foreign immigrants living in European Union countries (Soysal, 1993), 8 million of which were non-EU nationals stemming from North Africa, Turkey, Yugoslavia and the Indian subcontinent. This made up 2.5 per cent of the total EU population and 6.7 per cent of the EU labour force. Muslim populations are dispersed among European countries with 2 million in France, 2 million in Germany, 1 million in Britain and 500,000 in Spain (Hadar quoted in Fuller and Lesser, 1995: 75). The figures for migration have steadily increased: in the 1970s there were around 30,000 asylum seekers a year, but by 1992 there were 700,000 (Berthiaume, 1995: 4). However, this figure does not reflect the actual numbers that are granted permanent residency, nor does it reflect the fact that these numbers are in fact minor in relation to migration flows elsewhere in the world.

Although economic reasons have been the favoured justification for stemming immigration, they do, in fact, tend to play a secondary role to cultural or ethnic affinity. It is the perception of cultural incompatibility that forms the backbone of political debate on immigration. This is particularly relevant for Muslim communities. Cultural differences are intensified by the traditional and religious backgrounds of many Muslim migrants. For example, those coming from rural areas such as south-eastern Turkey do not assimilate easily into Western urban culture, alienating themselves from the society in which they live and in some cases embracing their traditional culture more adamantly.

Despite the pressure exerted by the growing tide of immigration, European governments have been slow in taking positive action to ease the integration process. A particular example is that of Germany which was the chosen destination of a great number of asylum seekers and economic refugees from the 1960s onwards. Riding on the anti-immigrant wave, legislation was passed in the 1970s to discourage immigration by denying work permits to migrants rejoining their families in Germany[14] as well as creating policies to encourage repatriation through awarding premiums, which had the effect of antagonizing immigrants. The political difficulty in attaining citizenship exacerbated their frustrations. However, following the increase in racist attacks in Germany in 1993, debate opened about the difficulty of attaining citizenship, resulting in a slight improvement in the regulations.

The 1990s also saw the growth of extreme right-wing political parties throughout Europe. Once again referring to Germany, the Republican Party increased in popularity from less than 1 per cent in 1989 to 8.3 per cent in 1993. At a more extreme level, neo-Nazi attacks perpetrated in 1992 in Mölln and a year later in Solingen resulted in the deaths of several Turkish immigrants. The problems encountered in Germany parallel the concerns of other European countries. In France, the dispute over the veiling of Muslim girls at school (*l'affaire foulard*) erupted in 1989 and again in 1994, provoking much controversy around cultural integration. Like Germany, France has also witnessed the increasing strength of the right-wing National Front led by Jean-Marie Le Pen who received 15 per cent of the vote in the French Presidential election of 1995 (Halliday, 1996: 185). Similarly, other right-wing parties in Europe are increasingly focusing their attention on the 'problem' of Muslim immigrants, discouraging the incentive for integration.

Nor is it only the parties of the far right that have come to regard continued immigration as a threat to the social fabric of European societies. Mainstream parties are equally adopting immigration policies that reflect these attitudes, moving in the direction of zero immigration. Nonetheless, the more pressing threat for the time being is the growth of racist and exclusionary inclinations, sustaining the rise of extremist groups that not only challenge the security of democratic regimes but also strain the relations between the countries of the Mediterranean Basin and Europe.

The EU's Mediterranean policy, focusing on development and encouraging investment, is guided by the need to stem the migratory flow. The Spanish EU Presidency in 1995, with the support of France and Italy, chose to focus on improving economic relations with the South which had to a large extent been overshadowed by EU expansion plans to the East. Eastern and Central Europe have over the past four years been promised twice as much money in loans and gifts as the countries of the South despite the South's projected doubling in growth in the next fifteen years.[15] While increases in trade figures alone will not be enough to secure the future of the countries of the Mediterranean Basin, without an improvement in the economic climate there can be no solid background from which to instigate other reforms.

In addition to improving the economic base, it will be necessary to encourage further democratization. With the end of the Cold War, human rights have arrived on the public agenda. Discussions on security have focused on the stabilizing influence of democracy. However, while Western governments criticize the tough security measures taken against Islamic opposition groups, they are challenged by ruling regimes to regard the repression of fundamentalist Islamic groups as a security necessity rather than a breach of human rights. In truth, while criticism is prevalent, actions against governments that blatantly disregard human rights are not taken. Should Western governments unequivocally support regimes against popular moderate Islamist movements, these opposition groups will formulate their policies accordingly. Most experts agree that the political, economic and cultural crises that elicited the rise of fundamentalist movements cannot be silenced in the long run by repressive regimes.

Addressing challenges from the Mediterranean Basin

Europe has recognized the neglect of the South in favour of East and Central Europe. Although the countries on the southern and eastern Mediterranean shore account for 209 million people, they are given only half the amount of aid that is received by the 110 million of Central and Eastern Europe. Additionally, in the present situation, prevalent trade interests are not protected sufficiently. The EU trade surplus with the

Mediterranean is twice that with the East. Recognition of these factors and the fear of increased pressures for migration, particularly towards the countries on the European side of the Mediterranean, have provoked the EU into greater action, promoting a 'Euro-Med' strategy. Prior to the establishment of the Euro-Med strategy, efforts made by Europe at addressing the problems of this region included the 4+5 Group (established 1990) for cooperation in the western Mediterranean between Southern European countries (Portugal, Spain, France and Italy, later joined by Malta) and the Arab countries of the Maghreb (Mauritania, Morocco, Algeria, Tunisia and Libya). This led to an Italian and Spanish initiative establishing the Conference on Security and Cooperation in the Mediterranean, which was to encompass not only the Mediterranean but the entire Middle East. It was intended to follow the mould set by the CSCE – involving the United States and Russia. Later proposals included the idea to establish links between the Arab Maghreb Union and the WEU or NATO similar to what had been done through the North Atlantic Cooperation Council. This was to assure commitment to improving security by both regions (Gaspar, 1994). However, neither of the initiatives has had great success thus far, owing partly to the immensity of their scope incorporating both European and Middle Eastern security complexes, and partly also to the lack of a clear common policy from the European states.

The relatively new Euro-Med strategy is heralded as a novel approach by the European countries at responding to the needs of the South. It has led to an agreement offering ECU 4.7 billion (US$6 billion) of aid to the twelve states on the Mediterranean Basin in the period from 1995 to 1999 and the decision to support 'association agreements' with the countries of the region.[16] Additionally, a conference in November 1995 was organized under the Spanish EU Presidency in Barcelona to elaborate on the particular needs of the region. Acknowledging that there could be no improvement in the economic climate even with the promised aid packages, attempts were made to encourage private investment through the improvement in the political state. Thus, the Barcelona Declaration was signed in which the signatories agreed to 'respect human rights and fundamental freedoms and guarantee the effective legitimate exercise of such rights and freedoms'. In view of the human rights records of the signatories, there is not much room for hope that changes will occur in the immediate future.

In the area of trade relations, it was hoped that the Barcelona conference would provide better opportunities for improving trade possibilities for the countries of the South. However, there is cause for pessimism here too as the countries of the Mediterranean Rim export primarily textiles, farm produce, and low-technology goods that compete with EU countries such as Spain, Portugal and Greece. The Barcelona conference additionally referred to the establishment of a free trade area by 2010 which would do away with barriers to trade in manufactures. However, in agriculture, where it would make a difference, the EU common agricultural policy will continue to protect its own, barring the entry of many North African crops.

In retrospect, efforts towards addressing problems emanating from the South have not had great success. First, this is due to the lack of a common sense of purpose from either Europe or the countries of this region. The primary uniting factor appears to be fear. For Europeans, it is the spectre of fundamentalism to the South and the potential migratory flows northward. For the Mediterranean Basin, it is the fear that Europe will not only close its doors but also return migrants who will worsen the already declining situations in their native countries. Secondly, it has been quite clear since the Gulf War that Western interests lie further east, where countries such as Saudi Arabia and Bahrain are also struggling with internal militant Islamic activity. And finally, although the difficulties of the South are becoming of greater concern to Europe, Eastern and Central Europe still command greater attention because of their role as the 'prodigal sons' (Boutros-Ghali, 1996).

Concluding remarks

Some scholars contend that Islamic fundamentalism is a phenomenon that will not simply disappear through the improvement of living conditions in the countries of the Mediterranean Basin. Although references are often made to the lack of employment opportunities and the difficult economic climates that alienate the poor and encourage the growth of Islamist movements, they believe it would be a mistake to assume that these are the sole reasons behind its appeal. While it is true that the common denominator in the region is that of steadily declining living standards, there is also the knowledge that a sense of inferiority was imposed both by Western colonizers and by the national elites' emulation of the West. The search for an authentic cultural identity remains paramount. This is particularly so as Arab nationalism utilizing the tools of Western secular thought is seen to have failed in the Arab world. As Edward Shirley states, 'Fundamentalism's greatest strength lies in the failure of secularized Muslims to create a solid, historically secure, and competitive identity' (1995: 33).

The means whereby change is to be effected have been modified. The *modus operandi* of Islamist groups no longer lies in spectacular *coups d'état* or assassinations but in amassing power through grassroots activity, building support upwards and achieving victory through the ballot box. While Khomeini's revolution was a top-down usurpation of power by the mullahs which began the re-Islamization process, in Algeria, Egypt and Turkey the emphasis is on Islamization through the building of a solid power base to pursue the democratic road to power.

However, the danger of emphasizing the cultural element is the effect it may have in diminishing the role played by political, economic and social problems. With regard to the developing situation in this region and European concerns of political fallout, policies undertaken should not seek to portray Islamic fundamentalism as a monolithic threat. Islam, in its many forms, is not *per se* a unifying force; however, it does become the rallying cry in response to the social and political ills faced by the region. Therefore, different movements will vary in moderation and should be regarded on a case-by-case basis. The strengthening of ties with the countries of the Mediterranean Basin and the encouragement of economic growth must not be at the expense of human rights. The latter should not become trampled in the name of cultural understanding or political expediency. While there can be no democratization if basic living standards are not met, it does not follow that an improvement in the economic climate will automatically provide for greater democracy.

Notes

1 The term 'South' is, for purposes of simplicity, used in this chapter to refer to countries on the southern rim of the Mediterranean stretching from Morocco to Turkey.

2 Zitouna University had existed for twelve centuries and had institutions linked to it upon which 25,000 to 27,000 persons depended (interview with Ghannouchi in Burgat, 1993: 55).

3 As Esposito (1994) points out, Saudi Arabia and Libya are both categorized as fundamentalist states. Saudi Arabia is a conservative monarchy with close ties to the United States. Libya, on the other hand, a socialist state led by a military dictator, is recognizably anti-Western. The same differentiation can be made in the form of Islam espoused by the two. The former adopts a conservative approach while the latter opts for a radical and revisionist interpretation.

4 The Islamic revolution in Iran was strongly deplored by Morocco and Tunisia but supported in Algeria (with reservations) and unequivocally so in Libya. On the question of Afghanistan, however, Algeria and Libya were only able to express guarded disapproval over the Soviet Union's intervention.

5 For a more complete assessment of the criteria that determine a 'pivotal state', see Chase et al. (1996).

6 The spelling of al-Jama'a al-Islamiyya varies in its transcription into English and is also often referred to as the Gamaat Islamiyya. For practical purposes, it will here be referred to in the shortened version, al-Jama'a.

7 Not only does this level criticism upon his present rule, but it also throws doubt on who would have been in a position to succeed Mubarak had the assassination attempt in Ethiopia in June 1995 been successful.

8 Prime Minister Erbakan expressed his wish in 1997 to revise the constitution by amending Article 24, protecting secularism. However, it is highly unlikely that this would be accepted by his coalition partner Ciller or the army.

9 Figures vary due to assimilation and intermarriage, but an estimate is 10 million to 15 million, with official Turkish figures much lower (Abramovitz quoted in Tunander, 1995).

10 Owing to internal disagreements among the various Kurdish groups, PKK activity has been concentrated primarily in Turkey. Ocalan has found it difficult to solicit the support of Iraq's 4.1 million Kurds and Iran's 5.5 million whose leaders distrust and disagree with his violent methods.

11 Although most Turks, including the former President Özal, and a good number of foreign observers maintain that the unstated reason for exclusion is Turkey's Muslim identity.

12 'Gentle' in relation to its earlier forays into Turkish politics.

13 Due to the lack of reliable information, figures vary from 60,000 to 80,000.

14 This was later revoked as it was seen to be creating a disaffected and unemployed immigrant underclass.

15 By the year 2025, the population of Turkey and Egypt are estimated to reach 100 million each while the member states of the Arab Maghreb Union (AMU), Mauritania, Morocco, Algeria, Tunisia and Libya, will amount to 127 million. The combined population of the afore-mentioned will equal that of the current European Union (Loescher quoted in Fuller and Lesser, 1995: 75).

16 However, the applicant states of Eastern and Central Europe will receive US$9 billion.

11 Security Implications of EU Expansion to the North and East

Esben Oust Heiberg

In the new international situation after the end of the Cold War, the European Union faces a new set of challenges that are in many respects more complex, diverse and fragmented than they were during the previous period. During the Cold War, the security of Europe was to a large extent taken care of by the US, but now there is an increasing need for the EU to take a more active part in its own security. The success of the Community during the last decades has also contributed to this. The Union's expanded role in trade and in international economic matters makes it increasingly difficult to separate the economic side of the EU from the foreign and security policy side.

In the last round of EU enlargement, all the new member states (Finland, Sweden and Austria) were firmly 'Western' countries with strong political, economic and social ties to the rest of the democratic, market-oriented Western countries. It was therefore relatively easy to negotiate and adapt these states to the EU as they were already at the same level of development as most of the other members. The three new member states had previously been neutral, but this was not seen as a problem as the EU did not have a defence component. Even though they had different reasons for being neutral, they had to a very large extent identified themselves with the 'Western camp'.

The next round of EU enlargement is different. The prospective members from the East were all part of the communist bloc and under the USSR's sphere of influence. During the Cold War period these countries developed different economies, governmental traditions and perceptions of themselves and the outside world. There have been great changes during recent years, but their history and political traditions are still very different. There are also a number of unresolved conflicts in the region that were suppressed during the Cold War and which have proved, and can prove again, to be explosive.

What is security? In the words of Barry Buzan, security is 'an essentially contested concept' and 'the nature of security defies pursuit of an agreed general definition' (1991: 14). Security is more easily defined and articulated when there is a clear threat. With an overarching threat such as communism, it was easier to identify the common interest of different states. Without such a threat, states will increasingly focus on their own national interest. Even neighbouring countries will have different perceptions of their national interest depending on factors such as geography, economic situation and resources, etc. Also what constitutes security for one state may become a source of insecurity for another.

The issue of security has become much more complex with globalization and increasing interdependence between states. These factors require states to increasingly cooperate and harmonize their work in order to have influence. Furthermore, the action of one state can have much greater repercussions internationally because of the close links that now exist with regard to trade and financial flows. Therefore a return to a more narrow national interest can be detrimental to the broader and longer-term interest of a larger region.

This chapter will start with a discussion on the main security organizations and look at how they operate and how they are increasingly adapted to accommodate greater European involvement in security matters. The enlargement processes of both the EU and NATO will also be addressed as they have important security implications. This will set the stage for the final section on security implications.

NATO, WEU and the EU

NATO has been the primary security organization for Western Europe since the Second World War. Through the US security guarantee, Europe has been able to integrate economically and politically without also having to establish independent military and defence capacities. However, the role of NATO has been increasingly questioned after the Cold War and there is a desire to raise the European profile in security and defence matters.

Partly as a result of this, the role of the WEU has slowly been strengthened. According to the Maastricht Treaty, WEU shall be the 'European pillar of the Atlantic Alliance'. The Treaty also opens the possibility that the EU can develop a separate defence identity and aspire to a 'common defence'. The increasing desire by the EU to gain a more prominent and stronger role in defence has also been recognized by NATO, and there are now attempts at building a European security and defence identity (ESDI) inside NATO, and closer ties have been established between NATO and WEU.

At the EU Amsterdam summit (1997) it was agreed that the WEU could be used to 'plan and implement the Union's decisions that had defence implications'. This includes areas such as humanitarian missions, peacekeeping and peacemaking operations (Petersberg tasks). Peter Ludlow (1997) states that 'as Petersberg tasks cover 95% of the post-Cold War security agenda, this change allows for an active EU role through the WEU in virtually every crisis that might arise'. It was also proposed to merge WEU with the EU, but there was not enough support for this. Such a move could have caused significant problems for the four neutral EU states.

Should the WEU be merged with the EU in the future, then it will be under the second pillar, the Common Foreign and Security Policy (CFSP), where there is an intergovernmental decision-making process. As a result, states can veto any proposal, thus making a strong and coherent policy more difficult. However, the fact that the EU would have a military organization at its disposal would be an important step in giving the EU the full powers available as an international actor and also a symbol of its role in international affairs.

Both NATO and WEU give a security guarantee to their full members. The WEU was established by the Treaty of Brussels (1948). Article V in this treaty provides for automatic intervention by the other signatories. However, the WEU lost much of its role with the establishment of NATO in 1949 and was only reactivated in 1984. By this stage NATO was firmly established as the defence organization for Western Europe, and had proved its worth and capability throughout the Cold War. The security guarantee in the WEU has therefore never been put to the test as it was seen as being taken care of by NATO. Article V in the Washington Treaty that established NATO does not have the same automatic intervention clause as the WEU, but during the Cold War it was taken for granted that NATO would intervene owing to the integrated command structure inside the Alliance.

WEU is dependent on NATO for the means and capability to take on missions outside the NATO framework. There are moves to combine the two organizations in a more effective way, where they can cooperate and complement each other. An important development is the combined joint task forces (CJTFs), which would enable the WEU to use European NATO forces and equipment in pursuit of the EU's CFSP. CJTFs are to be 'separable but not separate' capabilities that can be used by either NATO or WEU. However, operations under WEU auspices will be under monitoring by the North Atlantic Cooperation Council and thus the Americans will have a large say in the running of these operations. It can be argued that the CJTF concept removed the need for the WEU to duplicate the capabilities that already exist inside the Atlantic Alliance, but it also clearly reflects the dependence of the EU on NATO and therefore, in the end, on the US.

It is unlikely that the WEU will be able to develop into a strong military/defence component without the support of the US. Also, there does not seem to be the political will or the financial resources available to build and establish the security organizations required to take care of European security needs in the near future. The European states have difficulty in agreeing on how to proceed, and how to share responsibility. NATO is therefore likely to remain the prime security organization in Europe for the time being.

Today, the EU is often described as 'an economic giant and a political dwarf'. It has considerable economic power, but it lacks the ability to pursue a clear and strong foreign and security policy. In order to do this the EU will have to considerably develop CFSP (including a defence component).

There was some development with regard to the CFSP at Amsterdam. A planning unit to prepare foreign policy initiatives will be established under the Council of Ministers. It is hoped that such a planning unit will contribute to defining the security aims and goals of the Union. However, the European Council will still have to agree unanimously on the Union's foreign policy strategies, but the implementation will be done with majority voting amongst the foreign ministers.

The crisis in Bosnia, and NATO's role in the conflict, reflect the failure of developing a more coherent European capability to deal with 'European' problems. Bosnia is, strictly speaking, out-of-area for NATO. However, it was NATO and the US that had to take the leading role in dealing with the crisis, while the EU and the UN were put on the sideline.

For the US, it is also useful to have an organization like NATO that can be responsible for crisis management in these areas. There are likely to be strong reactions if the US acted unilaterally, whilst NATO gives them a European alibi for acting in and around Europe. Strictly speaking everything outside the NATO member states is out-of-area, but recent developments in the former Yugoslavia have shown that NATO is both able and willing to take on operations outside its formal area of responsibility.

Framework for EU enlargement

At the end of the Cold War the EC/EU established Europe agreements with many of the former Warsaw Pact states. These provide for comprehensive cooperation in political, economical, trade and cultural spheres. They also provide a framework for rapid progress towards free trade and closer cooperation (Cameron, 1995). At present there are twelve states that have such agreements. The possibility of enlargement to the East made a major step forward during the Copenhagen summit (1993) where it was agreed that 'the associated countries of Central and Eastern Europe that so desire shall become members of the European Union'. It was also agreed that a country must have stable institutions guaranteeing democracy, the rule of law, human rights and protection of minorities, a functioning market economy, and the ability to accept the obligations of membership, including the aims of political, economic and monetary union, before it would be considered for membership. At the Essen summit (1994) the pre-accession strategy was laid out for the associated states. This was meant to help the associated states prepare the ground for future membership and includes issues such as putting in place 'legislative and regulative systems, standards and certification methods compatible with those of the EU' as well as the acceptance of the *acquis communautaire*. There are also economic and political conditions that have to be fulfilled before these countries can join the Union, and in this way the EU encourages these countries to develop systems more similar to those inside the EU.

In 1993 the French proposed a Stability Pact for Europe (also known as the Balladour Plan). The plan is to contribute to stability in Europe by preventing conflicts from breaking out, and is not intended to deal with states that are already in conflict (Hübertz, 1996). Its focus is on the Central and Eastern European states and it encourages states to deal with questions that can develop into large-scale conflicts. Once these have developed into large political or military conflicts, the states are much more difficult to get to the negotiation table, and once such a crisis has broken out it will also to a much larger extent have an influence on other states' national interests and hence be much more difficult to solve. Such preventive diplomacy and problem-solving can inspire further cooperation between the states and help promote trust between neighbours who are still uncertain of each other's intentions.

In July 1997, the Commission presented its opinion on which countries from Central and Eastern Europe the EU should open negotiations with. These are Poland, the Czech Republic, Hungary, Slovenia and Estonia (Ludlow, 1997). The Commission stated that it would open negotiations with these countries within six months after the end of the 1996–7 IGC.

Enlargement to the East is occurring simultaneously with other major political initiatives and obstacles facing the EU. In itself, it will be difficult for the Commission to negotiate with six countries simultaneously as well as dealing with regular EU business. In addition there is the introduction of the EMU as well as a number of other problems, including unemployment, that the EU has to deal with.

The large financial contributions required for NATO enlargement are already a challenge, and it is unclear what will be the result if the electorate also have to pay large sums of money to get these countries into the EU. Enlargement is also likely to shift to the East the large funds that today are spent on various support programmes in Southern Europe. This is likely to meet with considerable opposition from the present recipients of support in Southern Europe.

These are just some of the challenges facing the EU: they will have to be solved rapidly or they could hamper the enlargement process. There is already talk in Brussels that the new members will not be able to join before 2005–10.

The 1996 IGC and its conclusion at the Amsterdam summit were intended to prepare the EU for further enlargement. This included re-organizing the institutions and making them more efficient and effective. However, the summit failed to come to agreement on institutional reform, and instead it agreed to have an intergovernmental conference one year before the total number of EU members passes twenty to discuss the composition and functioning of the EU institutions. This makes it more likely that the first round of enlargement will only take in a maximum of four new members in order to avoid passing this limit.

Taking in only a few new members each time is sensible as this will give the EU time to absorb the new members (either as full members, or more likely as some sort of membership in a variable geometry) and will enable it to focus enough attention on the new member state. Furthermore, there are twelve states with Europe agreements and these are all potential members. Accepting all in one block would create a clear dividing line in Europe, in addition to giving the EU an institutional shock. It would set a number of states clearly outside the EU and leave them with little hope of joining the Union. By taking in only a limited number of states it will continuously leave open the opportunity for other states to attain membership in the future and thus help to ensure that they strive to achieve developments that are compatible with membership. So until the EU makes clear that it has reached the limit of what it defines as Europe, there will not be made a clear dividing line between the 'ins' and the 'outs'.

NATO enlargement

Since the Cold War NATO has been 'restructured to enable it to participate in the development of co-operative security structures for the whole of Europe. It has also transformed its political and military structures in order to adapt them to peacekeeping and crisis management tasks undertaken in co-operation with countries which are not members of the Alliance and with other international organisations'.[1] It has now taken on a new momentum with its decision at the Madrid summit in July 1997 to invite Poland, Hungary and the Czech Republic to join the Alliance.

Together with the national defence organizations, NATO is in charge of much of the hard security in Europe. It is through the US security guarantee that Western Europe has been able to develop and prosper during the last 50 years and this has enabled the European integration process to go ahead without having been hampered (until now) by questions regarding foreign, military and security affairs. NATO has 'kept the Americans in, the Russians out and the Germans down'. However, it has now become an organization that is increasingly likely 'to be called on to keep the peace elsewhere than to defend its own territory' (*The Economist*, 1997b). It has also been argued that out-of-area operations will become the core of the North Atlantic relationship (Kissinger, 1995).

There has been surprisingly little argument surrounding the decision to enlarge NATO. It seems increasingly clear that the decision to enlarge was taken as a consequence of a domestic debate on national security in the US. In the aftermath of the Cold War, the role of NATO was increasingly questioned in Washington, and there was a growing feeling that Europe ought to pay more for its own defence. The internationalist camp realized that they needed to strengthen the support for US engagement in Europe and NATO enlargement was the best means of gaining this support. Enlargement also enlisted the support of the influential Polish-American lobby and other ethnic groups. Thus the issue of enlargement served two purposes: it gave NATO a new lease of life as well as enhancing President Clinton's re-election chances (MccGwire, 1997).

MccGwire further argues that 'we are paying lip-service to the inclusive concept of *co-operative security*, while focusing in practice on the exclusionary concept of security as *defence* against an *external threat . . .* we are focusing on the future security (for which, read defence) of a truncated Europe that will be coextensive with a yet-to-be-defined expanded NATO' (1997: 3). The West emphasizes defence as the most important means of guaranteeing security, but this makes cooperation difficult and can have adverse affects on the policies of Moscow who may see themselves forced to re-establish a stronger security network around Russia.

Joining NATO has large financial costs for the applicant states. Not only do they have to change the structure of their military forces to be more similar to NATO's, but they also have to update and change much of their military material to make it NATO compatible. This will have adverse effects on other aspects of the economy and will leave fewer funds for later adaptations to EU requirements and economic development.

There is also a large question of who will pay the Alliance's costs involved in enlargement. There is increasing uneasiness in the US Senate and Congress about paying the bill for enlargement. There are also tight and declining budgets in most of the EU states and this makes such contributions both difficult to finance and unpopular. So the enlargement process can be stopped by both security and economic concerns in the existing member states.

Furthermore, the economic and political costs connected with NATO enlargement can be a threat to later EU enlargement. Politically this is so because of Russian opposition and fear of encirclement. Economically, it is because after a NATO enlargement, there will be less money to spend on EU enlargement.

Russia and NATO enlargement

The decision to enlarge the Alliance has prompted fears of a Russian reaction. Russia is, and considers itself to be, a European power. The exclusion of Russia from discussions on European security and development can be very dangerous and a good relationship with Russia is crucial in order to ensure peace and stability.

Even though NATO and Russia have signed the Founding Act,[2] there is still fear of what the enlargement of NATO can mean for the long-term relationship with Russia. It can be a significant factor in reviving Cold War thinking (for example, spheres of influence) and result in the drawing of a new dividing line in Europe. Furthermore it might also result in a strengthening of the nationalist groups in Russia, thus undermining the *rapprochement* that we have been seeing over the last few years. There is a danger that NATO enlargement plays into the hands of Russian nationalists.

The decision in Madrid to invite three countries, Poland, the Czech Republic and Hungary, to join the Alliance has set a precedent and has left many Russians feeling that they have been left out. For the Russian politicians, led by Boris Jeltsin, the acceptance of the Treaty with NATO was a necessity in order to ensure continued support and aid as part of the reform process in Russia. However, there is a strong feeling among large parts of the political class and the population of being encircled. According to SIPRI 'in 1996 NATO expansion was opposed by almost the entire spectrum of the political elite and all significant parties in Russia' and there is little reason to believe that this has changed (SIPRI, 1997: 139). Furthermore, after their anti-enlargement rhetoric the Russian leaders are under strong domestic pressure to act.[3]

It is also important to remember that many Russians still see NATO as a Cold War actor which is directed towards Russia. Therefore NATO enlargement is by many perceived as a way to contain Russia rather than to promote peace and stability in Europe. This can make Russia feel increasingly isolated from Europe and increase its contacts with, for example, China or other states like Iran in order to counterbalance what it sees as an increasing threat from the West. The fear of encirclement can also make Russia more inclined to oppose EU enlargement.

It has been convincingly argued that Russia feels deceived by the West with regard to NATO expansion (Dannreuther, 1997). They thought that Partnership for Peace was a means to postpone NATO enlargement more or less indefinitely and thus accepted it. The Russians were therefore surprised at the speed with which enlargement took place and that it did so without consultation.

Even though the US administration does its best to justify NATO enlargement, there is still strong opposition to it in large parts of the US foreign policy establishment. Many see this as an ill-conceived and dangerous idea that will undermine the relations with Moscow, and in a letter to the US Secretary of State in 1995 a group of retired State Department officials stated that NATO enlargement will 'convince most Russians that the United States and the West are attempting to isolate, encircle, and subordinate them, rather than integrating them into a new system of collective security' (MccGwire, 1997: 2).

Security implications

Both EU and NATO enlargement are in response to a new international situation that emerged after the Cold War. The Central and Eastern European Countries (CEECs) look to NATO for military security and to the EU to ensure their economic development. However there is a strong link between the two, as strong economic development is difficult without security and security is difficult to achieve without a well-functioning economy. Ideally the two ought to be reconciled inside an EU enlargement, but this is difficult as long as the EU does not have a defence dimension. Furthermore, the states in the East still see the US as the best guarantor for their security, and based on historical experience they also fear the long-term interests and developments in Russia and Germany.

Lying between Russia and the reunified Germany, the CEECs fear the role of these two large European powers who have frequently carved up or fought over their territory. Russia is still recovering from the collapse of communism and is led by people who are eager to be on good terms with the West, but there are strong nationalist tendencies and desire for Russia to regain control over its 'near abroad'.

Germany is still firmly anchored into both the EU and NATO. With leaders that still remember the last war and are firm believers in European integration, Germany has so far accepted US domination in strategic matters and French political leadership in the EU. However, there is a growing assertiveness in the reunited Germany and it is already a dominant partner in the EU and is likely to become even more so when a new generation of political leaders takes over. This is one reason why many of the potential member states from the East look to the US and NATO to ensure their security.

The CEECs also want to join NATO as the EU does not have a credible defence organization. It can be argued that the new members will get increased military security through membership of the EU. This is because new members will be able to join WEU and thus also come under its security guarantee. Even if the new member states do not join the WEU, there is an implicit security guarantee in EU membership. This is through the EU's economic weight and its role in the international arena, which give the EU considerable leverage and clout. It is unlikely that the member states would accept an act of aggression against another member state as this would threaten the idea of a united and integrated Europe as well as the credibility of the Union. It would not be possible for the EU to allow this to happen if it is to retain its international prestige and role in global affairs.

In case of aggression against one of the member states the EU will be obliged to act, but it will only be within what is acceptable to Washington. Since it looks as if Europe will remain dependent on the US for its security for the foreseeable future, the new member states much prefer the US guarantee through NATO which both can protect them against Russia and also keep some of the larger European states at bay.

In the EU, hard security issues are presently organized on national lines but under the overarching defence pact within NATO. The US is, however, the final guarantor of European security. This worked well during the Cold War when it was clear both *what* and *who* the threat was, and until the collapse of communism the development of the EC was dependent on the Cold War nuclear security system.[4] The European NATO members allied behind the US and were willing to put past conflicts behind them in order to counter the communist threat from the USSR. With this threat gone, there has been a return to an emphasis on national interests when faced with new challenges and where history and old political ties have played a role.

Historically, the various EU member states have strong and varied foreign and security interests. States perceive their security interests in relation to their relative strength, economic base, military capability, geography and history. Thus the national perspective on security can vary considerably amongst the members of the EU. The states have a variation of political/economic ties with different countries and each want to maintain its allies. A result of this is that the interests of the member states easily conflict. This was not a big obstacle during the first decades of the EC's existence since the emphasis was on economic development, and differences on foreign and security policy were minimized owing to the overarching threat from the USSR during the Cold War. However, such links are resurfacing again and the member states are increasingly preoccupied with security issues. A good example of the various interests of the member states is the Yugoslav conflict.

Because hard security has been, and looks as if it still will be, to a large extent taken care of by NATO, it is possible that EU enlargement will follow NATO enlargement. In this way the EU will not get entangled in other countries that it will be difficult for them to defend without the US security guarantee. It will be difficult for the EU to enlarge to countries that are not members of the NATO Alliance as it will be very difficult to defend these in case of attack without the support of the US.

For the EU itself, enlargement both enhances and reduces its security. Enlargement can be very positive for the member states, but it can also deflect attention from other important areas to the detriment of security in that area. It can also alienate other states and thus lay the groundwork for later conflicts. Some of the present member states will feel that their security is diminishing as there will be less economic support and focus by the EU on their problems. This is particularly for the Southern European states, while, for example, Germany will feel that its security is greatly improved as it will no longer be on the border of the EU and will have gained important new markets and new member states that will have a more 'German' mentality.

In an increasingly globalized and interdependent world, states will have to be very large or pool some of their sovereignty into regional organizations such as the EU in order to have influence in international affairs. If the European states are to have a say, they will have to make the EU a strong organization that can participate in setting the global agenda. In order to achieve this it is also necessary that the states have a sense of shared political and security interests. But without a major threat it is difficult for the EU to define common objectives and what some see as increasing security may by others be seen as decreasing it.

From a military viewpoint enlargement will in the long run give the EU greater resources to draw on, but it also gives the EU a much larger territory to protect and one which does not in many places offer specific geographic advantages. It will draw the EU into much closer geographical contact with Russia and it will thus be of increasing importance for it to have a strong and coherent CFSP to deal with security issues. A possible benefit of expanding security guarantees to the East is that it may contribute to stopping the renationalization of defence in that region and thus help in defusing tensions. The former Warsaw Pact countries need to come into a stable security environment, otherwise they may start making bilateral alliances that could destabilize the region.

Politically, enlargement enhances the Union's international role. Also, the new member states from the East will gain considerably. The stability and economic development that is likely to come from EU membership will enhance the strength and stability of those countries and, with economic development and a higher standard of living, their internal stability will be improved. The new members will also have aligned themselves with like-minded powers and thus be under less political pressure. By being part of the Western security arrangements they will also have become part of a larger security area, and reduce some of the more direct and immediate threats. Furthermore, enlargement would also put Germany at the geo-graphical as well as the political core of the Union. Even though many of the new member states have historical reasons to fear Germany, they still have a similar mentality and look to Germany as an economic model.

This will further strengthen German influence in Europe. EU member-ship can also contribute considerably to the economic development of the new members. This would of course have to be handled carefully as full membership with the full application of the *acquis communautaire* would most likely destroy the uncompetitive industries in many of these countries. However, a gradual and sensible integration of these states into the internal market should benefit them enormously and create a better economic environment for both business and individuals. Economic development and EU legislation would also contribute to solving many of the environmental problems in the East that also constitute a threat to the citizens in the present member states.

Enlargement of the EU can also significantly contribute in the spheres of soft security. These countries need help to develop their economies and democracy, not just strengthen their military capability. This is where the EU can and ought to contribute. Through an EU enlargement these coun-tries would get access to a much larger market, become more attractive to invest in and become firmly part of Western Europe with the added security that this brings with it.

As long as there is no outer border for how far the European Union will expand, those outside are likely to at least strive for membership and try to gain preferential agreements. In this way, the area around the EU will be more 'stabilized' through their efforts to join and it will also be in the inter-ests of the EU to help these countries develop economically and politically as this will enlarge the security cordon around Europe. Economic progress is also important in giving citizens a greater stake in both economic and political development.

Enlargement of the EU to the East is likely to defuse a number of the potential conflicts there. This is through both economic development and participation in a greater European entity, but the opening of borders and increasing contacts across borders and between citizens are likely to foster greater understanding and reduce the desire to reconquer formerly lost territories. By decreasing the potential for conflicts in the East, there will be less threat or danger for the present member states. However, there will always be states that are on the borders of the EU and it is important to also help these develop, as instability in the border areas can spread to the EU.

Conclusion

This chapter has outlined some of the security challenges facing the EU with regard to eastward enlargement, indicating the embryonic state of the security arrangements in the EU and the WEU and their dependence on the US. The role of NATO and its enlargement has highlighted the problems faced in trying to establish a new security architecture for Europe and the destabilizing effects that NATO enlargement can have for Europe and EU enlargement.

The EU was able to develop owing to the US security guarantee, and it seems as though the US will continue to play a major role in European affairs. This makes it very difficult for the EU to enlarge without the (tacit) consent of the US. This is because EU enlargement outside NATO countries in the East may get the Union into conflicts where it might need US support. It is possible that the development of the CJTFs will help overcome this problem, and that the EU could eventually be capable of mounting its own operations. If EU enlargement to the East is confined to NATO members, the EU will have a role to play in contributing to political, democratic and economic development and thus promoting internal stability while NATO takes care of the hard security.

NATO has developed significant military means to deal with conflicts and has showed that it is willing to use these assets. The EU does not have this capability: it does play a role as mediator and aid giver, but with difficulty as some of the larger member states prefer to act unilaterally on what they see as issues of national interest.

At present the Russians are not part of any of the important security organizations in Europe, apart from OSCE, and the enlargement of both NATO and the EU is resulting in an increasing exclusion of Russia. It is therefore important to engage Russia actively in the new security arrangements in Europe, and ensure that Russian concerns are also taken into consideration.

This chapter opened by discussing the problems of defining security. Nothing is ever completely secure, only more or less so. Enlargement of the EU opens up the possibility to include many other European states in the Union and contributes to the stability as well as the economic and democratic development of these countries. By itself, EU enlargement will have considerable benefits for the involved parties, in both economic and political terms. However, there is a risk that it may also increase the Russian feeling of encirclement, particularly if NATO enlargement precedes EU enlargement. EU enlargement is also hampered by the Union's dependence on military support from the US, and thus the Union's ability to act will continue to be dependent on American agreement.

Notes

1 NATO homepage (http://www.nato).
2 Founding Act on Mutual Relations, Cooperation and Security between NATO and the Russian Federation, Paris, 27 May 1997.
3 See also discussion of this in Pierre and Trenin (1997).
4 Wallace as quoted by Ulf Sverdrup (1995).

12 The Future of Armament Cooperation in NATO and the WEU

Pierre de Vestel

The intergovernmental conference (IGC) for the revision of the Maastricht Treaty only addresses in a secondary manner the questions linked to the organization of defence markets and industries in Europe. The IGC should nonetheless play the role of catalyst by obliging European states, engaged for some years in a difficult process of defence market and industry integration, to accelerate their momentum.

The Europeanization of defence markets and industries figures among the most complex subjects of European integration. Through defence markets and industries, the problematic issues of political integration and more particularly the integration of the tools of sovereignty are posed. In effect, the evolution of the economic aspects of defence is animated by two closely linked processes, one political, the other economic. Few technological and industrial sectors will benefit from a similar correlation between political and economic considerations. The choice of a particular armament, its conception and production, and its eventual export are considered in many countries as constituting the attributes and conditions of sovereignty. Public policy, whether it be industrial and technological or concerning security and defence, contributes in profoundly affecting the technological, industrial and social dimensions of armament production.[1]

The relations between politics and economics are complex and vary from one country to the next. This complexity is further heightened by the multitude of levels to which the questions of defence economics are applied. Public authorities and businesses develop their strategies essentially at the national level. But they must reconcile their strategies with the necessity of cooperating on other levels – bilateral and multilateral (with European partners or transatlantic) or even wider, as part of institutions such as the WEU and NATO. Finally, defence ministries and businesses must be aware of the increasing globalization of technological innovation.

This chapter will not analyse the economic evolution that has affected defence markets and industries since the end of the Cold War. It will focus on the study of the political dimensions of the changes occurring in defence economics. In effect, Europeans are trying at present to build on the procedures and institutions that will be capable of encompassing and improving their cooperation in armament matters. It is this process that will be analysed through an analytical screen based on a more theoretical approach to the process of European integration. This should allow for the identification of dominant traits in the process of the Europeanization of defence economics, in this way indicating development perspectives in the medium term. The conclusions will evaluate the implications of these developments for the process of security and defence integration.

The growth of initiatives

The desire to integrate defence markets and industries in Europe, in some way or another, has been regularly expressed since the 1950s. In 1991 the French and German governments,[2] outside the Maastricht Treaty negotiations, proposed to create an agency of the WEU for cooperation in armament matters. In December 1992 the IEPG (Independent European Programmes Group), which was the only European body competent in matters of armaments, integrated into the WEU to give birth to the Western European Armaments Group (WEAG)[3] whose primary task is to negotiate the principles and operational modes required before presiding over the creation of a European armaments agency (EAA). In November 1994, during the Council of Noordwijk, the member states of the WEU approved the working principles of a European armaments agency. In the course of the same meeting, the defence ministers of the thirteen member countries of the WEAG agreed upon the creation of a permanent secretariat in the spring of 1995 for the EUCLID research programme. Paralleling the work of the thirteen member states of the WEAG, France and Germany announced at the Baden-Baden summit on 7 December 1995 their intention to create a French–German cooperation structure in armaments. It was soon evident that the partners of France and Germany, particularly the United Kingdom and Italy, regarded this move with a critical eye as it consisted of two countries anticipating the events and bilaterally usurping part of the role reserved for a European armaments agency. In March 1995, Britain and Italy proposed to France and Germany the joint creation of a larger agency. In January 1996, France and Germany announced the creation not of an agency but of a 'structure' to assemble and manage their bilateral armaments programmes. In March 1996 Britain, soon followed by Italy, announced its intention to join France and Germany in a quadripartite structure. Britain and Italy joined the initiative[4] on 12 November 1996 and the Organization of Cooperation in Armaments (OCCAR) was created.

At the same time, on 19 November 1996, the member countries of the WEAG adopted[5] a charter and a 'memorandum of understanding anticipating the constitution of the Western European Armament Organization'. Paralleling these institutional developments, discreet discussions were being pursued to try to define more precisely the guidelines that were to frame the functioning of these structures.

The complexity of the processes under way were even more accentuated by the fact that the European National Armament Directors (ENAD), who had already met in the context of the WEAG, were also negotiating, through bilateral means, the creation of new structures or the launching of armament programmes. They were also meeting their North American counterparts within the Committee of National Armament Directors (CNAD) of NATO. There, they were discussing transatlantic cooperation in armament matters.

These final months also saw the multiplication of positions taken by the European states in matters of security and defence in the perspective of the 1996–7 intergovernmental conference. The European Commission (1996b) made public a communication on the 'challenges that confront European industries linked to defence' (European Commission communiqué, 24 January 1996) in which it proposed to once again extend the application of the rules of governing public markets to the acquisition of military equipment. The European Parliament expressed the same desire although countries such as France and the UK wanted to keep questions of defence economics in particular, and defence in general, at the intergovernmental level.

The list of initiatives is impressive. It appears therefore that there is a will to establish an economic pillar of defence in Europe. However, in order to be more precise, one must note the diverging wishes that exist with respect to the form of organization and the political and economic objectives to be pursued within this pillar. The economic aspects of defence should constitute the third pillar of the future temple of European defence next to the pillars labelled 'common defence policy' and 'military tools' (baptized 'common defence' in the well-known phrasing of Article J.4.1 of the Maastricht Treaty). The construction of this third pillar has only just been initiated, as has the construction of the other two for that matter. The foundations already exist. They are made up of multiple intra-European agreements in matters concerning the production of arms, the research programme EUCLID and some more or less institutionalized structures. However, beyond the build-up of these first steps and the multitude of positions taken, it is difficult to draw out the predominant guidelines that will structure the organization of the defence economics pillar over the medium term.

Why integrate?

If the political wish to integrate markets and industries exists it remains to be analysed. After 35 years of aborted attempts and traditional rhetoric, it is doubtless not entirely inappropriate to ask the question 'Why integrate?' before asking 'How?'

In fact, three incentives seem to spur attempts at integrating defence markets and industries. The primary incentive is functional and aims at the improved economic management of the production, acquisition and export of military equipment at the European level. The second incentive is protectionist. It consists of organizing at a European level to confront an exterior threat, in this case that of the United States and its more competitive defence firms. The third incentive is political and is aimed at pursuing the construction of a political union of the European states. It depends on the will to capitalize politically on the different expressions of informal integration[6] that already exist and put them at the service of European integration.

Political capitalization

The notion of capitalizing politically on the various existing informal expressions of integration at the European level may seem obscure. In order to understand it, it is necessary to look back on the very nature of European integration. William Wallace (1990: 20) has noted that the dynamics of European integration depend both on the informal pressures exerted by free economic and social forces and on the formal channelling of these forces in specified directions. The Single European Act is the most significant example of this formal canalization of the various pressures exerted by multinationals and some governments to keep national markets open to competition in Europe. It has not only made it possible to deal with economic problems such as the improvement of the competitiveness of companies, but it has also allowed for the completion of the European Union's institutional and political construction, notably through the supranational management of the single market by institutions equipped with extensive competence such as the European Commission and the Court of Justice. The temptation is great, particularly at the European Commission, to apply this arrangement to defence economics. The latter, already marked by some informal integration (the numerous intra-European collaboration agreements), would do well to capitalize on these political and institutional opportunities.

   An analysis of the internationalization process, and above all the Europeanization of defence, reveals in effect a profound and growing tendency[7] by states and enterprises to cooperate with foreign partners. This movement increased in the 1980s. For example, it must be noted that there is an increasing propensity for states to conduct R&D projects of an international scope. Eurostat, the European Union's statistics office, has supplied interesting though incomplete statistics on the proportion of national defence R&D investments made to international projects. Such expenditures have been on the increase since 1983: the proportion of international R&D projects in defence R&D budgets rose between 1983 and 1991 from 31 to 38 per cent for Germany, from 10 to 23 per cent for the United Kingdom, and from 16 to 30 per cent for The Netherlands (Eurostat, various years). In France, the proportion of non-nuclear R&D conducted with international cooperation increased from 5.5 per cent in 1984 to 23 per cent in 1992.[8]

Economic management

The desire to better manage economic problems whose magnitude surpasses the capacity of individual states is the second motivating factor behind integration. European defence ministries have for many years faced a consistent increase in the cost of military programmes and the great dissipation of their efforts. In effect, in 1992, the member states of the Council of Europe and of EFTA developed 125 different armament models as opposed to the 53 different armament models in the same class developed in the United States alone.

The continual rise of programme costs is the principal inducement for European cooperation. The costs of developing arms systems grows in a remarkable manner with each new generation of arms. Between 1965 and 1986, the cost of the R&D phase of a fighter aircraft increased by 191 per cent in constant terms.[9] At the same time, the unit cost of fighter aircraft produced in the United Kingdom doubled every seven years.[10] This reflects a worrying trend for the military, the manufacturers, and the taxpayer.

The increase in programme costs, the duplication of R&D efforts and the limitation of series are not new developments in Europe. They have existed for decades, and a limited recourse to cooperation and an increase in defence budgets had been sufficient to address the problem until the end of the Cold War. Since then, the defence ministries of the European member states of NATO have seen their purchasing power in military equipment reduced by 34 per cent between 1987 and 1992 and 23 per cent between 1990 and 1994 in the area of R&D investment. The conditions are therefore present for encouraging a veritable explosion in the number and scope of armament materials agreements in Europe. One can surmise that international cooperation will be the rule in matters of new and large armament programmes, with national solutions left as the exception.

Increasingly, European states are going to have to select the technological sectors that they wish to master at a national level (fighter aircraft or nuclear technology as in France and the United Kingdom, for example) as well as selecting the sectors they wish to develop through more or less institutionalized cooperation with other states or through agreements with companies. Finally, they must choose the sectors in which states should rely on technological imports. The challenge for defence ministries is to increase cooperation agreements while improving their efficiency and profitability.[11] The stakes involved in the present negotiations concerning the construction of a genuine European armaments agency include the installation of management and organization procedures for cooperation agreements in armament matters that are capable of limiting costs. The discussions also concern the type and the nature of relations to be established between defence ministries and industries.

Collective protection

A third incentive is linked to the first two. As Phillipe Schmitter notes, in effect 'participants to an integration scheme will see themselves obliged to adopt common policies with regard to third parties independently of their original intentions. The members will be obliged to forge a common exterior position' (1969: 161–6). The presence of an exterior threat is a powerful incentive for several partners to unite on positions with common objectives. The partisans of rapid and deep integration have attempted to use the United States as the economic and technological bogey, making it the principal competitor or indeed the principal threat.[12] A corollary of this approach takes the form of 'fortress Europe' or, in its acceptable version, of 'European preference' policy as supported by France. This approach is inspired by the course followed in the commercial world with the estab-lishment of a uniquely European market in opposition to the two other 'blocs' – American and Japanese. The supporters of a European market closed to American arms and technology can count on the support of Euro-pean manufacturers who see in this option the opportunity not only to regenerate the legitimacy of the defence effort holding out against the US, but also the rebuilding at the European level of a protected area where close relations between manufacturers and defence ministries may be continued or renewed.

There are at least three arguments against such a scenario. The United States enjoys such a technological lead in defence matters that it seems very difficult, indeed unacceptable for financial reasons, to bypass a technological source of such importance. Moreover, this type of commer-cial confrontation will have repercussions for transatlantic relations in matters of security and defence. At present, all the European states wish to keep the United States involved in the management of security and defence problems in Europe. Finally, the competition of American defence firms may play a useful role in the maintenance of a competitive structure for arms production in Europe. Nonetheless, transatlantic relations remain ambivalent, marked simultaneously by cooperation and competition. Europeans will most probably follow their subtle but effective policy of resistance in the face of American competition. They will do this princi-pally through national practices that allow them to exclude or accept American industry in their markets depending on the circumstances.[13] As far as transatlantic cooperation is concerned it may be hypothesized that, in the future, technological exchanges between the United States and Europe are going to increase. Under these conditions, transatlantic relations are going to stabilize and become modified, directed towards technology rather than materials. The Joint Advanced Strike Technology (JAST) programme aiming to improve the technology behind the fighter aircraft of the future is open to European participation. The British are already involved in this project, since the project of the future vertical take-off and landing aircraft has been merged with JAST. The anti-aircraft defence system with an anti-ballistic capacity (MEADS) which should be deployed by NATO has incorporated, since its R&D stages, the United States at 50 per cent and France, Italy and Germany at the remaining 50 per cent.

Europeans must recognize the ambivalent, almost schizophrenic, nature of transatlantic relations. They are informed, on the European side, by the need to cooperate and simultaneously by the necessity to withstand American competition. The establishment of a European identity in the technical and industrial domains of defence makes this dilemma twice as powerful.

The Europeans should exist as technological and financial actors of sufficient size and cohesion *vis-à-vis* the United States. This will establish centralization in certain technological domains and particular arms programmes, as well as creating collective political procedures that can contribute to presenting a unified front in negotiations with the American partner. In the opposite situation, Europeans will present the image of a group of disparate states and enterprises in a position of relative weakness. This final hypothesis indicates what will result if the present situation is maintained. The European states must also develop the integration and the relative protection of their markets and their arms policies in a manner that is sufficiently flexible in order to avoid a direct confrontation with the United States.

Nonetheless, the future of transatlantic technological and industrial relations depends above all on the American attitude. The United States demonstrated in the 1970s and the 1980s that it was capable of effecting a large-scale policy of cooperation in armament matters under pressure from Congress. Two options coexist for the future. The first is that of a withdrawal of American needs and relative disinterest in cooperation with the Europeans. The second requires that the Pentagon[14] and the US administration be capable of pursuing a cooperation strategy with Europe for financial and strategic reasons. The unknown factor is the attitude of the United States Congress which plays a fundamental role in matters of international cooperation.

The role of the smaller European states

There exist numerous differences between the smaller European states. But they share two great demands in common and they have only one asset at their disposal. The two points in common are:

1 The desire not to be kept out of an eventual integration process of defence markets, for both political and economic reasons. This desire is apparent as smaller states are asking to participate in the OCCAR or even in their refusal to accord to this structure the status of a subsidiary to the WEU as France and Germany have requested.
2 The forwarding of the principle of 'fair returns' or industrial and technological compensation. However much big businesses and the larger states sometimes advise against it, this principle will not be abandoned, even if consensus is reached on the necessity to limit the difficulties herein. This question of fair returns is all-important for the defence enterprises of the smaller countries.

The small and medium European defence industries only yield a limited industrial and technological interest for French, British, German and Italian industries. More often, they are redundant. The small states have only one trump card in their deck: their domestic markets, even in a reduced form, are coveted by the larger states. What would be the attitude of these small countries with regard to an eventual 'European preference'? A European preference system as imagined by France does not have any chance of being accepted. On the other hand, a European preference system constructed progressively through cooperation programmes will elicit the support of different states as long as their businesses and their armed forces are associated with it.

This short analysis of the incentives and the conceptions of defence markets and industries integration has served to explain the positions and the ambitions of the various actors. The question that is now posed is that of the future in the short and medium term of these processes of market and industry integration. If one wishes to tackle the probable forms and modes of Europeanization, a first stage must be surmounted. This is the analysis of the European political integration process in matters of security and defence as it has developed until the present day and as it should be pursued in the middle term. It will define the political and institutional framework in which the integration of the defence economy should be inscribed.

In which framework should integration take place?

Debates over the Treaty of European Union, and more generally the development of the European Union, have shown that the process of European integration has not taken the form hoped for and imagined by the founding fathers of the European Community, or even that which the neo-functionalist theoreticians[15] thought indicative in the 1960s. The latter conceived of European integration as a progressive process of transferring national sovereignty to supranational institutions, a process marked by an almost mechanical progress towards increasingly closer forms of integration in a single institutional framework. It now appears that the integration process resembles more of a complex network of areas of cooperation and integration whose composition and functions vary, as is illustrated by the coexistence of institutions such as the European Union, the WEU, NATO, the research programmes EUREKA and EUCLID, the executive programme of the European Union, or even the European Space Agency, the Airbus consortium, etc. Flexibility, variable geometry and segmentation have become the principal characteristics of the process of European integration.

What kind of European armaments policy?

As far as defence economics are concerned, they are presently affected by two stages of the integration process. These are the coexistence of national industrial bases and national markets and decentralized cooperation composed of hundreds of international cooperation agreements. Returning to the idea of continuum, three potential developmental possibilities exist for the future. The two extreme scenarios are on the one hand the status quo (or the absence of Europe), and on the other the rapid integration of markets and industries in a unique framework. The progressive establishment of a large cooperation regime – of fifteen within the framework of the European Union and of thirteen within WEAG – or of a more limited one in the form of a hard core, is placed between these two extremes.

The absence of Europe

The status quo scenario consists of following the course taken for three decades – a course characterized by limited collaboration agreements according to specific arms and variable geometry (from bilateral agreements to larger agreements). It therefore consists of following the course of informal market integration without notable political intervention other than the continuation of discussions and a few initiatives that are more symbolic than substantial within a relatively weak European framework. The Europeanization and the internationalization process of markets and industries will continue in any case. But certain economic problems (the increase of costs and the reduction of budgets) will be resolved not at all or only partially, and rarely optimally. At the political level, returning to the image of a European defence temple with three pillars, this scenario signifies that the economic pillar of defence will resemble more of a heap of bricks than the rough outline of a column. At the present time, it appears that no important actors[16] wish to maintain the status quo and this scenario is only considered as a provisional fallback position if none of the agreements, even the limited ones, between European states are realized in the short term.

Federal or 'national' Europe

Opposing the *laissez-faire* policy, the federalist scenario or that of a European 'nation'[17] is certainly that which has been expressed the most clearly and implies the most active political intervention, a sort of 'Big Bang' in integration. It aims to integrate defence markets at the European level and to create supranational mechanisms for the management of these markets. The development of a true European defence industry under these conditions would forge a European identity of interests.

In this framework, as Ian Gambles has remarked in relation to security and defence in general:

> the integration of security promises not only to deprive the united state of one of the principal means of affirming a distinct sovereign identity on the international scene but also of endowing the nascent European entity with elements that are as

important for the formation of an identity as martial symbols, the military *esprit de corps* and the sharing of risks and losses. (1991: 15)

The suggestion of the European Parliament[18] and the Commission of creating a single market for armaments is one variation on this scenario. It is within an industrial and technological framework marked by numerous informal integration agreements, and marked also by the desire of some large enterprises to release themselves from national controls, that the European Commission is trying to capitalize politically on these informal integration processes and accelerate the momentum in defence policy denationalization. The communication by the European Commission (1996b) cited previously is revealing in this regard (European Commission communiqué, 24 January 1996). It was written following two meetings with defence industrialists. It addresses, in a principally economic manner, the problem of the organization of markets and industries. The repeal of Article 223 and the application of the rules of civil public markets to defence markets, even slightly adapted, that are proposed in this text (1996b: 20–1) will result in the creation of a single market of armaments, protected from the outside by customs barriers (1996b: 32–3) and managed as a last resort by the Commission and the Court of Justice.

The virtues of Article 223   The suggestion to repeal Article 223 will probably be moved outside the IGC, not only because the principal European states (France and Britain) refuse for political reasons to see Community rules govern these questions but also because this proposition is technically and strategically very difficult to put into practice. In effect, what would the consequences be of repealing Article 223? Two major problems are posed. On the one hand they concern the selection procedures for armaments, and on the other the maintenance of a competitive structure (with several competitors) at the supply level. In order for competition to prevail, clear and precise rules for the selection of armaments must be established. The choice of defence ministries should be made on common foundations, to be founded on 'objective criteria for selection and endowment' using the wording of the European Commission (1996b: 21) in a manner that will not penalize one manufacturer over another. Additionally, defence ministries must be made to respect these rules.

How does one define these objective selection criteria in military markets? In civil markets, characterized by numerous buyers, numerous manufacturers and relatively similar products, the buyer makes his choice essentially on cost. In the defence sector, on the other hand, the situation is different, since in most cases a lot of (sometimes very different) equipment is presented when there is an invitation to tender. Taking a recent example, The Netherlands and the United Kingdom had to choose between three competitors for their attack helicopter programmes: the not yet operational Eurocopter Tiger; the American Apache, which has been in service for ten years now; and the Italian Mangusta, in service for two years. The armed forces made their choice based on a complex combination of criteria that included operational performance, the total estimated cost of the programme over twenty to thirty years, the potential for mid-life updating, interoperability with existing equipment, etc. They also had to bear in mind technological, industrial and social considerations put forth by other ministries. In these conditions, how is it possible to guarantee that the buyer makes an objective choice on the basis of such subjective criteria? How can 'nationalist' or political choices be avoided, and on what premises can they be challenged by some supranational authority? The exercise appears impossible in all cases at the level of large arms systems. The situation may be different in certain sectors such as munitions, or even more likely with regard to dual-purpose equipment and services (civil and military: fuel, food supplies, etc.)

As far as the supply side is concerned, the introduction of competition between manufacturers would inevitably lead to a rapid process of concentration in the form of mergers, cartels, consortiums, etc. The authorities responsible for managing this single armaments market would rapidly find themselves confronting a dilemma:

1 Either maintain competition by preventing concentration among companies, and in this case being obliged to finance this competition following the American model.[19]
2 Or allow the development of European businesses in a monopoly situation: 'European champions' in an analogy with national champions. Such a decision could be justified in the name of global competition which accepts the building of European monopolies when market conditions are such that only European monopolies are capable of opposing foreign competition. In this case, regional blocs (North America, Europe or even Russia and Ukraine) would compete with each other in third markets via their regional industrial champions.

In the case illustrated, must one protect the European champions from foreign competition? Indeed, it is interesting to note that an opening of European defence markets to competition, leading to the emergence of national champions, associated with the protection of European companies (for example through the introduction of duty on imported armaments as proposed by the European Commission in 1988, or a strict European preference), would use a combination of liberalism internally and mercantilism *vis-à-vis* the rest of the world to build a European state and a European identity.[20] In addition to British opposition, which could well be joined by the Dutch, the Danish and probably the Italians and the Germans, two other consequences can be anticipated. The first concerns Europe. The European champions would have guaranteed sales, with the usual risks associated with monopoly situations: inefficiency, non-competitiveness, the dependence of buyer(s) on one manufacturer and little independence for governments in relation to economic considerations –

precisely the situation that the introduction of competition was meant to avoid. The second consequence is outside Europe and concerns trans-atlantic relations. In cases where the single European market in armaments was open to companies from outside Europe in order to avoid monopolis-tic situations, there would arise serious risks for European companies that are often less competitive than their American counterparts. In a word, by rescinding Article 223, Europeans find themselves in an uncomfortable and paradoxical situation of having to choose, in the name of competition, between the lesser of two evils: either a situation in which European champions have a monopoly followed by American reprisals, or the rapid de-stabilization, possibly even the demise, of European champions in the face of American competition.

Everything indicates that the rapid transfer of the format of a single market to an armaments market is difficult to envisage for technical reasons (the management of a competition policy), strategic reasons (whether or not to open to American enterprises) and political reasons (the questions of national sovereignty, of control and dominance in a single market of armaments).

A *regime for Europe*

Between the status quo and a federal or national Europe, the creation of a regime of cooperation in armament matters in Europe is without doubt the most realistic option if one is content with the political, operational and economic analyses that mark the cooperation process between European states. The member states of the WEAG have been working on the develop-ment of such a cooperation regime since 1993, as have the members of an expert group from the Council of the European Union[21] since July 1995. The outcome of these procedures, in any case those of the WEAG, should be the creation of a European armaments agency, the focus of a future European regime in cooperation matters.

In this domain, as in others, the notions of flexibility, of a hard core, and of variable geometry have made an appearance. The creation in 1995 of a Franco-German cooperation structure, later enlarged by Britain and Italy, can be interpreted as the vague desire to form a hard core. The other Euro-pean states, by contrast, wish to privilege a greater and more concerted approach in the future European armaments agency (EAA), in a manner that will guarantee the interests of all the states, the weakest included. Nonetheless it is probable that, parallel to the constitution of the EAA, the superposition of several forms of differentiated integration and variable geometry is inevitable in this domain,[22] in any case during the transition period of several years.

The European states will have to cooperate more and more with each other. This recourse to cooperation will be in a relatively constrained politi-cal and industrial framework which determines the political forms of inte-gration and limits the extent of possible changes as well as their speed.

Specific timing   Two factors reinforce the idea that the integration process will be long and difficult. The first is economic and is directed towards divergences among the defence economies of the European states. With regard to different countries, the defence industry exercises a variable influence in the economy and the society. In France and the United Kingdom, defence R&D dominates all other public investments of R&D and the acquisition of military equipment represents a very significant part of the capital expenditure of public authorities. In other countries, it is a marginal or medium expenditure, as in Germany. Furthermore, the organizational mode of the relations between the client and, at times, proprietor state and the manufacturers is even more disparate. The recent measure of restructuring of the defence industries and the armaments acquisition policy announced by President Chirac is directly inspired by the British example (privatization, restructuring, better cost control, recentring the armaments acquisition policy on the needs of the army and less on the needs of the manufacturers). If these measures are put into place, the French system for the acquisition and the production of armaments should be closer to that of the British. This is a *rapprochement* that will take many years (between five to ten) and should then facilitate closer technological, industrial and without doubt political cooperation between the two principal military powers in Europe.

The second constraint is linked to the fact that the common armaments programmes are veritable motors of integration for markets and industries. The assembly, by different defence ministries, of their armament needs and their financial capacities dictates the extent and the rhythm of the *rapprochement* between industries. The opportunity to harmonize armament needs and to initiate European cooperation will only present itself progressively in the course of the next two decades. In effect, it will require a minimum of two decades to see the European armies replace all of their equipment. The timing required by the armed forces gives an idea of the rhythm at which the integration of markets and industries may progress.

Can the industries wait several years, indeed a decade, before being reorganized and restructured? It would appear that the extent of the crisis that is affecting the defence industry in Europe is such that the arguments of the manufacturers are not capable of being heard. The stabilization of the sale of military equipment by European states since 1992 (with the exception of France)[23] after a fall of 35 per cent between 1987 and 1991, and the restructuring of enterprises, authorizes this relative improvement of the financial structure of defence industries. The improvement permits national public powers to envisage the future of the integration of markets and industries in a progressive manner[24] and no longer under the urgent pressure that was generally felt at the start of the 1990s.

Towards a European armaments agency?

It is once again up to the WEU to address the questions of armament production. At the end of long negotiations, which are not possible to summarize (Borderas, 1994) here, the members of the WEAG concluded by adopting a very progressive construction strategy for a European armaments agency. The creation of the Western European Armaments Organization (WEAO) is the first stage in this. This organization is limited to the secretariat of the EUCLID programme which has at present the judicial capacity, but not yet the financial, to make contracts with enterprises.

The members of the WEAG are still involved in long negotiations concerning the rules and the principles to put into practice in the future EAA. These principles will remain quite general in all likelihood and will inspire the principles already adopted by the action plan of the IEPG, that is to say, the opening of markets to competition. All the enterprises of the member states of the WEAG will be able to respond to invitations to bid, just as will the enterprises of the countries who will operate under the principle of reciprocity. Two principles could still be the object of disagreement among Europeans. The first concerns the modes (compulsory or by arbitration) of dispute regulation. The second concerns the necessity, or lack thereof, of recognizing the need to reinforce the industrial and technological base of European defence when a contract is awarded.[25] Whatever the final decisions may be, it appears that these principles will remain quite generous and that it will only be stage by stage that a European armament acquisition policy will be forged.

An analogy with the European Space Agency gives a rough idea of how the structure of the EAA may look in the coming years if it should be charged with the management of common research and infrastructure programmes. One may note that such an analogy allows for great flexibility between national and common programmes in a different framework from an institutional communitarian one and with a composition in terms of countries that does not match up with that of the Union. Consequently, it concerns a model of variable geometry far removed from those presently imagined within the framework of the Union.

The development of the EAA will probably occur in a progressive manner and according to four variables that are difficult to evaluate: first, the rhythm at which states transfer armament programmes to a European level, and more particularly the rhythm at which they will determine their common needs in armament materials, research infrastructure, telecommunication, intelligence, etc.; secondly, the state of advancement of a common European defence policy definition (an exercise currently conducted by the ten member states of the WEU); thirdly, the evolution of transatlantic relations; and finally, the evolution of a strategic context in Europe and more particularly the existence of external pressures that could accelerate European *rapprochement*.

Figure 12.1 allows one to visualize the place of the future European armaments agency and its context. Neither exclusive nor marginal, it should be situated in a position notably contested by national logic and by the tendency of states to favour bilateral accords as well as by the role that NATO and the United States play.

Level	Requirements	EU	WEU	NATO
Transatlantic	Joint programmes US–EU (MEADS)			NATO infrastructure Research programmes
	Limited transatlantic cooperation (JAST, X31)		Legal status for limited cooperation Complementary programmes	Legal status of NATO agency or projects
European	European programmes (FLA, Torrejon)	Dual-use research programmes	**European armaments agency** Management of CR CA Management of European research programmes Harmonization of requirements Mandatory programmes	
		Control of aid, cartel		
	Limited European cooperation	Common arms export policy	Complementary programmes Legal status for limited cooperation	Legal status of NATO agency or projects
National		KONVER Competition in dual-use products		

FIGURE 12.1   *The armaments market in Europe with three levels and three institutional actors*

Conclusion: will its function shape Europe?

The analysis of organizational modes and the adaptation of national models for the management of defence industrial and technological bases is evidence, particularly among the major European states, of the desire to keep the acquisition and production of armaments under national control. The national dimension is predominant but it has had to adapt. Obliged to cooperate, confronted with the globalization of the economy in general and the internationalization of defence industries and technologies in particular, and finally struggling with the reduction in defence budgets, national models of the development of industrial and technological bases of defence are emerging from the Cold War, both confirmed and modified.

The European states have together reformulated their forms of control for armaments production and acquisition, increasingly becoming more international. The relations that have been established between the national state and its national champions and the relations that the latter establish among themselves are most indicative of this. The major European states appeal to Europe to support the national dimensions incapable of facing alone the new technological and financial implications of defence.

The supranational alternative to this functional and intergovernmental vision of market and industry integration proposed by the Commission and the European Parliament is impracticable. The creation of a single market of armaments based on the model of a civil single market does not enjoy any significant political support. Furthermore, the technical and strategic obstacles inherent in this proposition appear insurmountable.

For the Europeans the present challenge is less in the futile denunciation of nationalism in the matter of armament acquisition than in the success of the progressive construction at the European level of defence markets and industries situated between national and transatlantic levels. This European dimension should ideally be attractive and capable of guaranteeing a reduction in costs, improving the quality of materials and contributing to the establishment of a European security and defence identity. The future European armaments agency should be an institution emblematic of this European dimension. It will develop in a difficult environment marked at times by the contradictory interests of European states and by the competition of transatlantic and bilateral cooperation in armament matters.

The multitude of initiatives and institutions has been apparent for two years. They have in common the fact that they are still in the embryonic stage as in the case of the WEAO or very vague such as OCCAR. The image that Europe offers at present is one of an abundance of initiatives that at times are unaware of each other, and at times are competing against one another, when they are not redundant. Some will see here a sign of good health, or at least signs of an awareness of the need to do something. But this desire to 'do something' rapidly collides with reality: the absence of consensus regarding objectives that should be pursued by a European armaments policy. The various states and institutions defend conceptions of European integration that are at times very different. This European ambivalence, which may make Europe seem non-existent in a strategic role, will be prolonged for a few years yet.

As long as the debate continues, a European idea of defence will have to remain functional and subsidiary: a level among others destined to generate operational industrial and financial advantages for the national states that have the ambition to closely control the integration process. The construction of this European dimension of defence economy will have to be progressive and flexible in view of the obstacles that it will meet, as well as the very significant disparities that exist between the national systems of armament acquisition, and additionally in the absence of consensus on the nature and the objectives of the European integration defence process. This flexibility and this progressiveness of the European construction has its advantages and its limitations. In the absence of a unified plan, or at least without clear objectives, the actors run the risk of constructing a multitude of institutions without much coherence, that is, seeing this process taken over by special interests.

John Kenneth Galbraith made the remark 25 years ago, concerning the American military-industrial complex criticized by Eisenhower, that 'the problem of military power is not unique: it is rather a formidable example of the tendency that an organization, when put in place, has of developing a life, a justification and a truth of its own. This tendency applies to all great bureaucracies, whether they be public or private' (1969: 19). Europeans find themselves today in a situation that the Americans recognized during the Second World War and at the time of the first phase of the Cold War when the American military-industrial complex was building its legitimacy, its organizational and reproductive models, and finally its role and its influence in US technological, foreign and defence policy. Europe fortunately should not have to experience either a world war or a new Cold War in the years to come.[26] Using an expression destined perhaps to enter into European political history,[27] it will have to construct its WEAO in the midst of the complex political integration process, still largely embryonic and marked by some confusion that is undoubtedly bound to last several decades. This should allow Europeans the opportunity to question their goals, objectives and modes of integration and thereby influence the course of European integration.

Notes

1 The defence industry of the European Union directly employs 600,000 people. Its turnover is around ECU 45 billion of which ECU 10 billion are for export. This turnover represents 1 per cent of Community GDP, the export of arms corresponds to 1 per cent of total Community exports, and 0.5 per cent of the active population is employed directly in businesses producing goods and services of a military character. The defence sector is classed in third position in the hierarchy of European industrial sectors when using employment as a basis for comparison. More significantly without doubt are the public investments in defence research and development (R&D), representing 19.5 per cent of total public investment in European R&D in 1993. Only the amounts received for research financed by university funds exceeds this amount (27 per cent) (European Commission, 1994: 133). For a more detailed description of the defence markets and industry see de Vestel (1994).

2 *Union politique: initiative franco-allemande sur la politique étrangère, de sécurité et de défense*, 16 October 1991. This proposition was incorporated by the WEU into its *Declaration of the Member States of the Western European Union who are also Members of the European Union on the Role of the WEU and its Relations with the European Union and the Atlantic Alliance*, Maastricht, 10 December 1991, paragraph 5. This question was once again addressed in the Petersburg Declaration adopted by the WEU Council on 19 June 1992.

3 The WEAG is composed of the same members as the former IEPG.

4 Other European states have expressed the desire to participate in this 'structure' whose status is yet uncertain, like that of all the missions for that matter.

These include The Netherlands, Belgium and Spain. The last should become the next member of this structure.

5 WEU Ostend Declaration, 19 November 1996.

6 By 'expressions of informal integration' must be understood the numerous relations that the European states, businesses and social actors establish among themselves and which contribute to create non-formalized solidarity and inter-dependence in institutions and/or through Treaties. Among the works devoted to the detailed analysis of the various dimensions of the European integration process, it is necessary to cite the outstanding work by William Wallace, *The Dynamics of European Integration* (1990). The tools of integration analysis – formal and informal, reactive and proactive – proposed by William Wallace in this work have been adopted in this chapter in an attempt to understand the form and details of the defence market integration process.

7 For a quantitative and qualitative analysis of the internationalization process of European defence see de Vestel (1995: 22–36).

8 General Commission of the plan *L'avenir des industries liés à la défense*, La Documentation Francaise, Paris, November 1993, p. 48.

9 Matthews, p. 62. For more details see Hartley (1991: 15).

10 Ainscow (1993). For the French situation see Hebert (1991: 113–42).

11 The evaluations circulating concerning international cooperation in armament matters are generally negative. Hartley and Martin (1993) offer, on the contrary, an authoritative and particularly balanced evaluation of the advantages and the disadvantages of cooperation agreements.

12 It appears that this anti-American argument is adopted more or less vigorously by defence manufacturers for economic reasons and by the French authorities on an economic and political basis. This conception of the international order where economic 'war' is conducted through military R&D budgets, replacing conventional warfare conducted with armed forces, is very well described and argued by Boyer (1994).

13 Article 223 of the Treaty of Rome, in this regard, plays an indispensable role by permitting European states to protect themselves from American enterprises.

14 In 1994, a high-level working group studied the propositions aimed at relaunching a policy of international cooperation. See 'DoD Arms Panel Aims at Global Cooperation' in *Defence News*, 23–9 January 1995, p. 26.

15 See for example Lindberg (1963).

16 The United Kingdom and France each represent a third of the production of military material and together 75 per cent of the R&D, followed at a distance by Germany (respectively 18 and 15 per cent) and Italy (8 and 4 per cent).

17 This notion of a European nation refers to the idea that Europe should dispose of the classical attributes of the national state in order to exist on the international stage (integrated security and defence policy, European army, etc.). Jean-Marie Guéhenno dismisses the possibility of seeing the establishment of a foreign policy and common security 'based only on the defence of European interests, which would return to the nationalist affirmation of a European identity, the ultimate foundation of a foreign policy' (1995: 29).

18 Dury/Maij-Weggen evaluation report on the work of the Reflection Group and the specification of the priorities of foreign policy in view of the IGC, adopted 13 March 1996.

19 The American Department of Defense has a policy of maintaining at least two manufacturers in each category of armaments in order to be able to benefit from competition between them and to mitigate against one of them defecting. In practice, the DoD is obliged in a certain number of areas to keep companies in existence artificially, in particular for major weapons systems like submarines or fighter aircraft, by financing all of the research and development phases of several different prototypes for each tender. In this manner, the company that loses the competition

will at least have enhanced its technological capability during the R&D phase of the prototype and maintained its research teams, and should be capable of surviving until the next invitation to tender. Can a similar system be imagined in Europe? It would probably be impossible for financial reasons.

20 M. Wolf (1995) stresses the role of mercantilism in the constitution of modern states and develops the idea that European integration has until now operated by combining liberalism within a precise space and mercantilism *vis-à-vis* the rest of the world. It has been possible to build a European identity both within an economic and political area protected by customs or other barriers (such as quotas), and *vis-à-vis* the rest of the world through an aggressive policy of exporting and defence of European trading interests. Within this framework, a European identity has been formed and a supranational institution has been responsible for defending collective interests *vis-à-vis* the rest of the world.

21 The European Union Council established in July 1995 a working group POLARM (for armament policy) which gathers the member states of the Commission to study the principles of a future European technological and industrial defence policy.

22 As an example, one must cite the project creating a community of Nordic interests in matters of armament production including Sweden, Norway, Denmark and Finland.

23 France deferred for six years the measures for industrial restructuring and the reduction of budgets that its partners undertook starting in 1990 (1985 for the UK). It is not the time for stabilization in France but rather time to undertake reforms too long postponed.

24 As such, it is interesting to note that the German Defence Ministry estimates that the industrial and technological base of German defence is not threatened despite a reduction in production of 50 per cent and 25 per cent in R&D expenditures between 1990 and 1994. ('Germany: surviving cuts', *Jane's Defence Weekly*, 25 March 1995, p. 38). The British authorities do not demonstrate any more anxiety than their German counterparts despite significant reductions between 1985 and 1992.

25 With the information available at present, it appears that the principal point of friction between Europeans concerns the notion of 'European preference'. The acceptance of 'European preference' in armament matters was considered by France as the condition *sine qua non* to participate in OCCAR. The United Kingdom and France found a compromise in November 1996 by specifying that European preference should be of paramount importance in the choice of an armament, all the while authorizing the purchase of material from another state as long as there is reciprocity.

26 A fortunate situation for the Europeans but a situation that singularly limits the possibilities of establishing a new defence organization in Europe.

27 This expression appeared in WEU and WEAG circles in 1995 to qualify the construction of a European dimension of armaments. See Assemblée de l'UEO (1995: 41–50).

13 European Foreign and Security Policy in the Future

Kjell A. Eliassen

A messy state of affairs is at least an accurate description for it avoids extremes of optimism and pessimism that serve no useful purpose.

[Ginsberg (1997: 31), speaking of the CFSP's progress]

This volume has addressed three particular aspects of the long-lasting drama of European political integration. First and foremost it has considered 'the screenplay', the chronological story from the 1985 Single European Act to the Amsterdam Treaty, and in particular the way it has been so difficult to develop this common political policy-making process parallel to the very successful European economic integration. Secondly, it has examined the main actors involved in this adventure; their interests, attitudes and actions at the IGCs and between. Finally, the book has analysed the consequences of the failures for wider European security interests, such as the enlargement of both EU and NATO to the East, the great Mediterranean challenge, the EU/WEU relationship, and armaments cooperation as the acid test of a willingness to cooperate.

The point of departure for this book was curiosity as to why political cooperation, and in particular foreign and security policy cooperation is so difficult when other aspects of economic and monetary cooperation have so far been a success. One basic factor has been revealed: the contradiction between, on the one hand, the unwillingness of the countries involved to give up enough of their own sovereignty in foreign and security policy to be able to create a well-functioning supranational CFSP within the context of the EU; and, on the other, the lack of success of the resulting national policies owing to the interdependency of European nation-states which requires a cooperative effort to solve the foreign and security policy issues confronting the Union.

This paradox is the main theme in Pinar Tank's chapter 'The CFSP and the Nation-State'. It has proven to be true both before the Maastricht Treaty (Chapter 3) and after the creation of the second pillar in the period up to 1997 (Chapter 4), and even seems to be the case following attempts at improving the functioning of the second pillar after Amsterdam (Chapter 5). The second part of the book illustrates that this is not only the case for countries sceptical to integration like Britain (Chapter 8), but also for integrationist states such as France (Chapter 6) as well as for the two most federalist minded countries, Germany (Chapter 7) and Spain (Chapter 9).

However, progress has been made in the last ten years and it is fair to say that some improvements in the institutional mechanisms were favoured by a majority of countries at the Amsterdam summit, but effectively blocked by the countries most sceptical to integration.

The third part of the book deals with some of the consequences these contradictions have for the foreign and security field of the Union as well as indicating the issues that are likely to present future challenges to the CFSP. We have in Chapter 10 illustrated the lack of a real initiative to solve some of the problems on the southern rim of Europe and the consequences this may have for the member states. Chapter 11 deals with the multiplication of problems given the introduction of even more member countries, and the final chapter addresses the difficulties of armaments cooperation among the member states.

In sum, we have in this book indicated the most important answer to this fundamental question of a lack of willingness to cooperate in the political field. We have found the reason to lie in the contradiction between the reduction in the sovereignty of the European nation-state and the inability to tackle the policy implications of this in the foreign affairs and security field. Below we will summarize and discuss some of the findings and perspectives taken up in the preceding chapters.

The CFSP screenplay

The basic theme in the CFSP screenplay is laid out in Chapter 2: the unwillingness of the member countries to establish supranational power within this policy field. As indicated in that chapter, already in the 1950s, prior to the European Community era, an attempt had been made to create a common European foreign policy, but with no success. Although there has been a forward momentum in subsequent years, inevitably influenced by integration in other fields, the will to devolve state sovereignty to the second pillar has been absent despite the recognition that greater interdependence requires integrated policy making in the domain of foreign affairs and security issues.

The three necessities addressed at the 1996 IGC were strongly advocated in Chapter 4 which deals with the years 1991–6. The analysis of Arnhild and David Spence shows that the existence of a procedural framework helps to create what they refer to as 'the reflex' required by policy makers to assess European interests and the likely benefits of common action in times of crisis. This framework consists of three categories: analytical, procedural and operational. The need for a planning unit is imperative and turned out at Amsterdam to be the simplest requirement to meet. There is still far from an effective solution to the questions of qualified majority, a European security and defence identity or the integration of foreign economic policy and CFSP which were all resolutely discussed during the IGC.

Chapter 4 showed how 'the EU proved unable to manage, let alone settle, the international issues it selected for joint actions', and indicated the main reasons behind the unwillingness of the member states to go beyond international cooperation within this field of policy making. Catriona Gourlay and Eric Remacle (Chapter 5) elaborate further on these reasons and tell the story of the CFSP through the Amsterdam summit. They focus mainly on the CFSP and argue that in these matters 'the European Union continues to oscillate between the French–German conception of a powerful Europe and the acceptance of US predominance in the post Cold War world order, and demonstrates parallel tensions between integrationists and intergovernmentalists.' They have perhaps a more optimistic view on the future functioning of the CFSP than do most of the other authors, but even they state that the CFSP is likely to remain limited to a few non-vital areas and that the EU in the foreseeable future is likely to 'remain largely a civilian power under the security umbrella of the US'.

The main characters: their interests, attitudes, actions and successes

In this volume we have investigated the interests and actions of four of the main actors involved in the CFSP process.

The most important, often difficult, and contradictory actor is France. Yves Boyer has in his chapter presented an interesting account of French foreign and security policy within the framework of the EU. He has particularly emphasized how domestic crises in France are affecting France's role in the CFSP process by noting that France's role has been decided by the government despite the relative disinterest of the public at large, for whom domestic issues are of greater concern.

According to Reimund Seidelmann (Chapter 7) Germany's role in the difficult, and disappointing, process of constructing a CFSP is important for three reasons. First of all, it must be noted that the contradiction is one that is to be found equally in other member countries. For even though Germany belongs to the strong supporters of integration in general, it cannot accept a reduction in the strong role of the US in NATO, or a weakening of its external defence identity or its defence industry. In sum, his argument is that 'there is no feasible strategy to stop or counterbalance Germany's new power. Control through integration means increasing Germany's net advantage, and continuation of the status quo means precisely not being able to control Germany's power. Even the most restrained and cooperative German policies can only lessen and not overcome this dilemma.'

Spain and Britain are to some extent two member countries on opposite sides of the spectrum in their support for increased integration in the Common Foreign and Security Policy area. Clarke argues (Chapter 8) that 'In looking at national approaches to European security after the Cold War it is difficult to resist the conclusion that Britain is a status quo power in a situation where the status quo is rapidly changing.' Britain has some very singular characteristics: it is strongly in favour of a strong defence, but extremely sceptical at the prospect that the EU should move towards a common European defence policy. Spain, on the other hand, is in the main-stream of EU foreign policy making, supporting a gradual approach towards a more effective and efficient CFSP.

Amsterdam: a rehearsal or a new beginning?

The main challenge before the Union today is the necessity of increased political cooperation in line with the success of economic and monetary cooperation. This need is further heightened by dramatic developments at the frontiers of the EU. The Amsterdam summit did not, however, manage to resolve fundamental problems related to the functioning of the Common Foreign and Security Policy. At Maastricht this issue had already been put on the agenda of the Amsterdam IGC. The focus of the negotiations in the IGC was, nevertheless, rather different (Ludlow, 1997).

In addition to the main paradox discussed in this book, of the lack of willingness to give increased power to supranational institutions in spite of the need for supranational solutions, there were other more specific events which influenced the negotiations and the outcome in Amsterdam. Both the nature of European security problems and the relationship between the three principal players, EU, WEU and NATO, had changed.

The nature of the conflicts in the post Cold War Europe was quite differ-ent and the new security agenda was much more complicated and complex than was thought in 1991. The rise of intrastate conflict after the fall of the Berlin Wall meant that security organizations had to rethink their strategies to meet the security needs of the new world order. Additionally, economic decline and the collapse of infrastructures began to be regarded as real security issues, perhaps better solved by organizations such as the EU. More and more, 'soft security' became as important as 'hard security'.

Meanwhile, the role of NATO has undergone changes, in part as a response to post Cold War security needs, and in part due to the substan-tially expanding membership of the organization. Closer integration in the relationship between WEU and EU has not materialized, as was assumed at Maastricht. This is partly a result of the changing role of the WEU from Maastricht up to the deliberations at the Amsterdam summit in 1997. These changes and the subsequent implications for cooperation in this field have been described in greater detail in previous chapters of this book, most notably Chapters 3, 4 and 5. These chapters also illustrate what have prob-ably come to be regarded as some of the most debilitating experiences that the EU member countries have undergone since 1991. These experiences arose from conflicts in which the EU has attempted involvement through the CFSP framework. The disastrous experience of the EU and its member states in the former Yugoslavia in particular has had an enormously nega-tive effect on the CFSP.

The result of this changed scenario in 1997 was that large steps and grand designs were not expected in the Amsterdam Treaty, as indeed turned out to be the case. Some of the countries could perhaps have wished for more dramatic changes, but they had little chance of success. What was achieved were only three new elements in the CFSP. First of all, there was one small step towards a much needed more efficient functioning of the CFSP through a central planning unit and the strengthening of the position in CFSP matters of the Secretary-General of the Council. Secondly, there was an inclusion of the Petersberg tasks in the definition of the scope of EU defence policy. Finally, the Treaty allowed a little more flexibility in the decision-making process by introducing constructive abstention and qualified majority voting in relation to the adaptation and implementation of joint actions or common positions, although subject to a veto right.

In sum, the Treaty of Amsterdam shows yet again that foreign and security policy diverges significantly from all other policy areas within the Union. Unlike the third pillar on justice and home affairs, the second pillar has not, thus far, suggested a slow evolution into the institutional set-up of the Community. The CFSP continues to run parallel to the Community and, as we have seen, has developed distinct institutional features differing from normal Community logic. This development also strengthens the inter-governmental nature of this policy area. The Treaty of Amsterdam leaves the underlying intergovernmental principles of the second pillar untouched. As such, the outcome of the IGC appears, at least for the impartial outside observer, only to keep in place the post-Maastricht status quo. But is this the whole truth about its functioning and the possibility for its future development?

What, if any, will be the implications of the changes in Amsterdam for the functioning of the CFSP after the Amsterdam Treaty has been ratified? The simplest answer is: not very much. If the new secretariat should have an effect, the ministries of foreign affairs in the member countries have to be loyal rather than continuously involved in competing analysis and planning activities. The effect of using the Secretary-General instead of a Ms/Mr CFSP responsible for foreign policy formulation and implementation depends, to a large extent, on the person who is chosen to fill the post in the future.

Regarding the future development of the CFSP, the Amsterdam Treaty will not mean that much. The most promising element in the Treaty is the new provisions for constructive abstention and qualified majority voting, if they can be expanded into a more general flexibility clause at a future IGC. During Amsterdam, this effort was blocked by the British. With an increased number of members and very different foreign and security policy ambitions, greater flexibility will become a must for any further develop-ment. As regards the WEU, its gradual inclusion into the second pillar seems, at the time of writing, an even more unlikely outcome.

Finally, if anything can be learned from the process of European inte-gration so far, and in particular the CFSP, it must be that Community integration is a long and time consuming process where the member states, and especially the large states, often have both the desire and the power to slow down the process rather than to speed it up. Thus the creation of a really well-functioning Common Foreign and Security Policy in the Union will remain a very difficult task for the future. We hope that this book has been constructive in indicating some of the reasons why.

Bibliography

Abdelnasser, Walid Mahmoud (1994) *The Islamic Movement in Egypt: Perceptions of International Relations 1967–1981*. London: Graduate Institute of International Studies, Geneva and Kegan Paul.

Abescat, Bruno (1996) 'La Cohorte des patrons devant la justice', *L'Express*, 11 July.

Abu-Amr, Ziad (1994) *Islamic Fundamentalism in the West Bank and Gaza*. Indianapolis: Indiana University Press.

AbuKhalil, As'ad (1994) 'The Incoherence of Islamic Fundamentalism: Arab Islamic Thought at the End of the 20th Century', *The Middle East Journal*, 48 (4).

Adenauer, Konrad (1967) *Erinnerungen*, vol. I (1945–1953). Frankfurt.

Ad Hoc Committee for Institutional Affairs (1985) *Report to the European Council* (SN/1187/85 (SPAAK 11). Brussels, 29–30 March.

Adviesraad Vrede en Veiligheid (1996) *Een nieuwe uitdaging: Europa 1996*. The Hague.

Agence Europe (1995a) no. 6452, Brussels, 31 March.

Agence Europe (1995b) no. 6462, Brussels, 14 April.

Agence Europe (1995c) no. 6474, Brussels, 5 May.

Agence Europe (1995d) no. 6484, Brussels, 19 May.

Agence Europe (1997a) no. 6941, Brussels, 24–5 March.

Agence Europe (1997b) no. 7018, Brussels, 17 July.

Ahmad, Feroz (1993) *The Making of Modern Turkey*. London: Routledge.

Ainscow, K. (1993) 'La Recherche de technologies à faible coût pour le futur aéronef de combat', *Défense et technologie international*, no. 14, June.

Ajami, Fouad (1995) 'The Sorrows of Egypt', *Foreign Affairs*, 74 (5): 72–88.

Alert (1996) 'A Security Role for the European Union', no. 10.

Aliboni, R. (1994a) 'Islam: Problems, Perspectives and Western Policies', in *Collection of Syntheses of Research Reports on Strategic Studies and International Politics: Military Centre of Strategic Studies*. Rome: Photolithography of the Center for Higher Studies of Defence. Ch. IV.

Aliboni, R. (1994b) 'South Mediterranean Countries and European Politics', in *Collection of Syntheses of Research Reports on Strategic Studies and International Politics: Military Centre of Strategic Studies*. Rome: Photolithography of the Center for Higher Studies of Defence. Ch. XVI.

Allen, D. (1996) 'Conclusions: The European Rescue of National Foreign Policy?', in Christopher Hill (ed.), *The Actors in European Foreign Policy*. London: Routledge.

Allen, D. and Smith, M. (1990) 'Western Europe's Presence in the Contemporary International Arena', *Review of International Studies*, 16 (1), January.

Alonso Zaldívar, C. (1992) 'El año en que acabó un mundo. La política exterior de España en 1991', in *Anuario Internacional CIDOB 1991*. Barcelona: CIDOB.

Alonso Zaldívar, C. and Ortega, A. (1992) 'The Gulf Crisis and European Cooperation on Security Issues: Spanish Reactions and the European Framework', in N. Gnessoto and J. Roper (eds), *Western Europe and the Gulf*. Paris: Institute for Security Studies.

Amnesty International (1996) *Memorandum: Proposals for a Strengthened Protection of Human Rights by the European Union in the Context of the Intergovernmental Conference 1996*.

ARENA (1995) *Enlargement to the East*. ARENA Conference Series, University of Oslo, December.

Assemblée de l'UEO (1995) *Le GAEO: la voie à suivre*. Document 1483, Paris, 6 November.

Auswärtiges Amt (1996) *Deutsche Ziele für die Regierungskonferenz*. Bonn, 26 March.

Ayata, Sencer (1996) 'Patronage, Party, and the State: The Politicization of Islam in Turkey', *The Middle East Journal*, 50 (1).

Baleanu, V. G. (1994) 'A Conflict of Contemporary Europe: Is it the Case that before there can be Europeans, there must be Europe?' Internet edition. gopher://marvin.stc.nato.int:70/00/secdef/csrc/europe.txt. Conflict Studies Research Centre.

Barbé, E. (1991) 'España y el Mediterráneo en el nuevo equilibrio europeo', in *Anuario Internacional CIDOB 1990*. Barcelona: CIDOB. pp. 75–82.

Barbé, E. (1994) 'Spanish Responses to the Security Institutions of the New Europe', in A. Williams (ed.), *Reorganizing Eastern Europe: European Institutions and the Refashioning of Europe's Security Architecture*. Aldershot: Dartmouth.

Barbé, E. (1995) 'European Political Cooperation: The Upgrading of Spanish Foreign Policy', in R. Gillespie, F. Rodrigo and J. Story (eds), *Democratic Spain: Reshaping External Relations in a Changing World*. London: Routledge.

Barbé, E. (1996a) 'Spain: The Uses of Foreign Policy Cooperation', in Christopher Hill (ed.), *The Actors in European Foreign Policy*. London: Routledge.

Barbé, E. (1996b) 'Spain: Realist Integrationism', in F. Algieri and E. Regelsberger (eds), *Synergy at Work: Spain and Portugal in European Foreign Policy*. Bonn: Europa Union Verlag. pp. 259–78.

Barbé, E. (1996c) 'The Barcelona Conference: Launching Pad of a Process', *Mediterranean Politics*, 1 (1): 25–42.

Barbé, E. (1997a) 'European Values and National Interests', in A. Landau and R. Whitman (eds), *Rethinking the European Union: Institutions, Interests and Identities*. London: Macmillan. pp. 129–46.

Barbé, E. (1997b) 'De la ingenuidad al pragmatismo: 10 años de participación española en la maquinaria diplomática europea', *Revista CIDOB d'Afers Internacionals*, no. 34–5: 9–30.

Barham, J. (1997) 'A Near Miracle of Resilience', *Financial Times Survey: Turkish Finance and Industry*. Friday, 12 December.

Baylis, John (1984) *Anglo-American Defence Relations 1939–1980*. London: Macmillan.

Benelux (1996)Memorandum, March.

Bennett, Peter and Gourlay, Catriona (1997) *The European Union's Common Foreign and Security Policy: The Policy Planning Dimension*. Brussels ISIS Briefing Paper 13, September.

Bennetto, Jason (1995) 'Paris Bomber Based in London' and 'Islamic Exiles Flocking to Safe Haven in London', *The Guardian*, 4 November.

Berberoglu, Berek (ed.) (1989) *Power and Stability in the Middle East*. London: Zed.

Bertelsmann Stiftung (1995) *Interim Report of a Working Group on CFSP and the Future of the European Union*. Munich, July.

Berthiaume, Christiane (1995) 'Asylum under Threat', *Refugees*, 3 (101).

Blair, Tony (1997) Statement to the House of Commons, 18 June.

Bloes, Robert (1970) *Le Plan Fouchet et le problème de l'Europe politique*. Bruges: College of Europe.

Bluth, Christoph, Kirchner, Emil and Sperling, James (eds) (1995) *The Future of European Security Policy*. Aldershot: Dartmouth.

Boissonat, Jean (1997) Interview, *Le Monde*, 28 January.

Bonino, Emma (1995) 'La Réforme de la politique étrangère et de sécurité commune: aspects institutionnels', *Revue du Marché unique européen*, 3: 261–78.

Borderas, M. (1994) *L'Agence europénne de l'armement: réponse au trente-neuviéme rapport du Conceil*. Document 1419, Assemblée de l'UEO, Paris, 19 May.

Boutros-Ghali, Boutros (1996) 'The Marginalization of Africa', *Mediterranean Quarterly*, 17 April.

Boutros-Ghali, B. (no date) 'The Marginalization of Africa', *Mediterranean Quarterly*. Articles from prevoius issues. Internet edition.

Boyer, Yves (1994) 'Technologies, défense et relations transatlantiques', *Politique étrangère*, Paris, no. 4: 1005–15.

Brundtland, Gro Harlem and Solana, Javier (1996) *NATO and our Common Security*. Norwegian Atlantic Committee, Security Policy Library 6/1996.

Bruni, Michele and Venturini, Alessandra (1995) 'Pressure to Migrate and Propensity to Emigrate: The Case of the Mediterranean Basin', *International Labour Review*, 134 (3).

Burgat, Francois (1994) *The Islamic Movement in North Africa*. Austin, TX: University of Texas Press.

Burghardt, Günther (1995) 'Politique étrangère et de sécurité commune: garantir la stabilité à long terme de l'Europe', *Revue du Marché unique européen*, 3: 261–78.

Buzan, Barry (1991) *People, States and Fear: An Agenda for International Security Studies in the Post-Cold War Era*, 2nd edn. Hemel Hempstead: Harvester Wheatsheaf.

Cahen, Alfred (1989) *The Western European Union and NATO: Building a European Defence Identity within the Context of Atlantic Solidarity*. Brassey's Atlantic Commentaries 2. London: Brassey's.

Cameron, Fraser (1995) 'The European Union and the Challenges of Enlargement', in *Enlargement to the East*. Oslo: ARENA, University of Oslo.

Cameron, Fraser (1997) 'Where the European Commission Comes In: From the Single European Act to Maastricht', in Elfriede Regelsberger, Philippe de Schoutheete de Tervarent and Wolfgang Wessels (eds), *Foreign Policy of the European Union: From EPC to CFSP and Beyond*. Boulder, CO: Lynne Rienner. pp. 99–108.

Carlsnæs, Walter and Smith, Steve (eds) (1994) *European Foreign Policy: The EC and Changing Perspectives in Europe*. London: Sage.

Cassandra (1995) 'The Impending Crisis in Egypt', *The Middle East Journal*, 49 (1).

Challenge Europe (1997) *1997: State of the Debate: The Uncertainties of Amsterdam*. European Policy Centre, no. 4, May/June.

Chase, Robert S., Hill, Emily B. and Kennedy, Paul (1996) 'Pivotal States and U.S. Strategy', *Foreign Affairs*, 75 (1): 33–51.

Chilton, Patricia (1995) 'Mechanics of Change: Social Movements, Transnational Coalitions, and the Transformation Processes in Eastern Europe', in Thomas Risse-Kappen (ed.), *Bringing Transnational Relations Back In: Non-State Actors, Domestic Structures and International Institutions*. Cambridge: Cambridge University Press.

Chilton, Patricia (1996) *The Defence Dimension of the IGC: An Alternative Agenda*. ISIS Europe Briefing 2, Brussels, March.

Chirac, Jacques (1996) Speech at the WEU Parliamentary Assembly, Paris, 3 December.

Chirac, Jacques and Jospin, Lionel (1997) Joint Press Conference Held by President Chirac and Prime Minister Jospin, Amsterdam, 17 June.

Church, George (1992) 'Across the Great Divide', *Time*, 19 October.

Clad, James C. (1994) 'Slowing the Wave', *Foreign Policy*, no. 95, pp. 139–41.

Clarke, Michael (1990) 'The Europeanisation of NATO and the Problem of Anglo-American Relations', in M. Clarke and R. Hague (eds), *European Defence Cooperation*. Manchester: Manchester University Press. pp. 29–33.

Clarke, Michael (1992a) 'A British View', in R. Davy (ed.), *European Detente: A Reappraisal*. London: Sage. pp. 90–7.

Clarke, Michael (1992b) *British External Policy-Making in the 1990s.* London: Macmillan/RIIA. pp. 183–4.

Clarke, Michael (1995) 'The Lessons of Bosnia for the British Military', in *Brassey's Defence Yearbook 1995.* London: Brassey's. pp. 51–2.

Cleveland, William L. (1994) *A History of the Modern Middle East.* USA: Westview.

Cohen-Seat, J. (1997) 'Le Pays est à bout', *Le Monde,* 12 June.

Commissariat Général du Plan (1993) *L'Avenir des industries liées à la défense.* La Documentation française, Paris, November.

Commission des Communautés Européennes (1990) *Avis de la Commission du 21 octobre 1990 relatif au projet de révision du Traité instituant la Communauté économique européenne concernant l'Union politique.* COM(90) 600 final, Brussels.

Commission européenne (1996) *Les Défis auxquels sont confrontées les industries européennes liées à la défense: contribution en vue d'actions au niveau européen.* COM (96) 10 final, 24 January.

Conference of the Representatives of the Governments of the Member States (1996a) *CFSP Decision-Making Procedures.* Doc. CONF 3824/96, 24 April.

Conference of the Representatives of the Governments of the Member States (1996b) *Security and Defence, Common Defence Policy and Common Defence, Article J.4 of the TEU.* Doc. CONF 3828/96, 26 April.

Conference of the Representatives of the Governments of the Member States (1996c) *Note from the Presidency.* Doc. CONF 3850/96, 24 May.

Conference of the Representatives of the Governments of the Member States (1996d) *Progress Report on the Intergovernmental Conference from the Presidency to the European Council.* Doc. CONF. 3860/1/96, 17 June.

Conference of the Representatives of the Governments of the Member States (1996e) *Presidency Introduction Note.* Doc. CONF 3868/96, 16 July.

Conference of the Representatives of the Governments of the Member States (1996f) *Memorandum by the United Kingdom, CFSP Planning Cell, Terms of Reference.* Doc. CONF 3894/96, July.

Conference of the Representatives of the Governments of the Member States (1996g) *Proposals for Treaty Amendments: Security and Defence, from the Finnish and Swedish Delegations.* Doc. CONF 3946/96, 8 October.

Conference of the Representatives of the Governments of the Member States (1996h) *Draft on the Flexibility from the Portuguese Delegation.* Doc. CONF 3999/96, 29 November.

Conference of the Representatives of the Governments of the Member States (1996i) *The European Union Today and Tomorrow: Adapting the European Union for the Benefit of its Peoples and Preparing it for the Future: A General Outline for a Draft Revision of the Treaties.* Doc. CONF 2500/96, 5 December.

Conference of the Representatives of the Governments of the Member States (1997a) *Draft on the Flexibility from the Italian Delegation.* Doc. CONF 3801/97, 15 January.

Conference of the Representatives of the Governments of the Member States (1997b) *Addendum to the General Outline for the Draft Revision of the Treaties.* Doc. CONF 2500/96 ADD. 1, March.

Conference of the Representatives of the Governments of the Member States (1997c) *Compilation of Texts under Discussion: An Effective and Coherent Foreign Policy.* Doc. SN 541/97 (C42), May.

Conference of the Representatives of the Governments of the Member States (1997d) *The Draft Treaty of Amsterdam.* Doc. CONF 4000/97, 12 June.

Conference of the Representatives of the Governments of the Member States (1997e) *Draft Treaty of Amsterdam.* Doc. CONF 4001/97, 19 June.

Conference of the Representatives of the Governments of the Member States (1997f) *Consolidated Draft Treaty Texts.* Doc. SN 600/97 (C101), 30 May.

Conferencia (1995) *La Conferencia Intergubernamental de 1996: Bases para una reflexión*, 2 March. Madrid: Ministerio de Asuntos Exteriores.

Conry, Barbara (1997) 'North Africa on the Brink', *Mediterranean Quarterly*, 8 (1): 115–31.

Council of Ministers of the Western European Union (1994) *Noordvijk Declaration*. 14 November.

Council of Ministers of the Western European Union (1995a) *Lisbon Declaration*. 15 May.

Council of Ministers of the Western European Union (1995b) *WEU Contribution to the European Union's Intergovernmental Conference of 1996*. Madrid, 14 November.

Cox, A. and Hartley, K. (1994) *The Cost of Non-Europe in Defence Procurement*. Executive Summary, Commission européenne, DG III, Bruxelles.

CREST Monography (1996) 'La Conférence Intergouvernmentale de 1996: Quelle perspective pour la politique extérieure et de sécurité commune?', April.

Crewe, Ivor (1985) 'Britain: Two and a Half Cheers for the Atlantic Alliance', in G. Flynn and H. Rattinger (eds), *The Public and Atlantic Defence*. London: Croom Helm. pp. 26–9.

Dannreuther, Roland (1994) *Creating New States in Central Asia*. Adelphi Paper 288, March.

Dannreuther, Roland (1997) *Eastward Enlargement: NATO and the EU*. Institutt for Forsvarsindustri, 1/1997, Oslo.

Davidson, Ian (1996) 'Nerve fails in Paris', *Financial Times*, 4 December.

de Charrette, Hervé (1996) Speech before the European Movement, Paris, 26 June.

de Charrette, Hervé (1997) Speech with French businessmen, Singapore, 14 February.

de Charrette, Hervé and Kinkel, Klaus (1996) Letter to Dick Spring, President on Office of the Council. 'Enhanced Cooperation with the Purpose of European Construction: The Franco-German Contribution within the IGC'. 17 October.

Dehaene, Jean-Luc (1996) Speech at the WEU Assembly, 4 June.

Deighton, Anne (ed.) (1997) *Western European Union 1954–1997: Defence, Security, Integration*. Oxford: European Interdependence Research Unit, St Anthony's College.

Delrapport til Europautredningen (1992) *Rapport fra en arbeidsgruppe nedsatt av Statssekretærutvalget for Europautredningen*.

de Rochebrune, Renaud (1996) 'Economie et Affaires: L'Aide Recule. Tant Mieux?', *Jeune Afrique*, no. 1826, 4–10 January.

d'Estaing, Valéry Giscard (1997) 'Après le naufrage d'Amsterdam', *L'Express*, 3 July.

Deutsch, Karl W. (1978) *The Analysis of International Relations*. Englewood Cliffs, NJ: Prentice-Hall.

de Vasconcelos, Alvaro (1991) 'The New Europe and the Western Mediterranean', *NATO Review*, 39 (5).

de Vestel, Pierre (ed.) (1994) *L'Industrie européenne de l'armement: recherche, développement, technologie, reconversion*. Dossiers du GRIP, Bruxelles.

de Vestel, Pierre (1995) *Les Marchés et les industries de défense en Europe: l'heure des politiques?* Cahier de Chaillot no. 21, Institut d'Etudes de Sécurité de l'UEO, Paris, November.

Diario (1996) 'Diario de Sesiones del Congreso de los Diputados. Comisiones', *Defensa*, no. 21, 6 June.

Dickey, Christopher (1995a) 'The Masks of Algiers', *Newsweek*, 12 June.

Dickey, Christopher (1995b) 'No Mercy, No Apology', *Newsweek*, 19 June.

Dictamen (1995) 'Dictamen de la Comisión Mixta para la Ponencia Europea en relación con el informe elaborado por la ponencia sobre consecuencias para España de la ampliación de la Unión Europea y reformas instituciones

(Conferencia Intergubernamental, 1996)', *Boletín Oficial de las Cortes Generales. Sección Cortes Generales*, Serie A, no. 82, 29 December.

Diedrichs, U. and Wessels, W. (1996) 'From Newcomers to Mainstreamers: Lessons from Spain and Portugal', in F. Algieri and E. Regelsberger (eds), *Synergy at Work: Spain and Portugal in European Foreign Policy*. Bonn: Europa Union.

Dini, Lamberto and de Charrette, Hervé (1997) 'Innover pour progresser', *Le Monde*, 25 March.

Document (1995) *Reflection Document on the WEU contribution to the Intergovernmental Conference on 1996*. Madrid, Ministerio de Asuntos Exteriores, 4 July.

Dorr, Noel (1996) Speech at the Institutional Affairs Committee of the European Parliament, 18 December.

Duncan, Andrew, Clarke, Michael and Stevens, David (1995) *Contingency Forces Available among WEU Member, Associate and Observer States*. London: Centre for Defence Studies.

Duquesne, Jacques (1996) 'La Société francaise en panne', *Ouest France*, 23 July.

Eaton, M. (1994) 'Common Foreign and Security Policy in Legal Issues of the Maastricht Treaty', in D. O'Keefe and P. Twomey (eds). Chancery Law Publishing.

EDIG (1995) *The European Defence Industry: An Agenda Item for the 1996 Intergovenmental Conference*. Memorandum by the European Defence Industry Group, Brussels, May.

Edwards, G. and Nuttall, S. (1994) in A. Duff, J. Pinder and R. Pryce (eds), *Common Foreign and Security Policy in Maastricht and Beyond*. London: Routledge.

Edwards, Geoffrey and Regelsberger, Elfriede (eds) (1990) *Europe's Global Links: The European Community and Inter-Regional Cooperation*. London: Pinter.

Edwards, Geoffrey and Spence, David (eds) (1997) *The European Commission*, 2nd edn. London: Cartermill.

Ehlermann, Claus-Dieter (1995) 'Différenciation accrue ou uniformité renforcée?', *Revue du Marché unique européen*, 3: 191–217.

Entretien (1990) 'Un Entretien avec M. Felipe González', *Le Monde*, 20 November.

Erlanger, Steven (1996) 'Making the Bosnia Deal Work: US Carrots and Sticks', *International Herald Tribune*, 5 February.

Esposito, John L. (1994) 'Political Islam: Beyond the Green Menace', *Current History*, January: 19–24.

European Commission (1994) *The European Report on Science and Technology Indicators 1994*.

European Commission (1995a) *Report of the Commission for the Reflection Group*. Brussels: Intergovernmental Conference, May.

European Commission (1995b) *Note d'information présentée par Monsieur le Président, Monsieur Oreja et Monsieur Van de Broek*. Brussels: European Commission, Séminaire de la Commission sur la Politique extérieure et de sécurité commune, 19 July.

European Commission (1996a) *Reinforcing Political Union and Preparing for the Enlargement: Commission's Opinion for the Intergovernmental Conference*. Brussels: European Commission, Doc. COM(96)90, 28 February.

European Commission (1996b) *The Challenges that Face European Industries Linked to Defence. Contribution with a View to Actions at European Level*. Brussels: European Commission, Doc. COM(96)10, 24 January.

European Commission (1997) *Composition, Organization and Functioning of the Commission: Contribution of the European Commission to the Intergovernmental Conference*. Doc. CONF 3839/97, 6 March.

European Communities Council (1992) *Treaty on European Union*. Luxembourg: Office for Official Publications of the European Communities.

European Parliament (1997) *Resolution on the General Framework for a Draft Treaty Review*. Doc. b4-0040/97, Brussels, 16 January.

Europe Documents (1991) *Conférence Intergouvernamentale sur l'Union Politique:*

Le *'communiqué conjoint' franco-allemand-espagnol*. Europe Documents 1737, 17 October.

Eurostep (1996) *A Global Foreign Policy for Europe*. Oxfam UK, May.

Eurostep (1997) *Planning for Global Foreign Policy*. Oxfam UK, February.

Evans, G. (1994) 'Cooperative Security and Intrastate Conflict', *Foreign Policy*, 96 (Autumn): 3–20.

Evcan, Sirma (1997) 'Respect for Human Rights is a Matter of Education and a Change of Mentality', *Turkish Daily News*, 15 September.

Fandy, Mamoun (1994) 'Egypt's Islamic Group: Regional Revenge?', *The Middle East Journal*, 48 (4).

Faria, F. and Vasconcelos, A. (1996) *Security in Northern Africa: Ambiguity and Reality*. Chaillot Papers 25, Institute for Security Studies, Paris.

Federal Trust (1995) *Security of the Union: The Intergovernmental Conference of the European Union 1996*. Federal Trust Paper 4, London, October.

Financial Times (1995) 'Financial Times Survey: Turkey', 12 June: 1–8.

Financial Times (1996) 'Financial Times Survey: Turkey', 3 June: 1–6.

Financial Times (1997a) 'Italy Breaks Ranks to Suggest EMU Delay', 26 March.

Financial Times (1997b) 'WEU Merger Plan on Agenda', 13 May.

Foreign and Commonwealth Office (1996) *Partnership of Nations*. March.

Forster, A. and Wallace, W. (1996) 'Common Foreign and Security Policy: A New Policy or Just a Name?', in Helen Wallace and William Wallace (eds), *Policy-Making in the European Union*. Oxford: Oxford University Press.

Freedman, Lawrence (1996) 'Wars of Necessity and Wars of Choice', in *Brassey's Defence Yearbook 1996*. London: Brassey's/Centre for Defence Studies. pp. 1–12.

French–German Foreign Ministers Seminar (1996) *Common Foreign and Security Policy*. Freiburg, 27 February.

Fricaud-Chagnaud, C. G. and Patry, J. J. (1994) *Mourir pour le roi de Prusse*. Paris: Publisud.

Fuller, Graham (1995) 'The Next Ideology', *Foreign Policy*, Spring: 145–58.

Fuller, Graham E. and Lesser, Ian O. (1995) *A Sense of Seige: The Geopolitics of Islam and the West*. USA: Westview.

Galbraith, J. K. (1969) *How to Control the Military*. New York: New American Library.

Gambles, I. (1991) *L'Intégration européenne de sécurité dans les années 90*. Cahier de Chaillot no. 3, Institut d'Etudes de Sécurité de l'UEO, Paris, November.

Gaspar, Carlos (1994) 'Europe and the Middle East: At the Crossroads', *NATO Review*, 42 (5).

GEIP (1988) *Action Plan on a Stepwise Development of a European Armament Market*. 9 November.

Gerges, Fawaz A. (1995) 'Egyptian-Israeli Relations Turn Sour', *Foreign Affairs*, 74 (3): 69–77.

Ginsberg, R. H. (1997) 'The EU's CFSP: The Politics of Procedure', in M. Holland (ed.), *Common Foreign and Security Policy: The Record and Reforms*. London: Pinter.

Gordon, Philip H. (ed.) (1997) 'The Western European Union and NATO's "Europeanisation"', in Philip H. Gordon (ed.), *NATO's Transformation: The Changing Shape of the Atlantic Alliance*. London: Rowman and Littlefield. pp. 257–70.

Grunert, Thomas (1997) 'The Association of the European Parliament: No Longer the Underdog in EPC?', in Elfriede Regelsberger, Philippe de Schouteheete de Tervarent and Wolfgang Wessels (eds), *Foreign Policy of the European Union: From EPC to CFSP*. Bonn. pp. 109–31.

Guéhenno, J.-M. (1995) 'Sécurité européenne: l'impossible statu quo', *Politique étrangère*, no. 1.

Haas, E. B. (1958) *The Uniting of Europe: Political, Social and Economic Forces, 1950–57*. Stanford: Stanford University Press.

Haas, E. B. (1967) 'The Uniting of Europe and The Uniting of Latin America', *Journal of Common Market Studies*, 5(4): 315–44.

Haftendorn, Helga (1986) *Sicherheit und Entspannung: Zur Außenpolitik der Bundesrepublik Deutschland 1955–1982*. Baden-Baden.

Halliday, Fred (1996) *Islam and the Myth of Confrontation*. London: Tauris.

Handl, Vladimir (1993) 'The West European Integration in the Political and Security Area and the Widening of the EC: A View from Eastern Europe', in Wolfgang Wessels and Christian Engel (eds), *The European Union in the 1990s: Ever Closer and Larger?* Bonn: Europa Union.

Hanrieder, W. F. (1978) 'Dissolving International Politics: Reflections of the Nation State', *American Political Science Review*, 72 (4): 1276–87.

Hanrieder, Wolfram F. (1995) *Deutschland, Europa, Amerika: Die Außenpolitik der Bundesrepublik Deutschland 1949–1994*. Paderborn.

Harries, Owen (1993) 'The Collapse of the West', *Foreign Affairs*, 72 (4): 41–53.

Hartley, Keith (1991) *The Economics of Defence Policy*. London: Brassey's.

Hartley, Keith and Martin, Stephen (1993) 'The Political Economy of International Collaboration', in Richard Coopey, Matthew Uttley and Graham Spinardi (eds), *Defence Science and Technology: Adjusting to Change*. Suisse: Harwood.

Hebert, Jean-Paul (1991) *Stratégie française et industrie d'armement*. Paris: Fondation des Etudes de Défense Nationale.

Heiberg, Esben Oust (1996) 'EU and Enlargement to the North and the East: What will this mean for a Common Foreign and Security Policy in the European Union?' Working Paper 1996/3 CEAS, Norwegian School of Management.

Heuser, Beatrice (1996) *The Transatlantic Relationship*. Chatham House Paper, RIIA, London.

High-Level Expert Group on CFSP (1994) *European Security Policy Towards 2000: Ways and Means to Establish Genuine Credibility*. Brussels, 19 December.

High-Level Expert Group on CFSP (1995) *European Security Policy Towards 2000: Ways and Means to Establish Genuine Credibility*. Brussels, 28 November.

High-Level Expert Group on CFSP, Subcommittee (1995) *The Industrial, Scientific and Technological Basis for Defence in Europe*. Brussels, 25 October.

Hill, Christopher (1993) 'The Capability–Expectation Gap, or Conceptualizing Europe's International Role', *Journal of Common Market Studies*, 31 (3): 305–28.

Hill, Christopher (ed.) (1996) *The Actors in European Foreign Policy*. London: Routledge.

Hill, Christopher and Wallace, H. (1996) 'Introduction: Actors and Actions', in C. Hill (ed.), *The Actors in European Foreign Policy*. London: Routledge.

Hirst, David (1995) 'As Night Falls, the Hideous Terror Begins', *The Guardian*, 15 November.

HMSO (1995a) 'Stable Forces in a Strong Britain', in *Statement on the Defence Estimates 1995*. London: HMSO. Cm 2800. p. 22, par. 234.

HMSO (1995b) *Statement on the Defence Estimates 1995*. London: HMSO. Cm 2800.

HMSO (1996) *Statement on the Defence Estimates 1996*. London: HMSO. Cm 3223.

Hocking, B. (ed.) (1998) *Foreign Ministry Reform*. London: Macmillan.

Holland, Martin (1993a) *European Community Integration*. New York: St Martin's.

Holland, Martin (1993b) *European Integration: From Community to Union*. London: Pinter.

Holland, Martin (ed.) (1997) *Common Foreign and Security Policy: The Record and Reforms*. London: Pinter.

Horsman, Matthew and Marshall, Andrew (1994) *After the Nation-State: Citizens, Tribalism and the New World Disorder*. London: HarperCollins.

Howe, G. (1996) 'Bearing More of the Burden: In Search of a European Common Foreign and Security Policy', *The World Today*, January.

HSFK/FEST/ISFH (1996) *Friedensgutachten 1996*. Münster: Hessische Stiftung für Friedens- und Konfliktforschung (HSFK)/Forschungsstätte der Evangelischen

Studiengemeinde (FEST)/Institut für Friedensforschung und Sicherheitspolitik an der Universität Hamburg (ISFH).

Hübertz, Unni (1996) *Fra Alliansepolitikk til Kollektiv Sikkerhet*. Hovedoppgave i statsvitenskap, University of Oslo.

Huntington, Samuel P. (1993) 'The Clash of Civilizations?', *Foreign Affairs*, 72 (3): 22–49.

Hurd, Douglas (1991) (writing as Foreign Secretary) 'No European Defence Identity Without NATO', *Financial Times*, 15 April, p. 15.

Imbert P. and Grilli, G. (1994) 'La Politique industrielle de l'ESA: le concept évolutif du juste retour', *ESA Bulletin*, no. 78, May.

Institut d'Etudes européennes Université libre de Bruxelles and Groupe D'Etudes politiques européennes (1994) *La Differenciation dans l'Union européenne*. Brussels, 10 December.

Irish Government (1996) *Challenges and Opportunities Abroad*. Dublin.

ISFH (1996) *OSZE-Jahrbuch 1996*. Baden-Baden: Institut für Friedensforschung und Sicherheitspolitik an der Universität Hamburg.

Isnard, Jacques (1996) 'La France tente d'obtenir un graud commandement régional de l'OTAN', *Le Monde*, 21–2 July.

Istituto Affari Internazionali (1996) *Revision of Maastricht: Implementation and Proposals for Reform. A Survey of National Views*. January–June, IAI, Rome.

Jane's Defence Weekly (1994) 'Global Update Special Report: Background to a Civil War', 2, pp. 3–6.

Jeune Afrique (1996a) 'Les Defis a Venir', no. 1830, 31 January–6 February.

Jeune Afrique (1996b) 'Le Temps du Maghreb et du Moyen-Orient: L'Algerie Revient en Force', no. 1830, 31 January–6 February.

Jopp, Matthias (1997) 'The Defence Dimension of the European Union: The Role and Performance of the WEU', in Elfriede Regelsberger, Philippe de Schouteheete de Tervarent and Wolfgang Wessels (eds), *Foreign Policy of the European Union: From EPC to CFSP*. Bonn. pp. 153–69.

Jospin, Lionel (1997a) Press Conference at the Franco-German Meeting, Poitiers, 13 June.

Jospin, Lionel (1997b) Speech, Conférence des Ambassadeurs, Paris, 29 August.

Juppé, Alain (1995) 'Quel horizon pour la politique étrangère de la France?', Speech for the 20th Anniversary of the Centre d'Analyse et de Prévision, Paris, 30 January.

Kelle, Alexander and Müller, Harald (1996) 'Germany', in Harald Müller (ed.), *European Non-Proliferation Policy 1993–1995*. Brussels.

Kinkel, Klaus (1996) 'Working Together to Build Europe's New Security Framework', *International Herald Tribune*, 24–5 December.

Kissinger, Henry (1995) *Diplomacy*. New York: Touchstone.

Kreile, Michael (1996) *Germany's Role in Shaping the New Europe: Architect, Model and Bridge*. Department of Political Science, Humboldt University Berlin, Working Paper 7.15, April.

Kupchan, Charles (1995) *Nationalism and Nationalities in the New Europe*. Ithaca: Cornell University Press. A Council on Foreign Relations book.

Lamers, Karl (1997) 'Les Cactus de l'union monétaire', *Le Figaro*, 23 January.

Lang, Jacques (1997) 'Je ne voterai pas le traité d'Amsterdam', *Le Monde,* 19 August.

Laursen, Finn (ed.) (1990) *EFTA and the EC: Implications of 1992*. Maastricht: EIPA.

Laursen, Finn (1992) 'Explaining the Intergovernmental Conference', in Finn Laursen and Sophie Vanhoonacker (eds), *The Intergovernmental Conference on Political Union*. Maastricht: European Institute of Public Administration.

Laursen, Finn and Vanhoonacker, Sophie (eds) (1992) *The Intergovernmental Conference on Political Union*. Dordrecht and Maastricht: Martinus Nijhoff and European Institute of Public Administration.

Laursen, Finn and Vanhoonacker, Sophie (eds) (1994) *The Ratification of the Maastricht Treaty: Issues, Debates and Future Implications*. Dordrecht and Maastricht: Martinus Nijhoff and European Institute of Public Administration.

Lemaître, Philippe (1997) 'Les quinze débattent de la mise en place d'une politique de défense commune', *Le Monde*, 25 March.

Le Monde (1996) 'L'été inquiet de Jacques Chirac', 23 July.

Le Monde (1997) 'L'euro favorisera la stabilité du système monétaire international', interview of Makoto Utsumi, Professor at Keio University in Tokyo, 18 March.

Lesourne, Jacques (1998) 'Vers une Europe anglo-allemande', *Le Monde*, 27 February.

Lesser, Ian O. (1993) 'North–South Issues in a Transatlantic Context', in N. Gantz and J. Roper (eds), *Towards a New Partnership*. USA: Rand Study/Institute for Security Studies of the WEU.

Libération (1996) 25 March.

Lindberg, L. (1963) *The Political Dynamics of European Economic Integration*. London: Oxford University Press.

Lodge, Juliet (ed.) (1989) *The European Community and the Challenge of the Future*. London: Pinter.

London Report (1981) Part II (12).

Lotter, Christoph and Peters, Susanne (eds) (1996) *The Changing European Security Environment*. Köln.

Ludlow, Peter (1997) *A View from Brussels*. Centre for European Policy Studies, Brussels, July.

Macko, Steve (1997) 'Algerian Terrorist Groups', *ENN Intelligence Report*, vol. 3, no. 065, 3 June.

Mandelbaum, Michael (1996) *The Dawn of Peace in Europe*. New York: Twentieth Century Fund.

Manin, Philippe and Louis, Jean-Victor (1996) *Vers une Europe differnciée? Possibilité et limite*. Paris: Pedone.

Marks, J. (1996) 'High Hopes and Low Motives: The New Euro-Mediterranean Partnership Initiative', *Mediterranean Politics*, 1 (1): 1–24.

Marlowe, Lara (1995a) 'Algeria: Ballots, Not Bullets', *TIME Magazine*, 27 November, 146 (22).

Marlowe, Lara (1995b) 'Egypt: Dying for Change', *TIME Magazine*, 11 December: 41.

Martial, Enrico (1992) 'France and European Political Union', in Finn Laursen and Sophie Vanhoonacker (eds), *The Intergovernmental Conference on Political Union*. Maastricht: EIPA.

Martin, L. and Roper, J. (eds) (1995) *Vers une politique de défense commune*. Paris: Groupe stratégique européen–Institut d'Etudes de Sécurité, UEO.

Matthews, Ron, *European Armaments Collaboration*. Suisse: Harwood.

MccGwire, Michael (1997) *NATO Expansion and European Security*. London Defence Studies 37, London: Brassey's/Centre for Defence Studies.

Mearsheimer, John (1990) 'Back to the Future: Instability in Europe after the Cold War', *International Security*, no. 1: 5–56.

Memorandum from Finland and Sweden (1996) *The IGC and the Security and Defence Dimension: Towards an Enhanced EU Role in Crisis Management*. Helsinki–Stockholm, 25 April.

Mesa, R. (1988) *Democracia y política exterior en España*. Madrid: Eudema.

Millon, Charles (1996) 'La France et la rénovation de l'Alliance Atlantique', *Revue de l'OTAN*, May.

Milward, Alan S. (1992) *The European Rescue of the Nation-State*. London: Routledge.

Ministerio de Asuntos Exteriores (1995) *Reflection Document on the WEU Contribution to the Intergovernmental Conference of 1996*. Dirección General de Asuntos Internacionales de Seguridad y Desarme. Madrid, 4 July.

Monar, J. (1997) 'The Financial Dimension of the CFSP', in M. Holland (ed.), *Common Foreign and Security Policy: The Record and the Reforms*. London: Pinter.

Mortimer, Edward (1992) *European Security after the Cold War*. Adelphi Paper 271, London: International Institute for Strategic Studies, Brassey's.

Mortimer, Robert (1996) 'Islamists, Soldiers, and the Democrats: The Second Algerian War', *The Middle East Journal*, 50 (1).

Moscovici, Pierre (1997) Speech at the Chambre de Commerce et d'industrie de Paris, 29 August.

Müller, Harald (ed.) (1996) *European Non-Proliferation Policy 1993–1995*. Brussels, pp. 103–28.

Myers, Julia A. (1993) *The Western European Union: Pillar of NATO or Defence Arm of the EC*. London: Brassey's.

NACC (1993) *Report to the Ministers by NACC Ad Hoc Group on Cooperation in Peacemaking*. Athens, 11 June.

NATO (1993) Press Release M-NACC-2(95)123: Meeting of the North Atlantic Cooperation Council. Follow-on to the 1993 Athens Report on Cooperation in Peacekeeping. Brussels.

NATO (1995a) *Study on NATO Enlargement*. Brussels.

NATO (1995b) *NATO Handbook*. Brussels: Office of Information and Press.

Nelsen, Brent F. and Stubb, Alexander C.-G. (eds) (1994) *The European Union: Readings on the Theory and Practice of European Integration*. Basingstoke: Macmillan.

Newman, M. (1996) 'Concepts and Confusions', in *Democracy, Sovereignty and the European Union*. London: Hurst & Co.

Newsweek (1995) 'They Will Never Come to Power', 19 June: 19.

Norgaard, O., Pedersen, T. and Petersen, N. (eds) (1993) *The European Community in World Politics*. London, New York: Pinter.

Nouvelles Atlantiques (1996a) 'OTAN/Espagne: Le gouvernement de Madrid cherche l'appui du parlement national pour negocier l'integration dans une nouvelle structue militaire alliée. Le probleme de Gibraltar', *Nouvelles Atlantiques*, no. 2486, 13 September.

Nouvelles Atlantiques (1996b) 'OTAN/Dialogue avec des pays de la Méditerranée', *Nouvelles Atlantiques*, no. 2858, 22 October.

Nuttall, Simon (1992) *European Political Cooperation*. Oxford: Clarendon.

Nuttall, Simon (1994) 'The Commission and Foreign Policy-Making', in Geoffrey Edwards and David Spence (eds), *The European Commission*. London: Longman.

Nuttall, Simon (1997) 'The Commission and Foreign Policy-Making', in Geoffrey Edwards and David Spence (eds), *The European Commission*, 2nd edn. London: Cartermill.

O'Keeffe, D. and Twomey, P. (eds) (1994) *Legal Issues of the Maastricht Treaty*. United Kingdom: Chancery.

Önis, Ziya (1995) 'Turkey in the Post-Cold War Era: In Search of Identity', *The Middle East Journal*, 49 (1).

Østerud, Øyvind (1991) *Statsvitenskap Innføring i statsvitenskapelig analyse*. Oslo: Universitetsforlaget.

Painton, Frederick (1993) 'From Banditry to Civil War', *Time Magazine*, 6 December.

Parlement Européen (n.d.a) Direction Générale des Etudes, Direction A, Division des Affaires Politiques et Institutionelles, *Fiche thématique no. 5 sur la Politique étrangère et de sécurité européenne (PESC)*. Brussels, successive updated versions.

Parlement Européen (n.d.b) Direction Générale des Etudes, Direction A, Division des Affaires Politiques et Institutionelles, *Fiche thématique no. 11 sur l'UEO, la sécurité et la défens*. Brussels, successive updated versions.

Parlement Européen (n.d.c) Groupe de travail du Secréteriat général, Task-Force Conférence intergouvenmentale, *Positions résumées des Etats membres et du Parlament européen sur la Conférence intergouvernmentale de 1996*. Luxembourg, successive updated versions.

Petersen, Nikolaj (1977) 'Adaptation as a Framework for the Analysis of Foreign Policy Behaviour', *Cooperation and Conflict*, 12: 221–50.

Pierre, Andrew J. and Trenin, Dimitri (1997) 'Developing NATO–Russian Relations', *Survival*, 39 (1): 5–18.

Pijpers, Alfred E. (1991) 'European Political Co-operation and the Realist Paradigm', in Martin Holland (ed.), *The Future of European Political Co-operation*. London: Macmillan.

Pinet, Hervé (1996) 'Le Temps des Hesitations', *Jeune Afrique Plus: Ou va L'Europe*, no. 1830, 31 January–6 February.

Politisches Lernen (1996) 'Was treibt die Bundesrepublik? Zur deutschen Außenpolitik', *Politisches Lernen*, Special Issue, no. 2–3.

Presse- und Informationsamt der Bundesregierung (1970–) *Weißbuch*. Bonn.

Public Hearing of the Subcommittee on Security and Disarmament (1996) *Towards a European Security Structure*. Brussels, 19 March.

Randsborg, Elisabeth (1996) 'Utland: Vanskelig Balansegang for Tyrkia', *Aftenposten*, 3 July.

Ranstorp, Magnus and Xhudo, Gus (1994) 'A Threat to Europe? Middle East Ties with the Balkans and their Impact upon Terrorist Activity throughout the Region', *Terrorism and Political Violence*, 6 (2): 196–223.

Regelsberger, Elfriede (1988) 'EPC in the 1980s: Reaching Another Plateau?', in Alfred Pijpers, Elfriede Regelsberger and Wolfgang Wessels (eds), *European Political Cooperation in the 1980s: A Common Foreign Policy for Western Europe?* Dordrecht: Martinus Nijhoff.

Regelsberger, Elfriede and Wessels, Wolfgang (1995) *Zero or Global Power*. Working Paper, NSM.

Regelsberger, Elfriede and Wessels, Wolfgang (1996) 'The CFSP Institutions and Procedures: A Third Way for the Second Pillar', *European Foreign Affairs Review*, 1 (1): 29–54.

Regelsberger, Elfriede, de Schouteheete de Tervarent, Philippe and Wessels, Wolfgang (eds) (1997) *Foreign Policy of the European Union: From EPC to CSFP*. Bonn.

Reichel, S. (1996) *The European Administration of Mostar: Objectives and Achievements July 1994–July 1996*. Unpublished Report to the Commission, 15 December.

Remacle, Eric (1991) *Les négotiations sur la politique étrangère et de sécurité commune de la Communauté européenne*. Brussels: series 'notes et documents', no. 156, April.

Remacle, Eric (1996) *La CIG, la PESC et l'UEO*. Brussels: Institut d'Etudes Européennes, Université libre de Bruxelles.

Remacle, Eric (1997) 'La CIG entre flexibilité et coopérations renforcées: perspectives pour l'intégration differencieée', in *La CIG et l'UEM après Dublin*. Brussels: Institut d'Etudes Européennes, Université libre de Bruxelles and Groupe d'Etudes Politiques européennes. pp. 23–32.

Remacle, Eric and Seidelmann, Reimund (eds) (1997) *Paneuropean Security Redefined*. Baden-Baden.

Report (1995) 'Informe del Grupo de Reflexión', SN 520/95 (reflex 21), Brussels, 5 December 1995.

Resolutions (1995) Implementation of CFSP from November 1993 until December 1994, *Official Journal*, C151, 19 June.

Resolutions (1996a) 13 March, *Official Journal*, C96, 1 April.

Resolutions (1996b) Implementation of CFSP from January 1996 until December 1996, Doc. A4-019397, Brussels, 28 May.

Resolutions (1996c) Implementation of CFSP from January 1995 until December 1995, *Official Journal*, C261, 9 September.

Resolutions (1997a) 16 January (Doc. B4 0040 97).

Resolutions (1997b) 13 March (Doc. B4 0266 97).

Resolutions (1997c) Coherence of the EC's Development Cooperation with its Other Policies, 10 June.

Reudy, John (ed.) (1994) *Islamism and Secularism in North Africa*. New York: St Martin's Press.

Rifkind, Malcolm (1995) 'The Future of European Security', *The Framework of United Kingdom Defence Policy*. London Defence Studies, Centre for Defence Studies, 30–1 December.

Risse-Kappen, Thomas (ed.) (1995) *Bringing Transnational Relations Back In: Non-State Actors, Domestic Structures and International Institutions*. Cambridge: Cambridge University Press.

Robins, Philip (1991) *Turkey and the Middle East*. London: Royal Institute of International Affairs, Pinter.

Rodrigo, F. (1995) 'Western Alignment: Spain's Security Policy', in R. Gillespie, F. Rodrigo and J. Story (eds), *Democratic Spain: Reshaping External Relations in a Changing World*. London: Routledge.

Roissonat, Jean (1997) Interview, *Le Monde*, 28 January.

Rollat, Alain (1996) 'Bons baisers de 1789', *Le Monde*, 14–15 July.

Rosenau, James (1970) *The Adaptation of National Societies: A Theory of Political Systems Behaviour and Transformation*. New York: McCaleb-Seiler.

Rühe, Volker (1996) 'Security In and For Europe', Speech at the RIIA, London, 22 November.

Rummel, Rudolph (1994) 'Power, Genocide and Mass Murder', *Journal of Peace Research*, 31 (1): 1–10.

Saferworld (1996) *Summary of CFSP and Defence Issues on the IGC Negotiations: Draft Amendments to the Maastricht Treaty*. London, November.

Sanders, David (1990) *Losing an Empire, Finding a Role: British Foreign Policy Since 1945*. London: Macmillan.

Sanguineti, Vittorio (1997) 'Turkey and the European Union: Dreaming West but Moving East', *Mediterranean Quarterly: A Journal of Global Issues*, 8 (1): 11–27.

Santer, Jacques (1995) 'Security and Defence of the European Union', *NATO Review*, 6: 3–9.

Schmitter, Philippe (1969) 'Three Neofunctional Hypotheses about International Integration', *International Organisation*, 23: 161–6.

Seidelmann, Reimund (1995) 'Towards a Common European Security Policy', in Christoph Bluth, Emil Kirchner and James Sperling (eds), *The Future of European Security*. Aldershot: Dartmouth. pp. 113–34.

Seidelmann, Reimund (1996a) 'German Foreign Policy and the European Order', in Reimund Seidelmann (ed.), *Crises Policies in Eastern Europe*. Baden-Baden. pp. 235–73.

Seidelmann, Reimund (ed.) (1996b) *Crises Policies in Eastern Europe*. Baden-Baden.

Seidelmann, Reimund (1997) 'Cost, Risks, and Benefits of a Global Military Capacity for the European Union', *Defence Economist*, no. 1.

Sharp, Jane M. O. (ed.) (1990) *Europe after an American Withdrawal*. Oxford: Oxford University Press, SIPRI.

Sharp, Jane M. O. (ed.) (1997) *Rebuilding War-Torn Societies: The Case of Bosnia-Hercegovina*. Harvard: Harvard University/CSIA.

Shirley, Edward G. (1995) 'Fundamentalism in Power: Is Iran's Present Algeria's Future?', *Foreign Affairs*, 74 (3): 28–44.

Simic, Predrag (1993) 'Eastern Enlargement of the EC', in Wolfgang Wessels and Christian Engel (eds), *The European Union in the 1990s: Ever Closer and Larger?* Bonn: Europa Union.

SIPRI (1995) *SIPRI Yearbook. Stockholm International Peace Research Institute.* Oxford: Oxford University Press.

SIPRI (1997) *Armaments, Disarmament and International Security: SIPRI Yearbook 1997. Stockholm International Peace Research Institute.* Oxford: Oxford University Press.

Sjoestedt, G. (1977) *The External Role of the European Community.* London: Saxon House.

Smeshko, Ihor P. Gen. Maj. (1995) *Partnership for Peace from a Ukrainian Perspective.* Paper to the 11th USNATO Annual Strategic Studies Conference, September.

Smith, Michael (1994) 'The Commission and External Relations', in Geoffrey Edwards and David Spence (eds), *The European Commission.* London: Longman. pp. 249–86.

Smith, M. (1997) 'The Commission and External Relations', in G. Edwards and D. Spence (eds), *The European Commission,* 2nd edn. London: Cartermill.

Smith, Steve (1994) 'Foreign Policy Theory and the New Europe', in Walter Carlsnaes and Steve Smith (eds), *European Foreign Policy: The EC and Changing Perspectives in Europe.* London: Sage.

Snyder, G.H. (1988) 'Spain in NATO: The Reluctant Partner', in F.G. Gil and J.S. Tulchin (eds), *Spain's Entry into NATO.* Boulder, CO: Lynne Rienner.

Solana, J. (1995) 'España y la UEO: la otra presidencia', *El País,* 31 October.

Soysal, Yasemin N. (1993) 'Immigration and the Emerging European Polity', in Svein S. Andersen and Kjell A. Eliassen (eds), *Making Policy in Europe.* London: Sage.

Spence, Arnhild (1994) *Enlargement of the European Union: A Step towards a Common Foreign and Security Policy.* NUPI Report 182, October.

Spence, Arnhild (1998) 'Foreign Ministries and the Gatekeeper Function in National and European Context', in B. Hocking (ed.), *Foreign Ministry Reform.* London: Macmillan.

Spencer, Claire (1993) *The Maghreb in the 1990s.* Adelphi Paper 274, London: The International Institute for Strategic Studies, Brassey's.

Stoessinger, J. (1973) 'The Anatomy of the Nation-State and the Nature of Power', in *The Might of Nations,* 4th edn. New York: Random House.

Strom-Pedersen, E. (1990) 'IEPG: Military Harmonization towards Common Procurement?', *NATO's Sixteen Nations,* 35 (6), October.

Stubb, Alexander (1996) 'Categorization of Differentiated Integration', *Journal of Common Market Studies,* 34 (2): 283–95.

Sverdrup, Ulf (1995) 'Enlargement', in *Enlargement to the East.* Oslo: ARENA, University of Oslo.

Taylor, Paul (1996) *The European Union in the 1990s.* Oxford: Oxford University Press.

Taylor, T. (1993) 'West European Defence Industrial Issues for the 90's', *Defence Economics,* vol. 4.

The Economist (1995a) 'Salaam, Welfar', 10 February: 16–17.

The Economist (1995b) 'Europe and the Maghreb Club Med', 2 September: 28.

The Economist (1995c) 'Europe's Far Right: Something Nasty in the Woodshed', 21 October: 39–40.

The Economist (1995d) 'A New Crusade', 2 December: 27–30.

The Economist (1995e) 'No Room at Europe's Inn', 9 December: 33–4.

The Economist (1995f) 'The Shape of the World. The Nation-State is Dead: Long Live the Nation-State', 23 December–5 January.

The Economist (1996a) 'Algeria: One Way Road', 17 February: 43–4.

The Economist (1996b) 'Springtime Means Wartime', 11 May: 33–4.

The Economist (1996c) 'Europe's Foreign Policy: The 15 at Sixes and Sevens', 18 May: 30–1.

The Economist (1996d) 'Turkey: The Elusive Golden Apple', 8 June: 3–18.

The Economist (1996e) 'Arab Summit: Déjà vu', 29 June: 42.
The Economist (1996f) 'No Turning Back', 29 June: 16.
The Economist (1996g) 'Turkey, Israel and the Arabs: Will It Last?', 29 June: 42–3.
The Economist (1997a) 'Algeria: Mayhem', 2 August.
The Economist (1997b) 'Bigger NATO, Safer World?', 12 July.
Thune, Christian (1985) 'Denmark and the Western European Union', in Panos Tsakaloyannis (ed.), *The Reactivation of the Western European Union: The Effects on the EC and its Institutions*. Maastricht: European Institute of Public Administration.
Tillinac, Denis (1997) 'Chronique d'un désanchantement. 1: L'Euphoric et le doute', *Le Monde*, 4 June.
Tsakaloyannis, Panos (1996) *The European Union as a Security Community*. Baden-Baden.
Tunander, Ola (1995) 'A New Ottoman Empire? The Choice for Turkey: Euroasian Centre vs. National Fortress', *Security Dialogue*, 26 (4).
Usher, J. (1997) 'The Commission and the Law', in G. Edwards and D. Spence (eds), *The European Commission*, 2nd edn. London: Cartermill.
Usher, Rod (1996) *TIME Magazine*, 22 July: 26.
Vandamme, Jacques and Mouton, Jean-Denis (eds) (1995) *L'Avenir de l'Union Européenne: élargir et approfondir*. Bruxelles: Presses Interuniversitaires Européennes.
Van Den Broek, H. (1994) 'The CFSP of the EU: An Initial Assessment', Speech at the Clingendael Institute, The Hague, 24 May.
Van Eekelen, Willem (1995a) *The Security Agenda for 1996. Background and Proposals*. CEPS Paper 64, Brussels.
Van Eekelen, Willem (1995b) *Defence Equipment Cooperation*. CEPS Working Document 96, Brussels, October.
Van Ham, P. (1997) 'The EU and WEU: From Cooperation to Common Defence?', in G. Edwards and A. Pijpers (eds), *The Politics of European Treaty Reform: The 1996 Intergovernmental Conference and Beyond*. London: Pinter.
Vanhoonacker, Sophie (1992) 'A Critical Issue: From European Political Cooperation to a Common Foreign and Security Policy', in Finn Laursen and Sophie Vanhoonacker (eds), *The Intergovernmental Conference on Political Union*. Maastricht: EIPA.
Vanhoonacker, Sophie (1997) 'From Maastricht to Amsterdam: Was It Worth the Journey for CFSP?', *EIPASCOPE*, Maastricht 1997/2.
Van Wijnbergen, Christa (1992) 'The Federal Republic of Germany and European Political Union', in Finn Laursen and Sophie Vanhoonacker (eds), *The Intergovernmental Conference on Political Union*. Maastricht: EIPA.
Védrine, Hubert (1997a) Conférence des Ambassadeurs, Speech made by the Foreign Affairs Minister, Paris, 28 August.
Védrine, Hubert (1997b) Interview, *Le Monde*, 29 August.
Vernet, Daniel (1994) 'Le Testament européen de Jacques Delors', *Le Monde*, 24 October.
Vernet, Daniel (1997) 'L'Europe dans l'engrenage de la monnaie unique', *Le Monde*, 19–20 January.
Viñas, A. (1981) *Los pactos secretos de Franco con Estados Unidos: Bases, ayuda económica, recortes de soberanía*. Madrid: Grijalbo.
Viorst, Milton (1995) 'Changing Iran: The Limits of the Revolution', *Foreign Affairs*, 74 (6): 63–76.
Wallace, Helen (1993) 'Deepening and Widening: Problems of Legitimacy for the EC', in S. García (ed.), *European Identity and the Search for Legitimacy*. London.
Wallace, Helen and Wallace, William (1996) *Policy-Making in the European Union*. Oxford: Oxford University Press.

Wallace, William (1971) *Foreign Policy and the Political Process*. London: Macmillan.

Wallace, William (1975) *The Foreign Policy Process in Britain*. London: Royal Institute of International Affairs.

Wallace, William (ed.) (1990) *The Dynamics of European Integration*. London: Pinter for the Royal Institute of International Affairs.

Wallace, W. and Smith, J. (1995) 'Democracy or Technocracy? European Integration and the Problem of Popular Consent', *West European Politics*, 18 (3): 137–58.

Webb, S. (1989) *Nato and 1992*. Rand Corporation, Santa Monica, July.

Weidenfeld, Werner (ed.) (1994) *Europa '96. Reformprogramm für die Europäische Union. Strategien und Optionen für Europa*. Gütersloh: Verlag Bertelsmann Stiftung.

Weidenfeld, Werner (ed.) (1996) *Neue Östpolitik: Strategie für eine gesamteuropäische Entwicklung*. Gütersloh: Verlag Bertelsmann Stiftung.

Weiler, J. H. H. (1997) 'Legitimacy and Democracy of the Union Governance', in G. Edwards and A. Pijpers (eds), *The Politics of European Treaty Reform: The 1996 Intergovernmental Conference and Beyond*. London: Pinter.

Weiner, Myron (1992) 'Security, Stability, and International Migration', *International Security*, 17 (3): 91–126.

Westendorp Report (1995) 'Progress Report from the Chairman of the Reflection Group on the 1996 Intergovernmental Conference'.

Wester, Robert (1992) 'United Kingdom and European Political Union', in Finn Laursen and Sophie Vanhoonacker (eds), *The Intergovernmental Conference on Political Union*. Maastricht: EIPA.

White-Spunner, Barney (1995) 'The Thin Blue Line: Britain's Military Contribution to the United Nations', in *Brassey's Defence Yearbook*. London: Brassey's for the Centre for Defence Studies.

Willaert, P. and Marqués-Ruiz, C. (1995) 'Vers une politique étrangerè et de sécurité commune; état des lieux', *Revue du Marché Unique Européen*, 3.

Wolf, M. (1995) 'The EU in a Liberal Global Economy', *International Affairs*, 71 (2): 325–8.

Zubaida, Sami (1993) *Islam, the People and the State*. London: Tauris.

Index